I0448247

Chapter

14

INTERNATIONAL TRAINING

INTRODUCTION

The US international military training program may be the most important security cooperation (SC) program the US has with another country. Long after a country purchases, utilizes, and disposes of US military equipment, what remains are the experiences the international military student (IMS) had during training. Through exposure to the American way of life and direct observation of US commitment to universal human rights concerns, the IMS comes to understand and appreciate American democratic ideals. The longest lasting and most valuable influence with a country is developed through the professional and personal relationships established by the IMS while training in the US.

There are many factors to consider in the US international military training program. This chapter will examine several of them, including:

- Legal authorities and regulations

- Training management organizations

- Training program development and implementation

- Types and categories of training

- Financial considerations

- Student administration

- Training program automation

LEGAL AUTHORITIES AND REGULATIONS

Today, the US international military training program consists of training under the security assistance (SA) program and an ever-increasing number of SC programs. All of this training must be authorized by federal law. When no other law authorizes an international military training event, then SA laws and regulations apply to that event.

Security Assistance Training

SA training includes training of foreign personnel authorized under the Foreign Assistance Act (FAA) and the Arms Export Control Act (AECA). Thus, the components of the SA training program are as follows:

International Military Education and Training

International Military Education and Training (IMET) is the cornerstone of SA training and is how most developing US partners begin their cooperative relationship with the US. The IMET program is authorized by the FAA, and the military departments (MILDEPs) are reimbursed from annual foreign operations appropriations. The IMET program aims to provide long-term strategic benefits to both the US and partner nations, particularly when the partner's limited defense funding would otherwise preclude training with the US military. For many different reasons, IMET receives a significant amount of oversight from the US Congress, resulting in constraints and reports not required for other training programs. Because of these factors, the IMET program deserves special consideration in any text of SA.

14-1

**International Military Education and Training Objectives**. The Defense Security Cooperation Agency (DSCA) Manual 5105.38-M, _Security Assistance Management Manual_ (SAMM), chapter 10, explains that the IMET program is a key component of security cooperation (SC), promoting regional stability and defense capabilities through professional military and technical courses and specialized instruction. IMET courses are provided primarily at military schoolhouses in the US, exposing the IMS to the US culture, military students, practices, standards, and professionalism.

Specific objectives of the IMET program include:

- Encourage effective and mutually beneficial relations

- Increased understanding between the US and foreign countries in furtherance of the goals of international peace and security

- Development of rapport, understanding, and communication links

- Develop host nation training self-sufficiency

- Improve host nation ability to manage its defense establishment

- Develop skills to operate and maintain US-origin equipment

On a broader scope, the dual objectives of supporting US regional security interests and the overall SC goal of supporting US foreign policy are always a consideration. All of the objectives stated above should be pursued simultaneously, with emphasis shifting progressively from operations and maintenance, to the independent management of in-country capabilities, and finally to preserving military rapport and understanding of the US. This ultimate state should be pursued as rapidly as possible, consistent with the achievement of overall objectives.

**Expanded-International Military Education and Training Program**. The Expanded-IMET (E-IMET) program was initiated in 1990. It is not a separate program from the IMET program, but a recognition that the IMET program needed to grow in response to a changing global political scene. Originally, the IMET program could only be used to train military/civilian personnel from a country's defense establishment. Through the E-IMET program, a broader eligibility of students is offered. Civilians who work in the country's non-defense ministries, legislators, and individuals who are not members of the government may be trained in E-IMET qualified courses, using IMET funds, if doing so would contribute to E-IMET objectives.

The objectives of E-IMET are to:

- Contribute to responsible defense resource management

- Foster respect for and understanding of democracy and civilian rule of law, including the principle of civilian control of the military

- Contribute to cooperation between military and law enforcement personnel with respect to counternarcotics law enforcement efforts

- Improve military justice system and promote an awareness and understanding of internationally recognized human rights

Additionally, E-IMET training is authorized in:

- Counternarcotics-related areas for defense civilians

- Teaching, developing, or managing in-country English Language Training (ELT) programs for defense civilians

- Maritime law enforcement and other maritime skills training for agencies which are non-defense or agencies which perform a maritime law enforcement mission

- Other maritime skills training provided to a country which does not have standing armed forces

All courses taught under the E-IMET program will be held in US military schools or will be conducted by Mobile Education Teams (METs). Many DOD education and training activities such as the Defense Resource Management Institute, the Defense Institute of International Legal Studies, and the Center for Civil-Military Relations aggressively support the E-IMET program. Courses must be certified by DSCA for E-IMET status.

International Military Education and Training Constraints. The SAMM, section C10.6.3, provides information on the types of training that can be provided under the IMET program. The intent is to preserve the integrity of SA as a military program, realize the maximum return on IMET funds expended in terms of utility and retainability of students, and limit police and intelligence training to purely military applications consistent with human rights considerations. Some types of training require a waiver approved by both the combatant command (CCMD) and DSCA. Waiver requests must be formatted in accordance with the SAMM, C10.F1.

Certain types of training are prohibited under the IMET program such as sniper training and foreign language training. For a complete list of types of training not provided by IMET see SAMM C10.T3. In addition, the FAA, section 660 and SAMM C10.6.4.4 through C10.6.4.5 prohibit using IMET to provide police training to military or civilian police if they perform a civilian law enforcement function. Military police training may be provided to non-police personnel but this requires a certification by the country that the IMS will not be used in a civilian law enforcement role for a minimum of two years following completion of training. The security cooperation office (SCO) must retain this certification for a minimum of three years.

Foreign Military Sales

Training can also be purchased via a Foreign Military Sales (FMS) case, funded by either host nation funds or USG funds such as FMFP.

Emergency Drawdown Authority

Training authorized by the FAA, section 506 applies when equipment is taken out of US stock and given to a country. This training includes how to operate and maintain the respective equipment.

Exchange Training

Exchange training is authorized either by the AECA, section 30A or the FAA, section 544: "Security Cooperation Training Managed by Security Assistance Personnel." Under this authority, the President may provide for the attendance of foreign military personnel at professional military education (PME) institutions in the US (other than Service academies) without charge, if such attendance is part of an international agreement. These international agreements provide for the exchange of students on a one-for-one reciprocal basis each fiscal year between the two military sevices participating in the exchange.

Security Cooperation Training Managed by Security Assistance Personnel

The US military conducts a wide variety of other SC training programs which are managed by the existing SA infrastructure. These programs are discussed more thoroughly in chapter 1 of this text, titled "Introduction to Security Cooperation." Significant SC training consists of:

- International Narcotics Control and Law Enforcement (INCLE) training authorized by the FAA, section 4891 to be funded by the annual foreign operations appropriations acts

- Counternarcotics training originally authorized by Public Law (P.L.) 101-510, 5 November 1990, section 1004, to be funded by subsequent annual DOD appropriations acts

- Counternarcotics training originally authorized by P.L.105-85, 18 November 1997, section 1033, to be funded by subsequent annual DOD appropriations acts

- Combating Terrorism Fellowship Program (CTFP) training authorized by *10 United States Code* (U.S.C.) 1051b to be funded by subsequent annual DOD appropriations acts

- Aviation Leadership program training authorized by 10 U.S.C. 9381-9383 to be funded by the United States Air Force (USAF)

- Training authorized under various memoranda of understanding in effect with the United States Coast Guard (USCG)

Other Training Not Managed by Security Assistance Personnel

The US military also conducts other types of international military training that are not managed by SA personnel. The latter need to be aware of these other programs although the details of these programs are outside the scope of this text:

- US military academy international students

- Special Operations forces training of international students primarily via Joint Combined Exchange Training (JCET)

- Various US government (USG) humanitarian assistance programs

- Caribbean support tender training programs conducted by the USCG

Regulations

In carrying out training management, the SAMM, specifically chapters 10 and 11, are used for overall general guidance. *The Joint Security Cooperation Education and Training (JSCET) Regulation* (AR 12-15; SECNAVINST 4950.4A; AFI 16-105) provides further direction in carrying out policies identified in the SAMM.. Each chapter of the JSCET begins with a DOD section followed by MILDEP-specific instructions.

TRAINING MANAGEMENT ORGANIZATIONS

There are many organizations involved in the management of international training. These organizations are geographically distributed in a variety of locations from Washington, DC to US embassies around the world. Refer to figure 14-1 as the US training management organizations are described.

Figure 14-1
Training Management Organizations

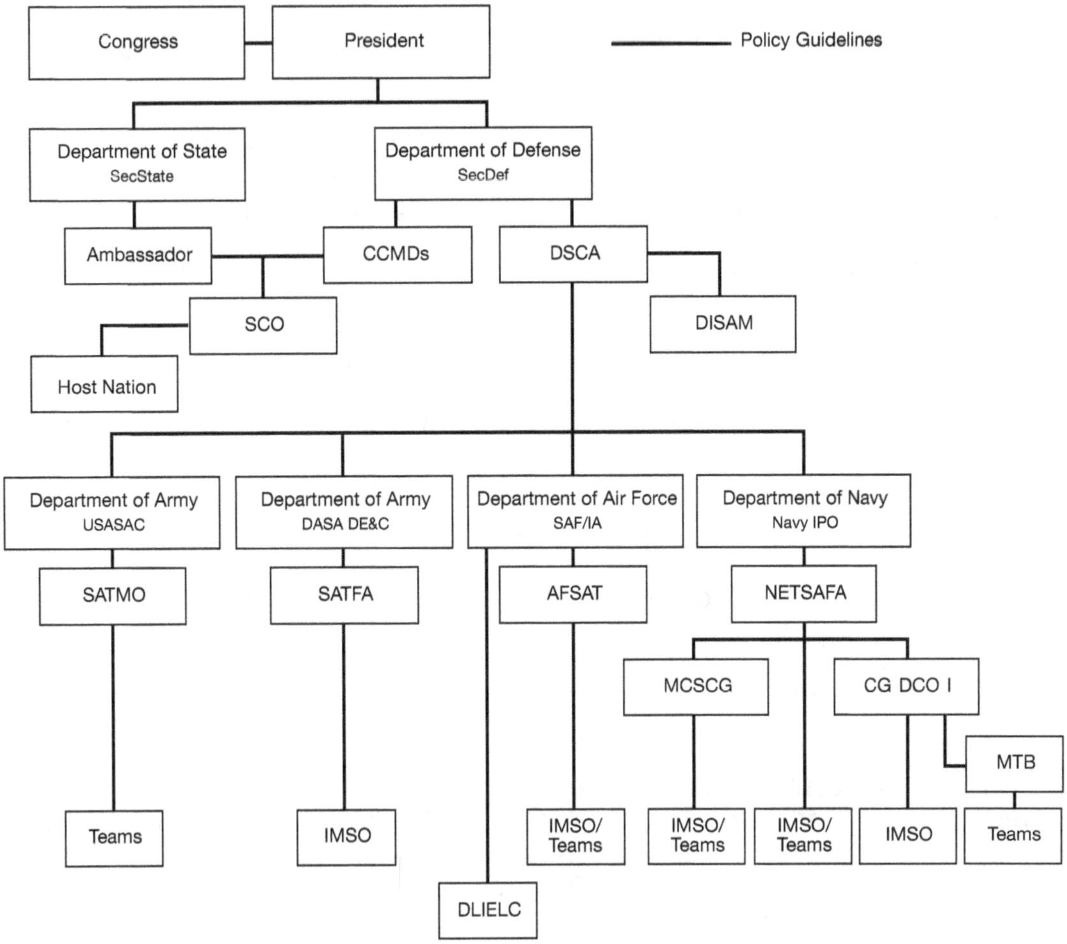

Training Policy

Training policy is guided by a small group of policy makers in the Washington, DC area. This section describes the role and relationships among these policy makers.

Department of State

The role of the Department of State (DOS) in training is basically the same as for all other aspects of SA; they decide a specific country's eligibility for training and the size and type of program to be authorized. The decision reflects an analysis of the country's needs by DOS in terms of US foreign policy and national security objectives. The concurrence of Congress is obtained by its approval in applicable legislation. After the analysis, decision, review, and legislative process is complete, the resulting SA program is given to DOD for implementation.

Department of Defense

Defense Security Cooperation Agency. Within DOD, the principal agency for implementation of the various international training programs is DSCA, which provides direction to the CCMDs and the MILDEPs. Policy coordination and support is provided by the Building Partner Capacity (BPC) division of the Programs (PGM) branch in DSCA. This office formulates policy for conduct of the SA Training Program (SATP), issues IMET program guidance, and exercises oversight of the US Field Studies Program (FSP). Matters involving conduct of the training program and approval authority for exceptions to policy rest with the individual country managers in DSCA regional operations divisions.

Military Departments

The MILDEPs, as designated Implementing Agencies (IAs), exercise execution oversight of international training and education solutions to country requirements to include fiscal management responsibilities across the various SC authorities. In most cases, the MILDEPs have delegated this responsibility to their respective training commands.

Department of the Air Force. Within the USAF, the Deputy Under Secretary of the Air Force for International Affairs (SAF/IA) is responsible for the policy direction, integration, guidance, management, and supervision of international programs and activities affiliated with the USAF.

As part of these general responsibilities for international training programs, SAF/IA functions include the following:

- Developing, coordinating, and issuing USAF-wide SA training policy and procedures

- Acting as the USAF representative and focal point for training policy and procedural issues

- Preparing any memoranda of agreement/understanding required for international training

- Monitoring the execution of approved training programs

- Acting as executive agent and service program manager for the Defense Language Institute English Language Center (DLIELC)

- Acting as the USAF focal point for policy matters involving the Inter-American Air Force Academy (IAAFA)

Department of the Army. At the Department of the Army, the Deputy Assistant Secretary of the Army for Defense Exports and Cooperation (DASA DE&C), within the Office of the Assistant Secretary of the Army for Acquisition, Logistics and Technology (ASA/ALT), exercises Army-wide oversight of all Army SA requirements to include training. DASA DE&C performs SA training policy and program guidance responsibilities through the Director, FMS Policy and Resources, to all Army agencies involved in the management and execution of Security Cooperation Education and Training Program (SCETP) requirements. DASA (DE&C)'s primary SCETP responsibilities include:

- AR 12-1, Security Assistance, Training, and Export Policy

- AR 12-15, Joint Security Cooperation Education and Training policy

- AR 12-7, Security Assistance Teams

- Coordinating with the HQDA G-3/5/7 and other HQDA offices as required on Chief of Staff, Army country/counterpart invitations for Army War College and Command and General Staff College attendance, Professional Military Education exchanges (PMEX) and country requests for SA Teams.

- Specific SCETP policy and procedural actions related to the management of international military students (IMS)

Department of the Navy. The Navy International Programs Office (IPO) provides centralized management for the Secretary of the Navy (SECNAV) of technology transfer, disclosure, SA, and international program policy. Navy IPO establishes policy, maintains oversight, deals with political issues, signs letters of offer and acceptance (LOAs), monitors and tasks subordinate commands in implementing the training program, and is the principal point of contact for foreign customers. With respect to international training, policy and oversight responsibility resides at the SECNAV level, while program execution is directed to the field level. Navy IPO has also issued specific guidance on how contractor-provided training is to be managed.

Training Implementation

Approved training programs are implemented through SA/SC specialized organizations out to the core DOD training activities.

Military Services

The five Military Service training activities are:

- The Air Force Security Assistance Training (AFSAT) Squadron, Air Education and Training Command (AETC) at Randolph AFB, Texas

- The Army Security Assistance Training Field Activity (SATFA), US Army Training and Doctrine Command (TRADOC) at Fort Eustis, VA

- The Naval Education and Training Security Assistance Field Activity (NETSAFA), Naval Education and Training Command (NETC) at Pensacola Naval Air Station, FL

- The Marine Corps Security Cooperation Group (MCSCG) at Fort Story, VA

- The Coast Guard Director of International Affairs & Foreign Policy (CG-DCO-I) at Washington, DC

Each of the training activities listed above is charged with planning and executing the Security Assistance Training Program (SATP) for its service. They manage all aspects of international training. Specifically, they program requested training, consolidate training requirements, and obtain and confirm course quotas. In addition, AFSAT, SATFA, and NETSAFA have been delegated MILDEP responsibilities for financial processes in funding training functions under the SATP. NETSAFA performs this function for all maritime services (Navy, Marine Corps, and Coast Guard).

United States Air Force, Air Force Security Assistance Training Squadron. AFSAT, as a component of the Air Education and Training Command (AETC), is the USAF's executive agent for all USAF-sponsored international training. AFSAT is charged with:

- Implementing all approved and funded USAF CONUS international training

- Monitoring the progress of training and the welfare of all USAF-sponsored IMS

- Supervising IMS administration and movement

- Sourcing and managing USAF Mobile Training Teams (MTTs) that provide OCONUS training as required by country needs/requests

- Administering and accounting for international training funds allocated for the training, administration, and support of IMS in CONUS and for Mobile Training Teams (MTTs) furnished from USAF CONUS resources

- Providing guidance for the implementation of the FSP for all USAF IMS in CONUS, approving fund estimates, and providing funds to support all USAF FSP activities

United States Army, Security Assistance Training Field Activity. SATFA, in the Deputy Chief of Staff for Operations, Plans and Training, G-3/5/7, at HQ, US Army Training and Doctrine Command (TRADOC), is responsible for brokering US Army-managed institutional training and PME solutions for country SCETP requirements across the various SC programs to include the central financial management and distribution of SC program funds to those Army CONUS activities executing training and PME for Army-sponsored IMS. SATFA's primary SCETP responsibilities include:

- Serves, in coordination with the Army Senior SAT Specialist at DASA (DE&C), as the primary point of contact for all Army institutional training and PME conducted under any SC authority

- Manages (programming through closure) valid Country/Program international training and PME requirements, by SC program, within US Army CONUS institutional training requirements and resourcing processes

- Coordinates with US Army training providers for the development of unique training to support the specific requirements of an FMS-purchased equipment/system that best meets the needs of the country

- Develops course costs annually for inclusion in the Army Training Military Articles and Services List (T-MASL)

- Provides guidance and direction to Army training activity International Military Student Offices (IMSO) and their leadership pertaining to any aspect of SCETP execution to include the US Field Studies Program (FSP)

- Coordinates with DLIELC the validated language laboratory requirements approved for execution and funding for all USG grant programs with the US Army Communications-Electronics Command (CECOM) action agent

SATFA coordinates training-related requirements with other Army major commands/activities to meet country specific needs. SATFA also coordinates the programming, scheduling, implementation, and funding of training provided by other major commands. Broad responsibilities for training within the US Army are as follows:

- TRADOC—All formal individual training

- Health Services Command—All medical training

- Army Materiel Command (AMC)—Technical training within the functional areas of AMC major subordinate commands; OCONUS SA training

- US Forces Command—Unit/collective training

- US Army Acquisition Authority ASA/ALT—Program Executive Offices (PEO)/Project-Program Managers (PM)—New Equipment Training; some technical training

United States Army Security Assistance Training Management Organization. The Security Assistance Training Management Organization (SATMO), which falls under United States Army Security Assistance Command (USASAC), is the interface between the US Army and the SCO for the conduct of overseas Army training supported by CONUS-based teams and the provision of training support and literature. SATMO's main functions include:

- Assisting SCOs in the development of in-country training programs

- Providing staff assistance to DASA DE&C, USASAC, and SATFA in developing FMS training packages

- Coordinating the planning and deploying of SA teams to include:
  ◊ MTTs
  ◊ Technical assistance field teams (TAFTs)
  ◊ Training assistance teams
  ◊ Quality assurance teams. In conjunction with this, SATMO assists field agencies in structuring these teams to meet customer needs and follows up on team visits.
- Coordinating the formation of TAFTs and field training services (FTS) services in support of country requirements
- Processing requests from field agencies for training documents, literature, programs of instruction, and information on training aids
- Ensuring all selected team members receive antiterrorism training

United States Navy, Naval Education and Training Security Assistance Field Activity. NETSAFA implements three separate but interrelated functions as the principal support and coordination activity for Navy training.

First, NETSAFA is the single point of contact between SCOs and USN training. In this role, NETSAFA has the lead in programming all USN-related training. It identifies available USN training programs to meet foreign training requirements, including reviewing Navy training plans and maintaining an interface with the Deputy Chief of Naval Operations in N1 (Manpower, Personnel, Training and Education) Community Managers to obtain training quotas. It oversees the submission of Navy course classified data to Navy IPO for release authority.

Second, NETSAFA is the chief agent of Naval Education and Training Command's (NETC) for SA. In this role, NETSAFA is responsible for managing international shore-based education and training conducted at Navy Education and Training Command activities.

Finally, NETSAFA is the principal support agent for the entire Department of the Navy (DON) international training program. In this role, NETSAFA prepares:

- Training "T" case LOAs
- Acts as "T" case manager or case administering officer for Navy, Marine Corps and Coast Guard cases
- Coordinates pricing
- Computes travel and living allowance (TLA)
- Interfaces with DSCA for IMET, CTFP, 1206, and other Security Cooperation Training Programs
- Authorizes the issuance of Invitational Travel Orders (ITOs)
- Financially administers the training program
- Provides billing services (except for USCG and Navy fleet commands)

NETSAFA is responsible for providing information technology support in the form of management information systems for publishing training program related documents and for conducting the annual IMSO workshop.

United States Marine Corps, Security Cooperation Group. On 2 Jun 2011 the Commandant of the Marine Corps announced the concurrent disestablishment of Security Cooperation Education and Training Center (SCETC), the reorganization and redesignation of the Marine Corps Training and Advisory Group (MCTAG), and the merging of both former organizations' functions into a new organization known as the Marine Corps Security Cooperation Group (MCSCG) effective 1 October 2011. The new MCSCG reports to Commander, Marine Forces Command.

This, in effect, establishes a coordinated Marine Corps security cooperation command that will have cognizance over all Marine Corps security cooperation less the security assistance functions performed by Marine Corps Systems Command (FMS sales of equipment, material, and related services). MCSCG is tasked with the coordination, management, execution, and evaluation of USMC SC programs and activities to include assessments, planning, related education and training, and advisory support to ensure unity of effort in building partner nation security force capacity and capability in order to facilitate USMC and regional Marine Forces component command security cooperation objectives. USMC Training and Education Command (TECOM) will play a key coordinating role in all things involving TECOM entities.

United States Coast Guard, International Affairs and Foreign Policy. The USCG is also a major partner in the DON international training programs. Policy, administration, and implementation of USCG training is conducted by the Coast Guard Director of International Affairs and Foreign Policy (CG-DCO-I). CG-DCO-I is responsible for training and education conducted at all USCG activities, coordinating USCG MTTs and ETSSs through its Mobile Training Branch (MTB), granting ECL and ranking waivers for USCG training, and coordinating USCG matters with other USN training activities. USCG training requirements are to be addressed to CG-DCO-I, with NETSAFA as an information addressee.

Combatant Commands

The CCMDs maintain directorates dedicated to SC functions, including international training. A list of the responsibilities of these directorates for international training is as follows:

- Provide training policy guidance

- Monitor, coordinate, and evaluate approved country training programs

- Assist the SCO

- Assist the defense attaché

- Assist embassy personnel in establishing and implementing country IMET and FMS training programs

- Provide training data and other inputs to the Joint Staff and the secretary of defense on special actions and studies pertaining to international training programs

- Recommend allocations and monitor student quotas for those courses/schools which MILDEPs designate as having limited quotas requiring CCMD determination of priorities

- Coordinate use of CCMD (component) assets in support of country training requirements

- Conduct SA briefings/orientations for SCO personnel

- Plan, coordinate, and conduct annual Security Cooperation Education and Training Working Groups (SCETWGs)

- Coordinate and approve all exceptions to policy requiring a waiver

In addition to the training provided from CONUS-based resources, the service components of the CCMDs are able to meet some international training requirements within their respective theaters. Nearly all types of training discussed later in this chapter may be requested through the CCMD:

- Formal school training

- On-the-job (OJT)/observer (OBS) training

- Ship crew training

Country requests for MTTs are frequently filled from CCMD resources. Service components may be required to provide escorts for orientation tours (OTs). Student processing for training from this source may be complicated by the fact the student will be transiting or residing in a third country while undergoing training, (e.g., Germany in the European and Central Command areas). Procedures for meeting these additional theater-specific requirements are disseminated to the SCO.

Security Cooperation Office

Since the international training program (IMET, FMS or other) is developed in country and IMS scheduled for training comes from the country, the SCO has an important role in managing international training. The international training management functions are normally assigned to a training manager within the SCO. The SCO training manager is responsible for assisting the country in identifying, planning, and programming US training that will meet host country requirements and then conveying those requirements. While in the planning phase, the SCO identifies the goals and objectives for the country, as far as training requirements are concerned, for the next two years in the Combined Education and Training Program Plan (CETPP). The SCO must also convey the specific course requests to the appropriate military service training activities, usually via e-mail. Upon relaying the training requests to the military service training agencies, the SCO must then monitor the Standardized Training List (STL) to ensure it reflects the training requirements that were requested. The SCO training manager must then accomplish all of the administrative tasks required to prepare and send the IMS to the US for training or to bring that training to the country via a training team. One of the most important administrative functions, although not the only one, for which the SCO training manager is responsible is the creation of Invitational Travel Orders (ITOs) for the students. In short, the SCO training manager must effectively manage a dynamic SC program that provides both professional military training and training in support of materiel acquired from the US.

Defense Language Institute English Language Center

DLIELC has a unique place in the overall scheme of international military training. DLIELC, although operating under the command and control of AETC, is responsible to all Military Service training activities for implementation of DODD 5160.41E, Defense Language Program (DLP). This directive describes and defines the DLP, including all foreign language training plus English Language Training (ELT). Basically, DLIELC is responsible for the conduct, supervision, and control of all ELT for international and US service personnel. DLIELC conducts General English Training (GET) and Specialized English Training (SET) to prepare IMS for follow-on training (FOT). In addition, DLIELC conducts many English language instructor/management courses and fields English language teams for in-country requirements.

Defense Institute of Security Assistance Management

The Defense Institute of Security Assistance Management (DISAM) is responsible for providing international training management instruction for US and international military, civilian, and US industry personnel. The trained US personnel perform international training management responsibilities in SCOs, the military service training agencies, DOD agencies, and at military training facilities and schools. Trained international personnel are normally the country training counterparts to the SCO training manager, as well as country embassy staff members in the US. Requests for DISAM course quotas, METs, ECL waivers, etc, from the international customer must be directed through the in-country SCO training manager to AFSAT with an information copy to DISAM.

TRAINING PROGRAM DEVELOPMENT AND IMPLEMENTATION

Each CCMD annually hosts a Security Cooperation Education and Training Working Group (SCETWG), usually between the months of March and June, to project IMET requirements for the budget year (the next fiscal year) and the planning year (the fiscal year following the budget year). SCO training managers attending these reviews present all training program requirements on behalf of the host nation and must be prepared to justify all requests in accordance with the SAMM, chapters 10 and 11. Representatives from agencies responsible for international training within Department of State (DOS), DSCA and the military service training activities attend these meetings to review and approve country program requests and to initiate programming and allocation actions for approved training courses. Any projected FMS training is also addressed during the SCETWG as well as CTFP and Regional Center events.

Combined Education and Training Program Plan

After discussions with host nation personnel, but prior to the SCETWG, each SCO completes a Combined Education and Training Program Plan (CETPP) which must be approved by the CCMD. The online Security Cooperation–Training Management System (SC–TMS), discussed in the training automation section of this chapter, is used to complete the CETPP in accordance with the preparation guidance found in the SAMM, C10.F3. DOS and appropriate DOD activities can access the CETPP to review each country's training goals and plans. This document provides vital information to ensure that military service training activities have all the information needed to plan and execute country-specific training programs.

Standardized Training List

Training requests are entered into the military service training computer systems by SATFA, NETSAFA, AFSAT, MCSCG, and CG-DCO-I. Each training track in a particular program is identified by combining the two-character country code, one-character implementing agency code, three-character case ID, three-character case line, four-character worksheet control number (WCN), and possibly a one-character suffix to identify a specific line of training within a training track that has multiple training lines (i.e. the training track identifier can be constructed as: CC-IA-CaseIDCase Line-WCN-Suffix. An example would be BN-B-14I001-2405). Sequential training programmed for the same IMS is indicated by an alphabetic suffix to the WCN and commonly referred to as a training line. Therefore, a training track can consist of one or more training lines. The consolidation of requested training is called a Standardized Training List (STL). There is an STL for each program (by fiscal year) and each FMS training case line a country has established with the US. See attachment 14-1 for an example of an STL.

Each military service training activity then coordinates the training request to confirm quotas and schedule report/start dates. Training quotas are assumed to be accepted once they have been confirmed on the STL for thirty days. Once quotas are confirmed, the actions described in the student administration section of this chapter can commence.

International Military Education and Training

Each year's IMET program is identified by country code, implementing agency (IA) code, and FY followed by the letter "I" indicating the Program Type is IMET (i.e., BN-B-13I).

5th Quarter

Because the budget for the annually-funded IMET program is not normally signed until months after that fiscal year has started, a determination was made that as long as IMET funds are obligated prior to the end of the fiscal year, they can be used for an IMS to start training prior to the end of the calendar year. Hence, the 5th quarter is training in the first quarter of a fiscal year (1 October–31 December) funded with money from the previous fiscal year's appropriation. Fifth quarter requests are discussed at the SCETWG and finalized through the end-of-year (EOY) reallocation process.

End-of-Year Reallocation

For many different reasons, a country may not be able to utilize their entire IMET allocation. Other countries may have additional training needs that their original allocation does not cover, or they may have unanticipated medical costs for an IMS that must be paid. An EOY reallocation process has been developed to address these circumstances. The time line and steps are spelled out in the SAMM, C10. T4. SCO training managers should remember that funds are reallocated in the order of "must pays" like outstanding medical bills, Invitational PME courses, and E-IMET courses with funds rarely available for technical training. Also, the military service training activities must have an available quota in the 5th quarter, and EOY requests must be identified in the current year's STL with a priority of "B."

Priorities

Another unique programming aspect of the IMET program is the assignment of priority codes to training lines to quickly identify whether the training can be funded. A priority code of "A" is assigned to training lines in the STL when country allocation is sufficient for the training. A priority code of "D" is assigned to other valid training lines in excess of the country allocation for which the country could provide an IMS if funds became available. The value of priority "D" training should not exceed ten percent of the country allocation. A priority code of "B" is assigned to training lines in the current year when EOY funds are being or will be requested. At the SCETWG, any priority "D" training lines for the current year must be resolved; either changed to priority "B" for an EOY request or deleted. The MILDEPs will not obtain quotas or authorize priority "D" training.

IMET training lines are implemented once a quota is confirmed and funded by the MILDEPs. Once the MILDEP provides authorization for WCNs via SC–TMS (and only upon receipt of this authorization) can the SCO prepare the Invitational Travel Order (ITO). Travel and Living Allowance (TLA) may be paid from the country's IMET program or paid by the sponsoring country. IMET-recipient countries are encouraged to enter into cost-sharing agreements by paying IMS travel and/or living allowances. This allows IMET dollars to most efficiently be expended against training tuition costs. The cost of medical care for any IMET IMS is funded by a medical line in the country's IMET program.

Foreign Military Sales, Host Nation-Funded Training

FMS training cases are developed between the MILDEPs and country representatives, with coordination by the SCO. If the training is in support of a materiel purchase, the materiel or systems command of the MILDEP providing the item may also be involved. No matter if the training on an FMS case is for training only or if it is in support of a materiel purchase, it is essential that the military service training agencies be made aware of the training requirement so that it can be programmed into the Standardized Training List (STL) and accounted for.

Once defined, FMS-funded training requests are also entered into the military service training activity's computer system by FMS case identifier, line number (i.e. BN-D-YCY989), and WCN. The FMS implementation procedures are similar to those for IMET. FMS cases do not normally include TLA as those are the responsibility of the country and are provided to the IMS directly without US involvement. FMS training cases may also include a medical services line to cover medical costs incurred by the IMS. Alternatively, the country may decide to have the bills for such services sent to the country embassy for payment, or the IMS may obtain health insurance. Arrangements must be made in advance to cover associated costs such as special clothing and personal equipment either by including such items in the FMS case or having the IMS or IMS's government pay for them upon issue at the training installation.

Total Package Approach

Military training provided to other countries through US DOD resources is a vital element of SC programs. Countries that purchase or otherwise receive US military equipment are encouraged to simultaneously consider the training requirements while planning for integrating the new equipment or weapons systems into their inventory. Failure to do so will result in needless delays in attaining and maintaining operational readiness once the new equipment arrives in-country. Thus, training should be viewed from the perspective of the total package approach (refer to figure 14-2) and given due consideration in every materiel purchase case.

Figure 14-2
Total Package Approach

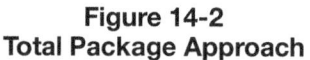

Professional Military Training
Technical Training
Flying Training
Specialized Training

CONUS-OVERSEAS
TRAINING

SECURITY
ASSISTANCE

SERVICES

MATERIAL

TECHNICAL ASSISTANCE

WEAPON SYSTEMS

Publications
Training Aids
Contract Administration
Management Services
Quality Assurance

End Item
Spares & Repair Parts
Follow-on Support

Planning and programming follow-on training support is an extremely important part of a viable training program. Those personnel involved in managing FMS programs should re-evaluate training requirements any time the procurement plan changes and coordinate training requirements in advance.

FMS training is provided through the normal FMS process either through a blanket line on the FMS case in support of that system sale or through a separate blanket order training case. Training should not be requested as a defined line on an FMS case or as a defined order case because changes are inevitable and would require case amendments or modifications. Blanket order cases provide much more flexibility, making them better suited to support a major weapon system purchase or an annual training program. The LOA process for training may require a lead time of six months or more from request through case implementation. Additional information on the LOA process for training is found in the JSCET, chapter 3, and in this textbook, chapter 5, "Foreign Military Sales Process."

**US Army Life-Cycle Management Commands**. More and more training is being included or embedded in USA FMS materiel cases managed by the various life-cycle management commands of AMC. However, the training lines are still developed, managed, and implemented by SATFA.

**US Navy Systems Commands**. The USN's three major systems commands, NAVSEA, NAVAIR, and SPAWAR have organic training managers who are responsible for training associated with that command's system sales. The NAVSEA, NAVAIR, and SPAWAR FMS case managers are responsible for the development of price and availability data for training provided by the FMS material prime contractor. When training under an FMS case includes USN resident training or contractor training other than the FMS material prime contractor, the FMS case manager will coordinate cost and availability data with NETSAFA. FMS case managers will coordinate with NETSAFA to ensure all training associated with the FMS case is properly programmed to allow for Invitational Travel Order authorization.

**US Air Force Life Cycle Management and Sustainment Centers**. The USAF also includes training in FMS materiel cases managed by their Air Force Life Cycle Management Center (AFLMC) and Air Force Sustainment Center (AFSC). These training lines are still developed, managed, and implemented by AFSAT.

Foreign Military Sales, Foreign Military Financing-Funded Training

Many SCO training managers and host nation personnel do not realize that a blanket order FMS training case can be funded with Foreign Military Financing (FMF) program funds. The value is that some of the constraints and restrictions placed on the IMET program do not apply to FMS training. For example, there would be no requirement to obtain a waiver for an MTT. Most importantly, this additional source of funds can provide for training that exceeds the country's IMET allocation. SCOs should attempt to influence the use of FMF funds to provide for support items (training, repair parts, etc.) as opposed to simply the acquisition of a new end-item with no support. Implementation of an FMF-funded case mirrors that of host nation-funded FMS cases except that USG funds are paying for the training. Sometimes, DSCA will approve payment of IMS TLA from the FMF-funded case.

Combating Terrorism Fellowship Program

The CTFP is developed and implemented quite differently from other training programs. First of all, the management of the program is highly centralized, with final approval for training (and the specific IMS attending) resting with the Defense Security Cooperation Agency/Programs/Building Partner Capacity office (DSCA/PGM/BPC). Each year, this office divides the CTFP appropriation into three "virtual" funding pots of money:

- Individual country allocations

- Invitational quotas issued by DSCA/PGM/BPC

- CCMD allocations used to further CCMD interests through regional seminars and other activities

Each year's CTFP program is identified by country code, implementing agency code, and fiscal year followed by the Program Type letter "B" (i.e. BN-D-13B). SCOs are provided guidance by DSCA/PGM/BPC as to the amount of CTFP country funding they are receiving each year and what invitations the country may receive for additional training. Similar to IMET and FMS training programs, CTFP training is programmed into the military service's training computer systems and will appear on the STL.

In order to proceed, the SCO must then nominate a specific candidate for the training and justify how this candidate's attendance would benefit US combating terrorism efforts. The nomination is submitted to the CCMD CTFP manager for approval and then forwarded on to DSCA/PGM/BPC for final approval. The entire nomination process is done online via SC–TMS, which will be discussed in the automation section of this chapter. Once approval is received, processing of the student is identical to IMET students.

For additional guidance and policy regarding the CTFP, refer to DOD Instruction 2008.28, DOD Policy and Responsibilities Relating to the Regional Defense Combating Terrorism Fellowship Program (CTFP).

Priorities

The CTFP also utilizes priority codes within its training lines identified on the STL. Priority codes associated with CTFP are used a little differently than priority codes associated with an IMET program as described above.

- A CTFP priority code of "B" indicates the training was paid for by CTFP and the training was provided by a Regional Center

- A CTFP priority code of "A" indicates all other training, not occurring at a Regional Center, which is paid for by CTFP

Other Security Cooperation Training

The SC training community is also responsible for managing training programs based on other legal authorities previously mentioned. While these other programs may change greatly from year to year, the resulting training requirements are handled much like IMET and FMS training requirements. To date, published guidance on the conduct of these other training programs has been limited only to message traffic. The existing SC training infrastructure is used to document, fund, and implement these training requirements. A pseudo LOA may be established to accomplish funded training. Thus, training can be identified by the SCO, formalized via the CCMD SCETWG process, entered into the training computer system by the military service training activities, and then implemented when the training quotas become available and funding is authorized.

Sanctions and Training Program Suspensions

Chapter 2 of this text, "Security Cooperation Legislation and Policy," provides information on sanction authorities. Political sanctions and Brooke Amendment economic sanctions result in IMET and FMF program suspensions. If a country falls under these sanctions, no new IMET or FMF-funded IMS may travel to the US or other locations to begin training. Normally, IMS who have already reported to training may continue their training for up to six months in order to complete the courses authorized on their ITO, but training may not be added or changed. However, Department of State reserves the right to shorten or lengthen this time period depending on the situation at hand. If a country is sanctioned for non-repayment of debt under Section 620q, FAA, only the IMET program is affected.

In addition to sanctions authorities, Congress has legislated that 110 percent of the amount of a country's unpaid parking fines or property taxes in Washington, DC and New York City be withheld from the country's IMET allocation until the bills are paid. [Section 643, P.L.110-161] While not eliminating the ability of the country to send IMS to training, it does reduce the available funds.

The consequences of a country being under sanctions must be addressed by the SCO. A country whose IMET program has been suspended no longer qualifies for the FMS incremental rate (Rate C) for tuition. Thus, if they wish to purchase training using their own host nation funds for an FMS case, the price of the training will be at the FMS full rate (Rate A). Cancellation penalties could be assessed against training for which the country had confirmed quotas but are now unable to utilize. A country with suspended IMET or FMF can still receive DOD program funds such as CTFP and counternarcotics programs.

DSCA maintains an informal list of sanctioned or suspended countries, but it cannot be distributed externally. DSCA country desk officers may release information concerning a country's status, but only to US citizen employees of the USG; contract personnel and Foreign Service National employees are not authorized to obtain this information.

Annual International Military Training Report

The foreign military training report, commonly referred to as the *Congressional Report on Military International Training* (CRMIT), is established by section 656, FAA, as an annual reporting requirement due by 31 January. The CRMIT contains substantial detail on each training activity: foreign policy justification and purpose of the training, number of foreign military personnel provided the training and their unit of operation, location of the training, aggregate number of students trained for the country, the cost, the operational benefits to US forces, and the US military units involved in the training. Through ITO issuance and MTT after-action summaries in the Security Cooperation–Training Management System (SC–TMS), SCOs provide CRMIT input. When directed by their CCMD and DSCA, they also conduct a final review for completeness. DSCA provides the data to DOS who strips out IMS names, excludes North Atlantic Treaty Organization (NATO), Japan, Australia, South Korea, and New Zealand data, and prepares the actual report for Congress. Sections 2 and 3 of the report are classified, but the rest of the report can be found at: http://www.state.gov/t/pm/rls/rpt/fmtrpt. Timelines for the report can be found in the SAMM, C10.T17.

TYPES AND CATEGORIES OF TRAINING

Consistent with US foreign policy, disclosure, technology transfer, and human rights considerations, international students are allowed to participate in a wide range of courses available through the military services training activities and DOD agencies. There are three broad categories of training that are offered to international countries or international organizations: English Language Training, Formal Training, and Specialized Training. Each category is described below.

English Language Training

The language difficulties encountered by some IMS continue to be a significant problem that hinders the effectiveness of training. It is imperative to recognize the need for an IMS to adequately understand English as most of the training that the US provides is conducted in English. The exceptions to this are the Western Hemisphere Institute for Security Cooperation, Inter-American Air Forces Academy, and the Navy Small Craft Instruction and Technical School, which conduct training in Spanish.

English Comprehension Level

The SCO training manager is responsible for ensuring that IMS meet all course prerequisites, including English Comprehension Level (ECL) requirements. ECL minimums are established and listed in the T-MASL for each course. The school has determined that an IMS with less than the minimum ECL would have great difficulty in successfully completing the course.

Prior to attending a US school, IMS must be tested both in-country by SCO personnel and at the first CONUS training location to determine their ECL rating. IMS from several native English-speaking nations are exempt from both in-country and CONUS English language testing. The requirement for in-country testing has also been waived for a number of other countries, although they will still be tested by the first CONUS training installation. IMS test scores are documented on the ITO. Each year, the Defense Language Institute English Language Center (DLIELC), located at Lackland Air Force Base, reviews the list of countries for which testing is waived and puts out an exemption message. Individual countries may be removed from the list by mutual agreement with DLIELC during the course of the year, but no additions will be made until the new list is approved and published.

For in-country testing, the SCO is responsible for appointing a Test Control Officer (TCO) to receive and safeguard the English language testing materials provided by DLIELC and to administer ECL tests to prospective IMS. The TCO must be a US citizen. Those who fail to achieve the required ECL when tested in-country may receive additional English language instruction in-country and be retested. In certain circumstances, a waiver may be granted if the prospective IMS is within a few points of the required ECL and there is sufficient justification. Requests for waivers are discouraged, since some degradation of comprehension and retention is bound to occur. These waivers are requested by the SCO from the military service training activities that are providing the training.

Oral Proficiency Interview

An additional requirement has been established, primarily for flight training programs, for an oral proficiency interview (OPI) to be conducted by DLIELC. This interview, to determine the English speaking and comprehension ability of the prospective IMS, takes place via telephone in the SCO training office between the IMS and DLIELC. If the IMS fails the OPI, a sixteen-week OPI prep course is available at DLIELC. The T-MASL will indicate the minimum OPI score required. As in the case of ECL scores, OPI waivers can be requested but are rarely approved.

General English Training

In those countries where little or no ELT is available, the SCO can program the IMS for General English Training (GET) at DLIELC prior to training at CONUS formal schools. The duration of GET depends upon the current ECL score of the IMS and the minimum score required for the training, but cannot be less than ten weeks. The primary purpose of GET is to raise the ECL of an IMS who has at least a minimum ECL of 55. A waiver must be granted by DSCA through the CCMD in order for an IMS to attend DLI with an ECL score below 55. Besides providing the IMS with ELT, DLIELC also has the capability to train language instructors and to assist in developing an ELT program for the country. Assistance in support of ELT in-country may be obtained by requesting a language training detachment from DLIELC to assist the country's ELT staff and faculty. A survey team from DLIELC can help the SCO determine the status of a country's ELT program and capabilities.

Specialized English Training

Although many IMS achieve the ECL specified in the T-MASL, they are unable to assimilate with sufficient speed the jargon that is so prevalent in subjects such as medical, electronics, or aviation training. To overcome this, DLIELC conducts nine-week Specialized English Training (SET) courses to familiarize the IMS with key words and phrases that they will encounter during their particular follow-on-training (FOT). DLIELC has developed SET for over forty subject areas in consultation with FOT locations. An IMS can be programmed for both GET and SET but will have to meet the minimum ECL prior to starting SET. If the IMS already meets his ECL requirement, SET may be programmed alone prior to FOT. Course requirements are expressed in the T-MASL to reflect the required ECL and whether SET training is required (R) or advised (A).

Sponsoring countries, SCO personnel, and DLIELC must continue to work together to eliminate the major problems associated with the English language program. These recurring problems are: inadequate language training in-country, lack of familiarization with technical terminology, and significant differences between the in-country ECL test score and the ECL test score at the first training location. It is also important to realize that acquiring an English language laboratory without providing for trained instructors, a lab manager, and English language materials will not help the country reach its ECL goals. SCOs should contact DLIELC for advice when planning a language lab acquisition.

Formal Training

Simply put, formal training is standardized training. The training location has conducted careful assessments, determined training goals, established methods and materials designed to achieve these goals, implemented training, and carefully evaluated the course to ensure training is carried out effectively and training goals are attained. Formal training is normally conducted at military educational and training facilities in the US and overseas.

Professional Military Education

PME includes the war colleges and the command and staff level schools (which are by invitation only for IMS) and other career development courses. For these types of courses, the host country is asked to provide only career personnel who meet the required rank/grade criteria.

Technical Proficiency Training

This category covers a wide range of courses including maintenance training, technical courses, and courses oriented toward developing a specific level of skill required to operate and/or maintain weapons systems or to perform required functions within a military occupational specialty. Training for officer and enlisted technicians and supervisors makes up the largest number of SC students. The country must have or intend to buy a particular system before technical training on the operation, maintenance, and repair of that system will be provided.

Flight Training

Flight training represents the highest cost training for international training programs and accounts for a large portion of USN, USAF, and USA training purchased by other countries. Because of the high costs associated with aircrew training, these courses can no longer be programmed under the IMET program; the bulk of such training is provided through FMS. The USAF coordinates all Euro-NATO fixed-wing flying training, and the USA is responsible for Euro-NATO rotary-wing flying training.

Specialized Training

Specialized training is tailored for the unique needs of the country. It can be a formal course that is modified to meet country requirements or something newly developed. The training can be provided in the US, overseas, or in the host country. Because specialized training is developed to meet the specific needs of the country, it requires more thorough communication to determine whether and how the US can meet those needs.

On-the-Job and Observer Training

Formal school training is frequently followed by a period of on-the-job, or hands-on training, to allow the IMS to gain proficiency in newly-acquired skills. Observer training is provided when no formal course covering the desired training is available or when it is impractical or otherwise undesirable for IMS to perform the tasks being demonstrated. An obvious example is medical training, where doctors and medical technicians who are not licensed to practice medicine in the US can benefit from observing US techniques and procedures. The SCO training manager must provide an OJT/OBS request which furnishes detailed information on the duration of training desired and the objectives to be achieved. Before such training can be confirmed, the military service uses this information to ensure that the training matches the needs of the country and can be provided from US resources. The availability of OJT/OBS training is limited due to the heavy commitments of today's active and reserve military components.

Orientation Tours

Orientation Tours (OTs) are provided under the SA training program to familiarize selected foreign officers with US military doctrine, techniques, procedures, facilities, equipment, organization, management practices, and operations. In addition to the purely military objectives to be achieved through OTs, they are intended to enhance mutual understanding, cooperation, and friendship between US forces and partner nations. This category of training includes distinguished visitor OTs for personnel of the rank of chief of staff of their respective military service. All OTs are conducted by the National Defense University (NDU) as short-term orientations not to exceed fourteen calendar days and require considerable detailed planning if they are to be effective.

An OT is programmed into a training program just like any other training, but there are requirements that must first be met. Prior to any proposal to country officials, which could be construed as an agreement to provide a tour, the SCO forwards the OT request to the CCMD, DSCA, NDU, and the MILDEPs with supporting rationale and justification for approval. An IMET-funded OT is programmed only after the SCO Chief attests to its importance to the country's efforts. To request an OT, the SCO forwards the OT request to the CCMD, DSCA, NDU, and the IA, with supporting rationale and justification for approval. OT requests are also included in the Combined Education and Training Program Plan (CETPP) for a country. Escort officers are provided from CONUS resources, although SCOs may fill this role in extenuating circumstances. Associated expenses are programmed and charged against the FMS case or the country's IMET program. These and other requirements are specified in the SAMM, C10.17.16.3 and the JSCET, chapter 12.

Exported Training

At times, it may be more expedient and cost effective to request that US personnel conduct training in-country (via a "team" of instructors) rather than to send a large number of IMS to the US or to a US military installation overseas. This is especially true when the equipment is no longer in the US inventory or when limited seats are available in the schoolhouse. SC training teams may be requested for a particular training task over a specific period of time. A few other advantages of exported training include the ability to tailor the training to fit the specific needs of a particular country as well as being able to train using the actual equipment which the country owns. Furthermore, it might be possible to use interpreters during training, at the country's expense, if a large number of students cannot speak English and it is determined that it will take too long for them to learn English at the level needed. If country and US personnel in country need help in identifying problems and developing training requirements and objectives, a survey team may be requested from the US military service as the preliminary step in the process. However, with or without a survey team, a request must be submitted which specifies the training objective, the number of personnel to receive training, skill levels to be achieved in each specialty area, equipment required and/or available, and the desired length of training. Such details, including constraints, are listed in the SAMM and the JSCET. All IMET-funded teams require a waiver approval from the CCMD and DSCA prior to programming.

However, there might be disadvantages with exported training that should be taken into account when requesting this type of training. A few disadvantages could be: more distractions for the students while training near home or the office, students do not get the opportunity to experience the US first hand, it might take longer for students to learn English if they revert back to their native language when not in class, and the equipment might not be available to train on in country.

SCO training managers must make every effort to identify all training team requirements at the SCETWG. With the current training personnel shortfalls in the armed services, there is little chance that out-of-cycle training team requests can be fulfilled.

**Mobile Training Teams (MTTs) and Mobile Education Teams (METs)**. MTTs and METs consist of DOD military and civilian personnel on temporary duty to train international personnel. The team members may be from CONUS or overseas units/organizations, and the training may be conducted in the CONUS or overseas using equipment owned by or allocated for delivery to the purchaser and recipient country. MTTs and METs are authorized for specific in-country training requirements, training associated with equipment transfer, or to conduct surveys and assessments of training requirements. They may normally be programmed for periods up to 179 days, including travel time. IMET-sponsored MTTs must be programmed to terminate on or before 30 September of the fiscal year in which they perform their duties. FMS-funded teams may span fiscal years, if necessary. An MTT that qualifies for E-IMET is normally referred to as a MET.

When the request message is received from the SCO and approved for programming, the CCMD and military service will verify that it has the capability to provide the training requested and "call up" the team. Verification involves identifying team members against the equipment and specialties involved, determining any pre-deployment training requirements for team members, and computing the costs.

Provisions must also be made in advance for purchasing associated tool sets, training aids, and other support items needed from the CONUS and having them in place in the country when the team arrives. Once in-country, the team reports to and comes under supervision of the SCO chief.

**Field Training Services**. FTS is the generic term for Extended Training Service Specialists (ETSS) provided from DOD resources and for contract field services provided under MILDEP contract from US industry sources. These teams provide advice, instruction, and training in the installation, operation, and maintenance of weapons, equipment, and other systems. FTS teams are normally programmed for a period of up to one year. Military members may be transferred on permanent change of station (PCS) orders without a permanent change of assignment when participating on an ETSS team. Requests for FTS under IMET and requests for FTS extensions must be justified by the SCO and submitted to the CCMD for approval on a case-by-case basis.

**Technical Assistance Field Teams**. TAFTs are DOD personnel deployed in a PCS status for the purpose of providing in-country technical or maintenance support to foreign personnel on specific equipment, technology, weapons, and supporting systems when MTTs and ETSSs are not appropriate for the purpose. Normally, TAFTs do not have training as a primary mission of the team. However, one must refer to the mission statement of the TAFT to see if the provision of training, formally or informally, is included. TAFTs may not be funded under the IMET program.

Classified Training

Attendance in classified courses or blocks of instruction is on a need-to-know basis. Each classified training request is subject to case-by-case approval, based on National Disclosure Policy (NDP-1), MILDEP implementing regulations, and existing security agreements between the US and the country. Refer to chapter 7 of this textbook, "Technology Transfer, Export Controls, and International Programs Security," for discussion of national disclosure policy and transfer of technology.

International Training

FINANCIAL CONSIDERATIONS

Tuition Pricing

The FAA and the AECA prescribe a multi-tier tuition pricing structure for training. The separate rates for the same course differ because various cost elements have been authorized by law to be excluded from some rates and others are charged only on an incremental cost basis. Furthermore, when a case is fully funded with US appropriated funds and/or FMS Credit (non-repayable), the FMS Full Rate is adjusted to exclude military pay and entitlements in accordance with the FAA. DOD policy for developing the tuition price for each military course of instruction is contained in DOD 7000.14-R, *Financial Management Regulation,* volume 15, section 0710. Currently, the SAMM chapter 10.14 identifies five tuition rate categories:

Rate A (Formerly FMS Full Rate)

The tuition price charged countries not eligible for any of the other rate categories below. These are full cost cash customers. This cost is about equal to what it costs the USG to send US students to the same course.

Rate B (Formerly FMS NATO Rate)

Countries with a ratified reciprocal training pricing agreement with the USG that are purchasing training via an FMS case are charged Rate B. SAMM C10.T.13 lists the countries and effective dates of the reciprocal agreements. Note that some of these countries are also eligible for Rate C.

Rate C (Formerly FMS Incremental Rate)

The tuition price charged to countries that are (1) currently authorized to receive IMET funds and using country funds to purchase additional training or (2) designated as a high income foreign country in accordance with the FAA (currently Austria, Finland, South Korea, Singapore, and Spain). If a country's IMET program has been suspended by political or economic sanction, it is no longer eligible for this rate. Rather, the Rate A (FMS Full) is charged.

Rate D

Training on a case financed with US-appropriated funds receives Rate D. FMS cases funded by US-appropriated funds include cases using Foreign Military Financing Program (FMFP) and Building Partner Capacity (BPC) program authorities. This rate is identical to Rate E except that the FMS administrative surcharge will be applied to it.

Rate E (Formerly IMET Rate)

The tuition price charged to countries when IMET program funds or other grant training program funds (e.g. DOS's INCLE or DOD's CTFP) are used.

Total Cost of Training

The total cost of training includes all associated costs to include the T-MASL tuition price, TLA paid to IMS, medical and dental costs, special clothing, and personal equipment items not included in the tuition, etc. Any of these articles and services to be furnished by the US training facility, which are not included in the tuition price, must be identified and included as specific items to be funded in the FMS training case, or reimbursed in cash by the student or the participating government. Authorized IMET expenditures include tuition, overseas and CONUS travel and baggage allowances, IMS living allowances while in training and IMET-paid travel status, and medical care. When specifically authorized by DSCA, on a case-by-case basis, these TLA costs can be included as a cost element on an FMS case funded by FMF grant funds. TLA costs are normally funded by the other DOD and DOS grant programs.

Cancellation Penalties

Because of the shortage of training quotas and the difficulty experienced by the military service training activities in adjusting to quota changes, DOD has instituted a penalty charge for IMS no-shows and for late-notice cancellations. Normally, country training programs are subject to a penalty charge of 50 percent of the tuition price of canceled courses if notification is not received more than sixty days prior to scheduled course start dates. The penalty is applied based upon determination by the MILDEP that lack of timely cancellation was the fault of the country. A pro rata charge of not less than 50 percent of the tuition price is assessed for IMS who fail to complete scheduled training due to illness, academic deficiency, or for disciplinary reasons. A cancellation penalty of 100 percent of the tuition price may be assessed if the training is provided by a contractor or a dedicated military service training activity that trains only international military personnel. It is very important to review each of the military service's cancellation penalty policy messages that are updated each year. Some courses identified in the messages are accessed 100 percent penalties no matter when the course is cancelled once it has been on the STL in confirmed status for thirty days. The policy messages can be found on the International Training Management web site (http://www.disam.dsca.mil/pages/itm/pages/messages/). Cancellation of 5th quarter IMET quotas also results in a 100 percent cancellation penalty fee.

STUDENT ADMINISTRATION

Even before a requested course of instruction has been approved, the administration of the student must begin. This administrative process can be separated into three distinct phases: pre-training, during training, and post-training.

Pre-Training Phase

The pre-training phase is the responsibility of the overseas SCO training manager in conjunction with host country counterparts. It begins with the selection of a prospective IMS.

Student Selection Criteria

Synthesizing DOD guidance on the type of person to be given preference for training under SA, one can construct a composite of student requirements:

- Leadership potential—Individuals who are in the future likely to occupy key positions of responsibility within the host nation's armed forces

- Retainability—Career personnel, in the case of professional level schools

- Utility—Persons who will be employed in the skill for which trained for a sufficient period of time to warrant the training expense

To broaden the IMS capability of the foreign military establishment, consideration should also be given to training persons with instructor ability, either as the prime reason for training, or as follow-on training to technical instruction.

SCO personnel are instructed to follow the above guidance and emphasize these criteria when projecting country IMET program requirements. Countries requesting FMS training apply the same criteria for the same reasons, i.e., proper and effective utilization of human and materiel resources.

Other aspects of the pre-training phase include: determining whether the IMS meets the physical and language prerequisites for the course or if additional English language training must be scheduled, ensuring physical/dental examinations are completed in accordance with policy, and verifying IMS has correct documentation to enter the US. Of particular importance is the screening, and possible Leahy Vetting, of the candidate IMS.

14-23

International Military Student Screening

For all US-sponsored training programs (regardless of funding), thorough and effective screening must be conducted by post on IMS candidates to ensure they have no history of involvement in human rights abuses, drug trafficking, corruption, criminal conduct, and/or other activities that are inconsistent with US foreign policy goals. It is up to each embassy country team to determine how that screening process will be conducted and then document the process in local standard operating procedures (SOPs). Normally, the following US organizations at post assist in the screening process: Human Rights Officer, Regional Security Officer (RSO), Drug Enforcement Agency (DEA), Consular Section, Pol-Mil, Defense Attaché Office (DAO), and other offices as appropriate. If an individual's reputable character cannot be validated, the individual will not be approved for training.

Leahy Amendment and Vetting

In addition to IMS screening requirements by post, increased Congressional interest in human rights violations worldwide has resulted in more stringent statutory guidance and limitations on training, especially that which is funded with US-appropriated dollars. The so-called Leahy Law or Leahy Amendment—after Senator Patrick Leahy of Vermont—was first enacted in 1997 as part of the annual appropriations act for State Department-managed programs, such as IMET. It prohibited use of appropriated funds for foreign security force units implicated in human rights violations unless the Secretary of State determined that the host nation was taking effective measures to bring those responsible to justice. Over the years, the Leahy Amendment has taken different forms and is now permanently in FAA section 620M which states that no assistance shall be furnished under the FAA or the AECA to any unit of the security forces of foreign country if the Secretary of State has credible information that such unit has committed a gross violation of human rights. Similar language occurs for DOD-funded training in the annual DOD appropriations act. The DOD Appropriations Act states that none of the funds made available by this Act may be used to support any training program involving a unit of the security forces of a foreign country if the Secretary of Defense has received credible information from the Department of State that the unit has committed a gross violation of human rights.

The purpose of the DOS and DOD Leahy Laws are three-fold:

1. To ensure that FAA and AECA-funded assistance and DOD Annual Appropriations-funded training do not support units of individuals who have committed a gross violation of human rights.

2. Encourage accountability and professionalism in foreign security forces.

3. Protect the US Government (USG) from accusations that the USG supports human rights abusers.

Once post has accomplished their local screening to validate a student's reputable character, depending on certain requirements such as if DOS or DOD funds are being used to pay for the training, post then submits the student's name and unit name via the INVEST system to Department of State (DOS) in Washington DC to be Leahy Vetted for gross violation of human rights. If an entire unit is being trained in country by a "team" of US instructors, the unit is Leahy vetted by submitting the unit and unit commander's name via INVEST to DOS in Washington DC. DOS's vetting process usually takes a minimum of ten days, upon which DOS will reply to post approving or rejecting the individual or unit to attend training. More details are in chapter 16 of this textbook.

DOS has implemented two policies in order to reduce the burden of work on the embassy country team and the SCO in regards to Leahy Vetting. First, for certain "fast track" countries, only embassy-level vetting is required for the SCO to continue processing the IMS. Second, the vetting is good for a one year period, so an IMS returning to the US for training within a year of vetting does not have to be vetted again. Detailed IMS screening and Leahy vetting guidance and information, including the fast track countries, can be found on the Security Assistance Network (SAN) under the training menu. Information on Leahy Vetting can also be found in the Security Cooperation Information Portal (SCIP) under SCO/COCOM > DISAM Presentations > SCM-O Course > Reference Materials > Leahy Vetting.

It is important for the country team at post to document the process for local student screening for reputable character and Leahy Vetting in local standard operating procedures (SOPs).

Medical Screening and Medical Coverage

The SCO must ensure that the student and any accompanying dependents are medically screened by a qualified physician and dentist to be sure they are physically fit to attend training and have no communicable diseases.

The SCO also must determine how medical coverage will be paid in the event the student and/or accompanying dependents get hurt or sick while in training. The five ways medical coverage can be paid for are:

1. Foreign Government Indemnification

2. FMS Case

3. Grant Program (cover student only)

4. Reciprocal Health Care Agreement (RHCA) or NATO/Partnership for Peace (PfP) Status of Forces Agreement (SOFA)

5. Commercial Healthcare Insurance

The SCO will identify on the student's Invitational Travel Order (ITO) the medical screening date as well as the means of medical coverage for the student and any accompanying dependents.

For detailed guidance on medical screening and medical coverage requirements, refer to the following two DSCA policy messages:

- DSCA Policy Memorandum 09-42, Medical Screening of International Military Students (IMS), Civilians, and Authorized Dependents

- DSCA Policy Memorandum 11-32, International Military and Civilian Students and Authorized Dependents Healthcare Coverage

Student Pre-Departure Briefing

The JSCET requires the SCO to provide each IMS with a thorough pre-departure briefing that is appropriate to the needs of IMS from that country. To assist in this effort, DISAM has prepared a pre-departure briefing that fulfills the JSCET requirement. It makes use of Internet-based materials and is available in English. The IMS pre-departure briefing is available online on the International Training Management (ITM) web site.

Arrival Message

It is absolutely essential that the SCO provides timely notification to the IMSO at the first training location regarding when and where the IMS will arrive. The JSCET requires that the training activity receives this notification at least two weeks before IMS arrival. If the IMS is to be accompanied by dependents, the notification must be received thirty days prior to IMS arrival. DSCA policy is that arrival messages will be provided via SC-TMS and appear on the SAN. Late or non-existent arrival messages continue to be a serious problem for the IMSO. If there are last minute changes, SCOs now have accurate point-of-contact information for all training activities on SC-TMS and should notify the IMSO immediately.

Invitational Travel Order

When authorized by the MILDEP, the SCO generates an Invitational Travel Order (ITO) using the Security Cooperation Training Management System (SC–TMS). An ITO is required for all IMS who are to receive US training. As it is their official proof of authorization, it is the most important document the IMS possesses. Attachment 14-2 is a sample ITO. DSCA has made ITOs mandatory for all IMS, even if the training is at a contractor training facility. Other student processing requirements are as specified in the JSCET.

During Training Phase

IMS receive essentially the same training as US students. In fact, although there are international-only courses, the majority of IMS are integrated directly into classes with US students. Courses can be conducted in a formal classroom setting, at a functional job site through OJT/OBS, through self-paced computer-assisted training, and/or through OTs. IMS training can take place in almost any location where US military personnel are based; nearly every DOD installation in the US has hosted an IMS at one time or another.

Although IMS are integrated into the US military education and training system as fully as possible, they still have many unique requirements. To assist the IMS while in training at a schoolhouse, the military services have directed that each installation or training activity involved in international military training designate an individual to serve as its International Military Student Officer (IMSO).

International Military Student Officer

IMSOs play a key role in international training. They serve as the training installation point-of-contact for all international training issues. Thus, the IMSO is responsible for ensuring that adequate billeting, messing, and all other IMS support requirements are satisfied. Most training activities with a large number of IMS have dedicated offices that handle IMS support issues. For training activities with smaller throughput, the IMSO function may be assigned as an additional duty or regionalized. The IMSO is truly responsible for the complete care, feeding, and well-being of the IMS while at the training activity. Included in these responsibilities is the important task of conducting the US Field Studies Program (FSP).

__United States Field Studies Program__. In accordance with DODI 5410.17, *US FSP for International Military and Civilian Students and Military-Sponsored Visitors*, commanders of DOD and military service training activities installations are responsible for establishing, operating, and administering a field studies program (FSP) for international students attending SA sponsored training at their installations. The intent of FSP is to provide students with a balanced understanding of US institutions, goals, and ideals, and to increase their awareness of how these reflect the US commitment to the basic principles of internationally recognized human rights. This is usually accomplished by taking international military students on field trips that cover specific topics identified in DODI 5410.17. Funds for conducting the FSP are generated by charges included in the training tuition price. Refer to chapter 16 of this textbook, "Human Rights and Related Concepts," for a further discussion of human rights.

Country Liaison Officers

Country Liaison Officers (CLOs) are assigned by the host country to be responsible for their IMS administration and discipline during training. CLOs are not normally in training themselves. They may accompany a particular group of students for a specified course of training, or they may be assigned on a more permanent basis with responsibility for all of their countrymen in training. If no CLO is assigned for a particular country, that country's senior student at each training installation is assumed to be in charge of his country's personnel in training for required administrative or disciplinary actions. The next level of command is assumed to be the country's defense, military, Army, Navy, or Air Force attaché or ambassador assigned to the US. If student disposition is in question, US channels of communication go from the IMSO at the schoolhouse, through the military service training activity, and then to the SCO for resolution of problems and/or clarification of the sponsoring country's desires.

Post Training Phase

To close the loop, the SCO training manager or representative should debrief the IMS when they return from training, thus performing a quality assurance check on the IMS's training experience. The retainable instructional material (RIM) issued to the IMS will be shipped from the training activity to the SCO. SCOs are advised to keep a log of when RIM is turned over to the country to be provided in turn to the IMS. Likewise, the IMS academic report will be sent to the SCO to be forwarded to the country and student. The SCO is responsible for monitoring the utilization of an IMS upon return to country, especially if the IMS was trained under the IMET program. Additionally, at select training locations, IMS who are completing their training and returning home are requested to complete a DOS IMET survey.

TRAINING PROGRAM AUTOMATION

SC training managers use multiple automation systems for the successful management of training programs. These tools include: the ITM web site and the SAN (with access to SC-TMS). The ITM web site can be used by training personnel worldwide and most training personnel also have access to the SAN. SCOs and IMSOs use the SC–TMS system on the SAN. International customers use the ISANweb. Military service training agency program managers primarily use the Defense Security Assistance Management System–Training Module (DSAMS TM). Figure 14-3 illustrates the automation tools available and who uses them.

Figure 14-3
Training Program Automation

International Training

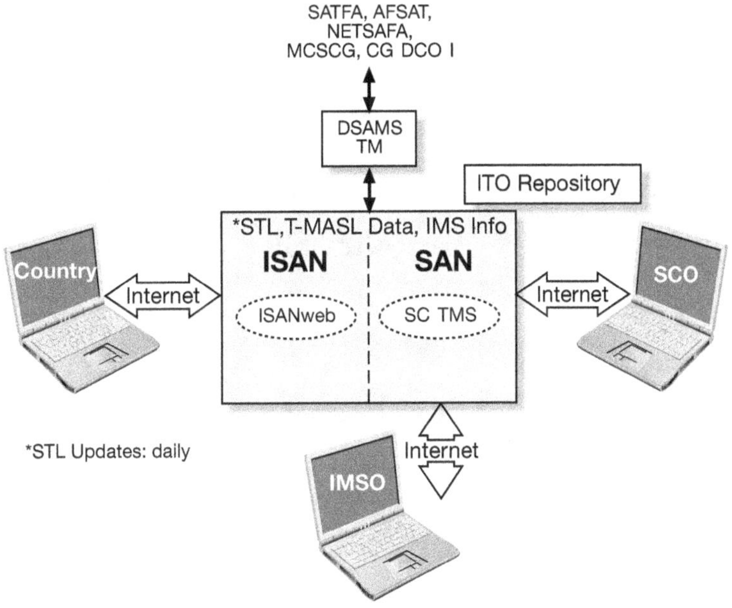

International Training Management Website

The DISAM–hosted ITM web site is available at http://www.disam.dsca.mil/itm/. It is an invaluable tool for those involved in international training, providing one-stop access to a large collection of SA/SC training materials: all current and relevant references, policies, messages, guides, or other helpful publications. The intended users are SCOs, IMSOs, DOD/MILDEP/military service training managers, IMS, and international training managers.

Security Assistance Network

The SAN is an internet-based, controlled access system used by SCOs, IMSOs, international purchasers, and other members of the DOD SA community worldwide. It contains the SA training program for each country as well as T-MASL and training location information. All SCOs and IMSOs must use the SAN and its components to perform their assigned SA training management functions. Rosters for CCMD, military service training agencies, DSCA, and DLIELC points-of-contact are available via the SAN training menu. SA training personnel access the SAN via the Internet. SCO support on the SAN is provided by the CCMD user group administrator, but requests for assistance can also be directed to DISAM. See appendix 1 of this textbook, "Security Assistance Automation," for further information on the SAN.

SC–TMS for IMSOs

IMSOs have access to certain functions within Security Cooperation–Training Management System (SC–TMS) based on the IMSO role type. IMSOs are able to see and manage training as well as IMS at their schoolhouse location. Functions available to the IMSO within SC–TMS include:

- Review course data and course descriptions contained in the MILDEP T-MASL database

- Input information about their schoolhouses (location information)

- Input specific information about their courses that are important for IMS (international notes)

- Input specific information on individual IMS including IMS travel and training status

- Submit IMS arrival/enrollment and completion/departure reports

- Maintain point-of-contact and detailed training location information

SC–TMS for SCOs

SC–TMS for SCOs provides an online view function for SCO training managers and instant access to the data that is entered by the IMSO. Functions available to the SCO through SC–TMS include:

- Access training data online (i.e., Standardized Training List [STL])

- View remarks entered by IMSOs and MILDEPs

- View current status of IMS

- Enter Student Information

- Create Invitational Travel Orders (ITO) and ITO Amendments

- IMS Arrival Information

- SCO POC Information

- Access IMSO point-of-contact and location information

- Submit the CTFP IMS nomination form

- Prepare the CETPP

ISANweb

The ISANweb provides training program information on the SAN to host nation training counterparts, giving them access to the very same country training data to which the SCO has access. The SCO training manager must request access from DISAM for host country counterparts via the SAN user menu and provide specific detail as to what training information should be made available.

Defense Security Assistance Management System Training Module

DSAMS TM is the DOD joint SA training management system for use by military service organizations. T-MASL information is loaded into DSAMS and made available on the SAN. Training requests by the SCO training manager are also programmed into DSAMS TM. Once quotas are confirmed, ITO authorizations are passed via DSAMS to the SAN. The SCO training manager can then view and act upon the information in SC–TMS. DSAMS provides significantly enhanced functions for military service country training program managers and increases information flow between SCOs and military service training activities.

SUMMARY

Training has been called the people side of SA/SC. People fly airplanes, drive tanks, and conn ships. People install, test, calibrate, and repair equipment. People manage information systems, fill requisitions, devise force postures, and implement operational plans and strategies. As long as people engage in all these activities, individual training will remain a long-lasting and indispensable part of US SA and SC efforts.

REFERENCES

Department of Defense

DSCA Manual 5105.38-M, *Security Assistance Management Manual* (SAMM). Chaps. 10 and 11. http://www.samm.dsca.mil/.

AR 12-15; SECNAVINST 4950.4A; AFJI 16-105, *Joint Security Cooperation Education and Training Regulation*.

DODI 5410.17, *United States Field Studies Program (FSP) for International Military and Civilian Students and Military-Sponsored Visitors*.

DSCA Policy Message 09-42, *Medical Screening of International Military Students (IMS), Civilians, and Authorized Dependents*.

DSCA Policy Message 11-32, *International Military and Civilian Students, and Authorized Dependents Healthcare Coverage*.

United States Air Force

AFSAT, *USAF International Military Student Officer Handbook*.

United States Navy

NETSAFA, *US Navy International Training Catalog*.

NETSAFA, *International Military Student Officer Handbook*.

United States Marine Corps

MCSCG, US *Marine International Military Student Officer Desktop Guide.* MCSCG, *Security Cooperation Education and Training Desktop Guide.*

United States Coast Guard

CG-DCO-I, *International Training Handbook.*

Defense Language Institute English Language Center

DLIELC, *Catalog of Materials, Courses, and Support Services* (Published Annually).

DLIELC Instruction 1025.7, *Planning & Programming S.A. English Language Training.*

DLIELC Instruction 1025.9, *Management of DLIELC Oral Proficiency Interview* (OPI).

DLIELC Instruction 1025.15, *English Comprehension Level (ECL) Test Guidelines.*

English Language Training Support for SCOs Handbook

Defense Institute of Security Assistance Management

SCO Training Management System User's Manual

BANDARIA COUNTRY STL

Case Identifier / Sfx MASL	Name / MASL Title	AN SC	ECL	Dur	Loc	Report Dt	Start Dt	End Dt	ITO#	TLS Sec	Pri	Est FY	UPrice	T+LA	Other	Total Cost	FS	Stu Clr
BN-B-12I001-0001 MED											B							
A B365003	MEDICAL COST-CONUS-IMET	MF		0	B834					P U	A	2012/1	$0	$0	$0	$1,890	U	
B B365003	MEDICAL COST-CONUS-IMET	MF		0	B834					P U	B	2012/2	$0	$0	$0	$0	U	
C B365003	MEDICAL COST-CONUS-IMET	MF		0	B834					P U	D	2012/1	$0	$0	$0	$315	U	
BN-B-12I001-1101 IMS											B							
A B171805	IF PREPARATORY COURSE	AA OFF	80	8w	703					P U	D	2012/3	$42,435	$24,528	$0	$66,963	U	
B B171806	ICAF	AA OFF	80	42w	705					P U	D	2012/4	$32,202	$92,906	$0	$125,108	U	
BN-B-12I001-1123 IMS HADIN VULKE						OFF 02			BNB12I0011123		B		80					Secret
A B171131	FA OFF ADVANCED PREPARATORY-ALLIED OFFICER	AB OFF	75A	3.4w	061	21-Nov-11	28-Nov-11	20-Dec-11		C U	A	2012/1	$2,459	$7,454	$0	$9,913	F	
B B171680	FIELD ARTILLERY CAPTAINS CAREER	AB OFF	75A	24.6w	061	03-Jan-12	04-Jan-12	22-Jun-12		C S	A	2012/2	$7,578	$15,329	$0	$22,907	F	
BN-B-12I001-1125 IMS MOHAMMED ALANEZI						OFF 02			BNB12I0011125		B		85					Secret
A B171772	SIGNAL CAPTAINS CAREER PREP-INTERNATIONAL	AB OFF	80A	1.8w	113	27-Dec-11	03-Jan-12	13-Jan-12		C S	A	2012/2	$2,258	$6,176	$0	$8,434	U	
B B171771	SIGNAL CAPTAINS CAREER	AB OFF	80A	20.4w	113	17-Jan-12	17-Jan-12	06-Jun-12		C S	A	2012/2	$7,710	$12,241	$0	$19,951	U	
BN-B-12I001-1126 IMS																		
Sfx B141755	AIRCRAFT STRUCTURAL REPAIRER	EB ENL	70A	15.2w	552	10-Jan-12	17-Jan-12	01-May-12		C U	A	2012/2	$2,990	$12,765	$0	$15,765	U	
BN-B-12I001-6163 IMS											B							
B B175281	COMBAT CASUALTY CARE	EM OFF	80A	0.8w	767	01-Oct-11				S U	A	2012/3	$1,709	$447	$0	$2,156	U	
C B175292	OBS MED/HEALTH/HYG-CONUS	EM OFF	80	4w	081					P U	A	2012/3	$1,744	$3,913	$0	$5,657	U	
A B175481	ADVANCED TRAUMA LIFE SUPPORT	EM OFF	80A	0.6w	767					S U	A	2012/3	$1,269	$5,568	$0	$6,837	U	
Programmed totals for SATFA													$366,417	$820,033	$0	$1,188,655		
BN-D-12I001-0001 MED											D							
A D365003	MED IMET ESTIMATES - SVC	MF		53w	D000	01-Oct-11	01-Oct-11	30-Sep-12		C U	A	2012/1	$0	$0	$0	$1,015	U	
B D365003	MED IMET ESTIMATES - SVC	MF		53	D000					C U	B	2012/1	$0	$0	$0	$0	U	
C D365003	MED IMET ESTIMATES - SVC	MF		53	D000					C U	D	2012/3	$0	$0	$0	$175	U	
D D365998	MED CIV FACILITY - SVC	MF		0w	D000	01-Oct-11	01-Oct-11	30-Sep-12		C U	A	2012/1	$0	$0	$0	$0	U	
E D365995	MED MIL FACILITY - SVC	MF		0w	D000	01-Oct-11	01-Oct-11	30-Sep-12		C U	A	2012/1	$0	$0	$0	$0	U	
F D365997	MED IMS INS POLICY REVIEW - SVC	MF		0w	D000	01-Oct-11	01-Oct-11	30-Sep-12		C U	A	2012/1	$0	$0	$0	$0	U	
G D365996	MED FLT PHYSICAL - SVC	MF		0w	D000	01-Oct-11	01-Oct-11	30-Sep-12		C U	A	2012/1	$0	$0	$0	$0	U	
BN-D-12I001-1200 IMS											D							
A D171011	INTL OFF SCH (FOR AWC)	AA OFF	80A	6w	DMAX			18-May-12		P U	A	2012/3	$15,910	$12,474	$0	$28,384	U	
B D171010	AIR WAR COLLEGE	AA OFF	80A	44w	DMAX			18-May-12		P U	A	2012/4	$36,450	$42,338	$0	$78,788	U	
BN-D-12I001-0300 TEAM																		
A D307011	DLI MTT	KL		15w	DAOTEAMS	03-Feb-12	03-Feb-12	18-May-12		C U	A	2012/2	$0	$0	$157,550	$157,550	U	
B D307011	DLI	KL		15w	DAOTEAMS	03-Feb-12	03-Feb-12	18-May-12		C U	A	2012/2	$0	$0	$0	$0	U	

ATTACHMENT 14-2
SAMPLE INVITATIONAL TRAVEL ORDER INTERNATIONAL MILITARY EDUCATION AND TRAINING

Invitational Travel Order (ITO) for International Military Student (IMS)

1. ITO Number: BNB11I0011044   2. Country/Organization: Bandaria   3. Date:10-May-11

The U.S. Government hereby issues this ITO for the IMS herein named to attend the course(s) of instruction herein listed, subject to the terms and conditions contained herein, and as may be amended by competent authority. This ITO is the only document that will be used and is valid only for the IMS entering U.S. training under the Foreign Assistance Act of 1961, as amended, or the Arms Export Control Act.

Definitions of acronyms and abbreviations contained in this document, and instructions for completing this form are provided in the Joint Security Cooperation Education and Training Regulation, JSCETR / Joint Security Assistance Training Regulation, JSATR (SECNAVINST 4950.4A/AR 12-15/AFI 16-105). This computer generated, letter format ITO is authorized in accordance with the Security Assistance Management Manual (SAMM), DoD 5105.38-M.

4. Issuing Security Cooperation Organization (SCO).
   a. Name of Organization: Office of Defense Cooperation (ODC) Bandaria
   b. Mailing Address: Unit 4095-PSC 80
                APO, AE 09765-1005
   c. E-mail Address: SCO@san.osd.mil

5. Program Type: IMET: 1-Year Intl. Military Education and Training BN-B-11I001

6. IMS Information.
   a. Surname: VULKE
      First Name: HADIN
   b. Sex: MALE
   c. Country Service Rank: MAJ
   d. U.S. Equivalent Rank/Pay Grade: O4
   e. Country Service: Army
   f. Country Service Number: OF100096
   g. Date of Birth: 10-Jan-58
   h. Place of Birth: HARARE BANDARIA
   i. Passport Number: 382956
   j. Country of Citizenship: BANDARIA
   k. Visa Number: A0000867
   l. Visa Type: A-2

7. Invitation.
The Secretary of the Department of the Army invites the IMS listed in Item 6 of this Order, to proceed from BANDARIA to FT BENNING, GA 31905, reporting on 04-Apr-11 for the purpose of commencing training listed in Item 8 of this Order.

8. Authorized Training: No additional training to that specified in this order will be provided.
Case: 11I001
   a. WCN: 1044A 107807.1   MASL: B121182   Title: AIRBORNE
      Military Service Course No: 2E-SI5P/SQI7/O   School: INFANTRY SCHOOL
      Location: FT BENNING GA 31905   Report Date: 04-Apr-11   End Date: 29-Apr-11
Case: 11I001
   b. WCN: 1044B 107807.1   MASL: B121179   Title: ARNG PRE-RANGER COURSE
      Military Service Course No: PRE-RANGER   School: ARNG WARRIOR TRNG CTR
      Location: FORT BENNING GA 31905   Report Date: 06-May-11   End Date: 04-Jun-11
Case: 11I001
   c. WCN: 1044C 107807.1   MASL: B121181   Title: RANGER
      Military Service Course No: 2E-SI5S-5R/011   School: INFANTRY SCHOOL
      Location: FT BENNING GA 31905   Report Date: 03-Jun-11   End Date: 05-Aug-11
*****Last Line*****

9. Funding.
   a. Fund Cite: 021 108110I11 A5788 0N100BN1 21TO 6007Q ARMY 6IRC71BC7BN11I 20000888 021001

10. Language Prerequisites:
   b. IMS completed In-country English Language Testing as follows:
      ECL Exam No: 36B   Date Completed: 07-Feb-11   Score: 77

11. Security and Student Screening:
   a. Human Rights, Security, and Medical Screening have been completed in accordance with SAMM Paragraph C 10.3.4 and JSATR Paragraph 10-41 for IMS listed in item 6 of this order.

12. Conditions:
   a. Dependents. Dependents are not authorized by U.S. authority to accompany the IMS or join the IMS while in training.

   b. Medical Services.
   (1) IMS:
     a. IMS under IMET.
     2. NON NATO IMS. Charges for outpatient and inpatient care, immunizations and medical examinations are chargeable to the IMETP and will be forwarded to the appropriate MILDEP for processing.
   (d) Medical Examinations.
     1. Medical Examination, to include HIV Test, was completed on 21-Mar-11.

   c. Participation in Hazardous Duty.
   IMS is authorized to participate in hazardous duty training.

   d. Physical Fitness Training.
   Participation in physical fitness training is required. Check TMS MASL Course Description, International Notes, and Prerequisites for prerequisite physical fitness requirements.

TMS generated ITO # BNB11I0011044   Page 1 of 2

    e. Leave.
      Upon completion of training, IMS is not authorized leave, and will proceed immediately as
      directed to home country.

    f. Living Allowances.
      Living allowance is authorized during period covered by this order, from day of departure from,
      to day of return arrival in , excluding period covered by leave, in
      accordance with SAMM Table C10.T3, and is chargeable to the fund cite in Item 9 of this Order.

    g. Travel.
      Travel covered by this order, overseas and CONUS, is chargeable to the fund cite in Item 9
      of this Order.

    h. Travel by POV.
      IMS is not authorized to travel by POV.

    i. Baggage.
      Training is 12 to 23 weeks in total duration: IMS authorized 3 pieces, not to exceed 50 pounds
      (22.7 kilograms) each.

13. Terms:
    a. Prior to departure from home country, the IMS and dependents listed herein are required to
      be medically examined and found physically acceptable in accordance with the health provisions
      of the Immigration and Nationality Act (8 USC 1182(A)(1)-(7); Public Health Service, Department
      of Health and Human Services, 42 CFR Part 34, Medical Examination of Aliens, and 42 CFR Part
      71, Foreign Quarantine; applicable U.S. MILDEP regulations; and other U.S. laws or DoD
      directives and regulations which may be enacted from time to time.
    b. The home country will ensure that the IMS has sufficient funds in United States dollar
      instruments to meet all expenses while in route to, and for the first 30 days of
      training pending receipt of applicable pay and allowances by the IMS.
    c. IMS will be responsible for custodial fees and personal debts incurred by self or family
      members. IMSs unable to meet these financial obligations may be withdrawn from training
      and returned to home country.
    d. The IMS will bring adequate uniforms and work clothing for field duty or technical work.
      U.S. fatigue uniforms and footwear will be purchased by the IMS in the event that the country
      work uniforms are inadequate. When flying training is involved, required special flight
      clothing and individual equipment will accompany the IMS, or provisions will be made by the
      home country or the IMS to obtain the use of all necessary equipment prior to start of
      training. The IMS will also possess adequate civilian clothing for off-duty wear.
    e. The Government of the United States is responsible for IMS travel which is part of the
      training program and for which costs are part of the course tuition.
    f. The IMS will comply with all applicable U.S. Military Service regulations.
    g. The United States may cancel training and return to country IMSs who violate U.S. law
      or Military Service regulation or who are found otherwise unsatisfactory. The IMS government
      will be alerted to such action in accordance with U.S. MILDEP regulations.
    h. The Government of the United States disclaims any liability or financial responsibilit
      for injuries received by the IMS listed herein while in transit to and from the training
      installation, while undergoing training or while in leave status, and any liability or
      financial responsibility for personal injury claims or property damage claims resulting
      from the IMS action.
    i. The IMS will participate in flights of U.S. military aircraft as required for scheduled
      course(s) or as specified in U.S. MILDEP regulations.
    j. The acceptance of this order by the host country constitutes agreement that an IMET
      funded student will be utilized, upon return to the host country, in the skills for
      which he was trained for a period of time sufficient to warrant the expense to the U.S.
      Government, in accordance with the SAMM, Chapter 10.time sufficient to warrant the expense
      to the U.S. Government, in accordance with the SAMM, Chapter 10.

14. Implementing Authority:
    a. MILDEP Authorization: 0246355   b. Date: 01-Apr-11

15. Special Conditions/Remarks:
    Upon return from training, IMS will report to ODC-Bandaria when notified, for debriefing,
    processing of travel voucher, and issuance of retainable instructional material.

16. Distribution:
    INFANTRY SCHOOL
      FT BENNING, GA 31905
    ARNG WARRIOR TRNG CTR
      FORT BENNING, GA 31905
    INFANTRY SCHOOL

17. ITO Authorization:
    a. Signature of U.S. Authority Authenticating Orders: John C. Smith, Major, US Army
    b. Title: Training Officer

☐☐

A COMPARISON OF FOREIGN MILITARY SALES AND DIRECT COMMERCIAL SALES

INTRODUCTION

In today's global economy, nations and international organizations have numerous choices among the various military systems produced throughout the world. The selection process must consider many factors such as: system cost, performance, delivery schedule, life cycle logistics support, interoperability, and industrial utilization as well as the political relationship with the selected source nation. International purchasers establish their own prioritized source selection criteria to evaluate the relative benefits and shortcomings of each system under review.

If the customer is an ally or friend of the United States (US), often the prospective purchaser will consider one or more US defense systems in their global source selection process. The Department of Defense's (DOD's) official position regarding the customer's selection is clear. The DOD prefers that allies and friendly nations choose to purchase US systems rather than foreign systems. The reason for the US preference relates to the various political, military and economic advantages derived from the US and its friends using the same military equipment.

Although DOD officially prefers that allies and friends select US systems, the DOD is generally neutral regarding the customer's choice to purchase by means of foreign military sales (FMS) or direct commercial sales (DCS). Under law, most US military systems may be purchased through either the FMS process or through DCS. The preceding chapters in this text provided a thorough explanation of the FMS process. This chapter will compare the FMS process to the DCS process.

The purpose of this chapter is not to promote one procurement method over the other. In reality, which acquisition method is best for a particular customer depends on a number of considerations. The purpose of this chapter is to examine the various areas that should be considered in making the FMS or DCS decision. By understanding these factors and applying them to a customer's specific situation, a better decision can be made regarding which method offers the best approach for a particular acquisition.

FOREIGN MILITARY SALES ONLY ITEMS

Although most defense items or services can be purchased through either FMS or DCS, in limited instances, technology or security concerns may require that sales of specific items be restricted to FMS only. The *Security Assistance Management Manual* (SAMM) C4.3.5 outlines the process for designating a particular sale or military item as FMS only. Four general criteria are used to determine if a sale is required to proceed through the FMS process. The criteria are (1) legislative/Presidential restrictions; (2) DOD/military department (MILDEP) policy, directive or regulatory requirement, e.g., the National Disclosure Policy; (3) government-to-government agreement requirements; and (4) interoperability/safety requirements for US forces. These criteria, particularly DOD/MILDEP policy, can be further understood by considering four possible elements:

1. US political/military relationship with the end-user. The geopolitical situation and security relationships are taken into account when considering the appropriateness of FMS-only. The

inherent strengths of FMS or DCS licensing methods are also considered in selecting the method that best suits the interests of US and the foreign purchaser within the context of existing world security circumstances.

2. Sale of a new or complex system or service. FMS-only may be recommended:

   - To maximize the purchaser's ability to assimilate the technologies and manage its acquisition/logistics

   - For enhanced interoperability and cooperation between US and purchaser's military forces

   - For end-items or services that require complex systems integration with other combat systems

   - For end-items or services that require access to sensitive US government (USG) databases, libraries, or software-source code

   - For end-items or services that require end-use monitoring (EUM) or on-site accountability

3. Diversion and exploitation of defense systems technologies. Security of sensitive technologies is an area of particular concern that requires greater scrutiny in the transfer process. Defense systems and munitions that are not particularly complex or sensitive, but still require enhanced control to prevent proliferation to rogue states or terrorist organizations, represent another area where FMS may be more appropriate than DCS.

4. Feasibility of separating weapon system components into FMS/DCS elements. At times, purchasers may desire all or a portion of a sale to be DCS. It is possible to separate the FMS-only aspects of a purchase from the portion that can be DCS.

The Arms Export Control Act (AECA) gives the President discretion to designate which military end items must be sold exclusively through FMS channels. This authority is delegated to the Secretary of State and executed by DOD through the Defense Security Cooperation Agency (DSCA) in close coordination with the Defense Technology Security Administration (DTSA) and the MILDEP responsible for the end item. DTSA monitors this process through its involvement with the Department of State (DOS) in reviewing commercial export license requests. The DOS will not issue a commercial export license for sales restricted to FMS only. In the absence of an export license, the only remaining method to procure US defense articles or services is the FMS process. Historical examples of FMS only items are man-portable air defense missiles, certain cryptographic equipment, precise positioning service and airborne early warning and control systems.

DIRECT COMMERCIAL SALES PREFERENCE

In instances where the USG is neutral regarding purchase by FMS or DCS, policy permits US defense firms to designate a preference that a sale of their products or services be on a DCS basis. When a company receives a request for proposal from a country and prefers a direct commercial sale, the company may request DSCA issue a DCS preference for that particular sale. Approved DCS preferences are valid for one year and are held within security cooperation offices (SCOs) and at the item manager level to allow screening of future letters of request. If the applicable implementing agency (IA) receives a request from the purchaser for a DCS preference item, the IA notifies the purchaser of the DCS preference and advises the purchaser to contact the applicable company directly.

Support of a DCS preference is a "best effort" commitment by the DOD. This means that any failure on the part of the IA to comply with the DCS preference will not invalidate any resultant FMS transaction. Items provided on blanket order lines and those required in conjunction with a system sale's total package approach (TPA) do not normally qualify for DCS preference. Customers that will be funding the purchase using Foreign Military Financing Program (FMFP) funds may be required to purchase by FMS. The Director, DSCA, may also recommend to the DOS that it mandate FMS for a specific sale.

COMBINATION OF FOREIGN MILITARY SALES AND DIRECT COMMERCIAL SALES

The comparison of FMS and DCS is generally intended to evaluate the circumstances of a particular procurement to determine which method offers the greatest advantages. However, policy permits an overall sale to be separated into an FMS portion and a DCS portion. This means that an entire sale does not have to be FMS simply because there is an FMS only component to the sale. The FMS only portion can be sold through the FMS process while the remainder of the sale proceeds on a DCS basis. Close coordination is required to ensure that the FMS only portion and the DCS portion will interface seamlessly upon delivery to the customer.

In regard to FMS material or services support for DCS, the DSCA Director issued policy memorandum 09-32, "Responses to Industry Requests for FMS Support Relating to DCS." This memorandum (see attachment 15-4) states that advance planning and coordination are essential in any situation where industry anticipates requiring both DCS and FMS elements in order to fulfill the terms of a DCS contract. Industry is reminded they are not authorized to make commitments on behalf of the USG. Industry should inform the foreign purchaser of FMS articles or services required to support the DCS purchased equipment. Examples of types of FMS support for DCS include airworthiness certification, training in US military schools, aircraft ferry or other transportation services, or the provision of FMS only articles or services. The foreign purchaser should then submit a Letter of Request (LOR) early in the DCS process to obtain the required FMS support.

SUSTAINMENT SUPPORT

Initial acquisition of a major system is just the beginning of what is required to support the system throughout its life-cycle. These systems will often be active in the customers' military inventory for more than a decade. Over this period of operational utility, a significant investment will also be made in the form of sustainment support. The method utilized to initially acquire a defense system does not obligate the purchaser to obtain sustainment support for that system through the same original acquisition method. Systems acquired by DCS are eligible to obtain FMS sustainment support for common support items. Likewise, systems acquired by FMS can be supported by DCS if the purchaser desires, with the exception of any FMS-only sustainment items.

UNITED STATES GOVERNMENT SALES SUPPORTING DIRECT COMMERCIAL SALES

The AECA, section 30, permits the USG to sell defense articles and services to US companies in connection with a proposed direct commercial sale. Sales may be made to a company incorporated in the US that has an approved export license. To be eligible, the US company must intend to incorporate the item(s) or service(s) being purchased from the USG into end items being sold to a foreign country or international organization. Services may include transportation, installation, testing, or certification directly associated with the sale. Per SAMM C11.T9, the sales must meet the following criteria:

- The end item must be for the armed forces of a friendly country or international organization

- The articles would be supplied to the prime contractor as government-furnished equipment (GFE) or government-furnished materiel (GFM) if the end item were being procured for the use of the DOD

- Any services provided must be performed in the US

- The articles and services are available only from USG sources or are not available to the prime contractor by other commercial methods at such times as may be required to meet the delivery schedule

A unique sales agreement is used by the USG for the sale of defense articles and/or services to US companies. The SAMM table C11.T11 outlines the information included in the sales agreement. Payment is required upon signature of the sales agreement. If there is an increase in the cost, the company is required to make additional cash payments to fund the costs. To allow for planning and marketing, IAs are authorized to provide cost and delivery data to authorized potential companies in advance of execution of a sales agreement. Such data are identified as estimates that are not binding on the USG.

CONCURRENT FOREIGN MILITARY SALES AND DIRECT COMMERCIAL SALES NEGOTIATIONS

For most defense articles or services, the customer has the choice to purchase by either FMS or DCS. However, it is the policy of the USG to not compete with US industry for foreign defense sales. As a result, the USG normally will not provide foreign governments with a Letter of Offer and Acceptance (LOA) to sell when it is known that a DCS contract has been requested or is already being negotiated. Any exception to this policy must be approved by DSCA.

If the purchaser obtains FMS data and later determines they should request a commercial price quote, the purchaser should cancel the LOR prior to requesting commercial data. If an LOA has been offered and the purchaser then solicits formal bids from private industry for the same item, the IA should query the country as to its intentions and indicate that the LOA may be withdrawn. If the purchaser requests FMS data after soliciting bids from contractors, the purchaser must supply information to the IA showing that commercial acquisition efforts have ceased before any FMS data is provided.

FOREIGN MILITARY FINANCING PROGRAM FUNDING

Foreign Military Financing Program (FMFP) funding (if available), is generally required to be utilized through the FMS process. The reason for this requirement is that FMFP funds are grant funds provided by the USG in order for the recipient country to enhance their national military capabilities. In general, there is an expectation that the FMS process will achieve a greater level of expenditure efficiency and capability effectiveness than may be consistently obtained through customer negotiated DCS arrangements. However, FMFP funding can, in certain circumstances, be used to fund DCS contracts. Under law, only ten countries are eligible to use FMFP funding to finance DCS contracts. The ten countries are: Israel, Egypt, Jordan, Morocco, Tunisia, Turkey, Portugal, Pakistan, Yemen, and Greece.

Although ten countries are eligible to use FMFP funds in DCS contracts, all FMFP financed purchases must be approved by DSCA on a contract-by-contract basis using *Guidelines for Foreign Military Financing of Direct Commercial Contracts* and the contractor certification provided at http://www.dsca.mil. Commercial contracts financed with FMFP must be valued at $100,000 or more and are intended for the procurement of nonstandard items (items that do not have a national stock number and are not currently being used by DOD). Offset costs are prohibited from being included on a FMFP financed DCS. Additionally, the prime contractor must be incorporated or licensed to do business in the US unless DSCA has approved an offshore procurement per the procedures in SAMM C9.7.2.7.3.

COMPARISON CONSIDERATIONS

Relationship Considerations

Under FMS, the customer is entering a direct government-to-government relationship with the USG. In fact, the customer is purchasing directly from the USG. Depending on the political climate, this can be viewed as either an advantage or a disadvantage. Some nations and international organizations desire the association implied by the FMS interaction. Other governments, where the popular view of the US is not as positive, may desire to distance themselves from the USG and enter into a DCS arrangement with a US contractor. In this situation, public opinion may view a relationship with US industry more favorably than the direct government-to-government relationship inherent in FMS.

The USG is involved in approving both FMS and DCS. For FMS, DSCA consults with the DOS for approval to develop new FMS cases. For DCS, the contractor must apply to the DOS to obtain an export license. In either method, the DOS makes the final decision to authorize military defense sales.

Under the AECA, both FMS and DCS must be notified to the US Congress if the proposed sale meets or exceeds the statutory dollar thresholds. The statutory notification requirements are essentially the same for both FMS and DCS and can be found in chapter 2 of this textbook.

Figure 15-1
Foreign Military Sales and Direct Commercial Sales Relationships

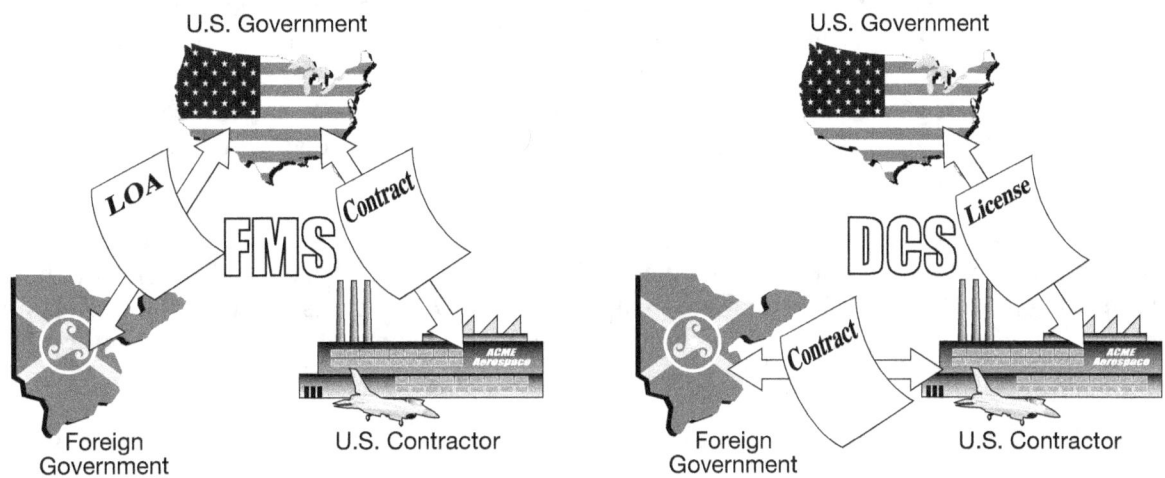

All sales of defense articles or services, FMS or DCS, must promote US strategic and foreign policy interests. This determination is made for DCS in the licensing process and for FMS in the internal coordination process of preparing an LOA. Although it rarely occurs, the USG always reserves the right to terminate a DCS export license or an FMS LOA and to halt the actual export deliveries of FMS items or DCS licensed items, when doing so is determined to be in the national interest of the US.

Other relationship considerations are decisions of technology transfer and disclosure of classified information, as discussed in chapter 7 of this text. Under a DCS arrangement, industry must apply for a license and then await the normal governmental technology transfer and disclosure process to render a decision. While industry representatives may advocate for a favorable decision with the various stakeholders, industry is external to the actual decision making process. Some industry representatives have stated that the FMS process may offer a more efficient method for technology transfer and disclosure advocacy for sensitive defense transfers. Under FMS, the DOD IA engages with the DOD technology transfer and disclosure infrastructure to advocate for the proposed sale. In this way, proposed FMS transfers garner an element of internal government sponsorship, whereas proposed DCS may have only external industry sponsorship.

Management Considerations

The FMS process is executed by US DOD civilian employees and active duty US military personnel. The direct involvement of DOD personnel in managing the procurement and delivery of a foreign purchaser's programs leads to robust communications throughout the LOA life as many day-to-day program issues are identified, evaluated, and resolved. Often, this level of communication and personal interaction is viewed as a catalyst to building stronger overall military-to-military relationships.

In DCS programs, contractor personnel can be expected to be very knowledgeable about their products. Defense contractors typically employ individuals that possess extensive experience with the DOD and often include individuals with prior active duty experience in the US military. In spite of this, many customers value the direct interaction with DOD civilian and active duty US military personnel offered through the FMS process.

Lead Times

Generally speaking, defense articles that are in production can be procured more quickly via commercial channels than through the FMS system. The FMS acquisition process involves the development, review, and acceptance of the LOA, plus the assembling of requirements for economic quantity or consolidated purchasing cycles, as well as contract negotiations, and production lead times. In the FMS process, an individual customer's priorities must be integrated into the overall DOD acquisition priority.

By contrast, after the company obtains the export license, the DCS system only involves contract negotiations and production lead times. In general, industry prepares its proposal more quickly than the USG prepares the LOA. Under DCS, the customer negotiates their own priority with industry. Industry may be capable of accelerating their processes for commensurate financial compensation. It is also possible that governments with a well-developed purchasing capability can negotiate sales contracts more quickly than DOD which is bound to the structured Federal Acquisition Regulation (FAR) process.

For secondary and support items, the DOD may maintain an inventory. In cases of an emergency for the purchaser, if the materiel is available in DOD inventories, it may be possible for the FMS purchaser to achieve faster delivery through shipment from DOD stocks or through the diversion of items that are under production for DOD. Contractors normally do not produce items in anticipation of sales and generally do not maintain an extensive inventory of defense articles.

Contract Issues

Whichever procurement method a foreign government decides is best for its situation, some basic form of legal agreement is required. The contract process has several areas that should be evaluated by prospective customers.

Under the FMS system, purchases for foreign governments are made by a well-established DOD contracting network. DOD is committed to procuring FMS defense articles and services under the same contractual provisions used for its own procurements. This system is designed to acquire the required quality items at the lowest price from qualified sources and to provide for contract administration. In fact, FMS and DOD orders are often consolidated to obtain economy-of-scale buys and therefore lower unit prices. Although DOD's procurement process offers these benefits, the foreign purchaser will be charged an appropriate fee in the LOA for the contracting and administrative services provided by DOD.

In DCS, the customer assumes contract negotiation and management responsibility. These activities represent overhead management costs to the customer in addition to the actual contract cost. Although it is not necessary for a purchaser to fully duplicate the DOD contracting network in order to make an efficient commercial purchase, the size and skill of the purchaser's contracting staff may be a limiting factor in the quantity and complexity of DCS procurements. Numerous contractors and subcontractors may be involved in supplying the entire package for a major weapon system. As a result, multiple DCS contracts may be necessary to make the total system procurement. The capability and capacity of the purchaser's indigenous procurement system must be evaluated.

Contract Negotiation

Governments with extensive business ties to the West, and which are knowledgeable of US law and financing, may perceive additional flexibility in DCS. The greater degree of flexibility in contracting is possible because US industry has no structured, regulatory guidance, such as the FAR, that must be followed as is the situation in FMS. Customers may wish to participate actively in tailoring the procurement process by fixing delivery schedules, negotiating fixed prices, including special warranty provisions and ensuring that designated penalties are stipulated for contractor failure to comply with the contractual agreement. Other flexible arrangements that may be negotiated into a DCS might include a used equipment trade-in or a sale involving a barter arrangement as partial payment.

The USG assumes responsibility for the procurement of FMS items. It determines the contract type, selects the contract source, and negotiates prices and contract terms with individual contractors. These negotiations are conducted on the same basis as procurements for DOD purchasers. Under FMS, the foreign purchaser trusts the USG to negotiate a contract that will meet the customer's needs.

The USG generally purchases directly from as many original manufacturers as possible, thereby minimizing the purchase price. This approach avoids going through a single prime contractor to procure various items from subcontractors and therefore also avoids the associated prime contractor price mark-ups on subcontracted components. Unless a country's purchasing staff is sufficiently large and skilled, a comparable procurement approach of purchasing direct from subcontractors cannot be duplicated in DCS.

Contract Administration

Under FMS, contract quality assurance, inspection, and audit services are routinely provided and are included as standard components of the overall FMS price.

For commercial contracts, the purchasing government must assess the total resources it must maintain in order to monitor production, evaluate modifications, provide for improvements, and ensure contract compliance. A large number of highly educated personnel well trained in international commerce, quality assurance, and audit processes may be required to perform such functions.

For DCS, rather than placing customer personnel throughout the US to perform contract administration functions, it may be more cost effective to acquire this support from the USG. It is possible for the customer to purchase contract administrative services for a DCS under a separate FMS case with the Defense Contract Management Agency (DCMA).

Financial Considerations

The issue of the total FMS cost in comparison to the total DCS cost is frequently a factor considered by the purchasing government. It is difficult to predict whether it would be more or less expensive to employ the FMS system or direct commercial channels for any particular acquisition. The differing contractual pricing and financing approaches, as well as variations in the total package content, make cost comparisons between FMS and DCS quite difficult.

Estimated Price Versus Final Price

The FMS system provides for estimated prices and estimated payment schedules. The final price of an FMS item or service generally will not be known until after it is delivered. The final price is determined by actual USG contract cost and other authorized FMS charges that are applied under the provisions of US laws and regulations.

The fact that the final LOA cost is generally lower than the initial LOA price estimate is a distinctive feature of the government-to-government FMS agreement. A multi-year DOD analysis of LOA prices revealed that final LOA costs generally fall below initial LOA estimates. While this is an interesting observation, the customer cannot count on their particular LOA overestimating the final cost.

DCS prices, on the other hand, typically provide a fixed price with a fixed payment schedule. Unlike FMS, DCS allows the customer to know the final price at the time of contract signature.

Support Package Differences

Under the FMS system, the USG includes all support equipment, spare parts, training and publications in the TPA. In DCS, the contractor may also develop a support package for the primary item. Depending on the factors used to develop these support packages, the actual content of the support packages may differ. As such, there may be significant cost differences in the FMS offer versus the DCS proposal even though both contain the same type and quantity of primary items.

In DCS, contractors may be able to achieve cost saving by offering other than DOD military standard configurations. It is important for the customer to understand that any deviations from typical DOD configurations could limit interoperability as well as cooperative logistics follow-on support from DOD. The cost savings achieved in the initial acquisition of a nonstandard DOD configuration may be quickly outweighed by the added cost of sustaining a nonstandard system.

Contract Price Factors

In situations where there are two or more manufacturers competing for the foreign business, DCS contract prices may be less than FMS prices. This may be possible because the manufacturers may be willing to agree to fixed prices which are below the normal profit margins allowable under DOD contracting regulations. Price advantages under DCS also may be possible during times of rapid inflation in the US, especially if the contractor has the ability to make quick deliveries from rapid new production.

The FMS process has the potential to offer lower contract prices primarily through larger quantity buys achieved by grouping DOD and multiple FMS requirements into a single procurement. Additionally, DOD may already have priced contracts in place for DOD that can also be used to support new FMS requirements. Typically, DOD has procured the same or similar items under other contracts. With this knowledge and experience, the DOD may be in a more informed position in the negotiation process. The FAR permits DOD, under certain contracting conditions, to require the contractor to substantiate their bid with supporting cost or pricing information. This is an important factor to ensure that a fair and reasonable price is being paid for the articles or services under contract.

Cash Flow Requirements

Direct commercial contracts generally require a relatively large down payment, payable at the time of contract signature. The size of such down payments varies with circumstances and the level of contractor risk. For FMS cases, the initial deposit required at the acceptance of an LOA is generally somewhat lower than commercial contract down payments. For items which have a substantial production period, the phased progress payment system used for FMS may distribute the payment burden beyond the payment requirements of commercial contracts. These possible differences in payment terms should be evaluated as part of the purchaser's procurement decision.

One special feature of the FMS system involves the potential use of cross-leveling agreements. Cross-leveling agreements allow country funds which are on deposit in the FMS trust fund to be moved to and from special holding accounts, or moved between separate FMS cases, thereby maximizing the use of country funds. Cross-leveling can be accomplished by two methods. In the first method, customer financial personnel conduct their own analysis to provide cash transfer direction to the USG. In the second method, the customer authorizes the USG, by written agreement, to conduct automatic cross-leveling to balance funds requirements among all FMS cases. Cross-leveling is in contrast to direct commercial contracts, which stand alone and typically provide for fixed prices with fixed payment schedules, but with no provision for the movement of funds between individual contracts. In short, cross-leveling under FMS provides the advantage of flexibility to the purchaser to meet changing requirements, whereas commercial sales offer the advantage of providing a final price at the time of contract signature.

Non-recurring Cost Application

The AECA requires a charge for a proportionate amount of any non-recurring costs (NC) of research, development, and production of major defense equipment sold through FMS. By contrast, DCS is exempt from these NC costs, so in this regard, it appears that DCS has an advantage. However, for customers desiring to purchase via FMS, a provision exists to potentially waive the application of NC under FMS. The purchaser can request a NC waiver when:

- Standardization benefits result to the US from the sale

- Cost saving benefits accrue to the US as a result of economic quantity purchases

- Loss of sale would occur if waiver is not granted

Waiver requests must be made by the country on a case-by-case basis and must be submitted prior to acceptance of the FMS LOA. More information on the NC waiver process is in the SAMM, C9.6.3.

Other Costs

The issue of other costs in both commercial contracts and FMS agreements requires clarification. As stated in section 3 of the LOA standard terms and conditions, the USG conducts the FMS program on a non-profit basis. Except for specific statutory exemptions, all USG expenses for FMS program performance must be recovered from the purchaser. The FMS administrative surcharge and contract administration services costs that are added to the basic price of an FMS agreement recover the cost of:

- Sales negotiations

- Case implementation

- Case management

- Contract negotiation

- Contract management

- Financial management

- Processing reports of discrepancy

- Case reconciliation/closure

SAMM table C9.T2 outlines the types of activities the DOD may perform that are funded by the FMS administrative charge. Collectively, this set of activities funded by the FMS administrative charge is referred to as the standard level of service.

For FMS, the LOA price includes the base cost that the USG paid for the item or service plus the other authorized charges necessary to recover the full cost to the USG. Although the USG does not make a profit from FMS, the price paid to DOD contractors does include a fair and reasonable profit for the contractor. However, the amount of contractor profit is limited by the provisions of the FAR. The full contract cost, including contractor profit, is paid via the LOA.

Conversely, the profit ceiling for commercial contracts is established by the marketplace. The purchasing government will not normally have access to information which reveals how much general and administrative costs or overall contractor profit is included in a direct commercial contract. US firms typically add administrative costs as part of their equipment unit prices, whereas FMS administrative costs are identified as a separate item on the FMS agreement. More information on FMS financial management is contained in chapter 12 of this text, "Financial Management."

Other Comparison Considerations

Evaluating the relative advantages or disadvantages of conducting a sale by FMS or DCS can be complex. In addition to the relationship, management, and financial issues, there are other factors that a purchaser must also examine.

Production Priority

There are many defense articles produced by US industry using production equipment provided by DOD or in USG-owned facilities. Such production equipment and facilities are made available to the contractor to fulfill DOD requirements including FMS requirements. Contractors may use such facilities and equipment for DCS only with USG approval and only when there is no adverse impact on DOD requirements. Except in times of crisis, the prioritization of the use of such equipment or facilities generally is not a problem.

The USG has established an industrial priority system to resolve conflicts in production priorities. Each US defense program is assigned a specific priority based on the program's relative importance to the USG. The USG uses its relative need for a system to settle production conflicts rather than leaving such resolution to the discretion of contractors. FMS equipment normally is purchased together with US equipment, and thereby shares the US industrial priority. DCS involves independent contracts that do not automatically receive the same production priorities as DOD procurements.

Another consideration involves GFE or GFM. Such items are generally incorporated by the contractor into larger systems which are then delivered to either DOD or a foreign government. Contractor access to GFE or GFM in support of DCS could have a significant impact on the capability of a contractor to make a direct sale. By contrast, under the FMS system, DOD coordinates delivery of GFE or GFM directly to the prime contractor for both US and FMS requirements. As identified earlier in this chapter, under certain conditions, US companies may be eligible to procure items or services from the DOD to support a DCS program.

If GFE and GFM components are not available directly to a contractor, the foreign purchaser could acquire them under FMS procedures and provide them to the contractor for incorporation in the end item. This procedure, of course, would make a commercial acquisition more complex for the purchaser and would require careful coordination of both the commercial and the FMS transaction.

Follow-on Logistics Support

An important consideration in the purchase of US defense articles involves the nature of the follow-on support that will be required from US sources. If the items being purchased are also being used by the US military, and are known to require substantial logistical, technical, and training support, an FMS purchase may offer support advantages. FMS permits the purchaser to capitalize on US experience and existing USG logistics inventories and training facilities. Under a cooperative logistics supply support arrangement, the DOD spare parts inventory can be drawn upon in support of the purchaser's requirements, and this can be accomplished by customer submission of requisitions for individual parts. In effect, the DOD logistics structure serves as procurement staff for the purchaser by procuring required individual items from the current US sources.

There are some US contractors who also are capable of providing full logistics support for the items which they sell. Corporate reputations depend on good performance and, where contractors have the capability of furnishing such support, the results can be expected to be as stated in their contracts.

The DOD may provide follow-on support for end items acquired through DCS. However, DOD's ability to support DCS items may be limited when equipment configurations differ. Also, if the manufacturer only uses commercial part numbers to identify items without cross-referencing to DOD national stock numbers, USG support will be greatly complicated and support delays may result.

Logistics support is frequently facilitated by the FMS purchaser's ability to use DOD information and data transmission systems such as:

- International Logistics Communication System (ILCS)

- Supply Tracking and Reparable Return/Personal Computer (STARR/PC)

- Air Force Security Assistance and Cooperation Center (AFSAC) Online

- Security Cooperation Information Portal (SCIP), including the Navy Community

- Federal Logistics Data (FED LOG)

- Federal Logistics Information System Web Search (WEBFLIS)

DOD also has dedicated security cooperation staffs and in-country SCOs to facilitate the administration of the FMS program. Per SAMM C2.1.8, the SCO can also provide limited support to industry. For DCS activities, the SCO's role is primarily a facilitator during industry's marketing phase rather than aiding in actual program execution (as the SCO does in support of FMS). More information on FMS logistics support is contained in chapter 10 of this text.

Nonstandard Items

Nonstandard items are those that the DOD has never used or no longer actively uses in its own operations. Standard items can become nonstandard items as DOD phases out certain items, models or configurations, replacing them with other items, models or configurations. Historically, DOD has not performed well at providing nonstandard item support. This is because DOD does not retain the logistics infrastructure in place to support items which it does not use itself. DOD has improved in this area by implementing commercial buying service (CBS) support for nonstandard items, i.e. contracting out nonstandard support. CBS support for nonstandard systems or components is usually provided via an FMS case. In general, DCS has provided better support for nonstandard items.

Training

Training is a key element to successfully operating and maintaining today's high technology military equipment. The DOD has established training resources to support its own training needs. Under FMS, customers can access many of these training resources. Although the DOD does acquire contractor training in certain circumstances, some types of military training are simply not available through commercial sources such as access to DOD's unique training ranges. On the other hand, the customer may require some form of tailored training that is not available from DOD. As an example, DOD training is normally conducted using only the English language. If the customer required training in its native language, contractor training could be an alternative training source.

Classified Items

The FMS process ensures all security provisions are in place for sales of classified items, and it also provides for required purchaser agreements to protect US concerns and to ensure the proper use of the article or service. In DCS arrangements, before an export license for classified material may be granted, security agreements establishing appropriate security measures must be executed between the purchasing government and the USG. The requirement for a security agreement is determined during the US review of the license request.

RANGE OF CHOICES

In comparing the FMS system to the DCS system, it is important to realize that the decision regarding a potential procurement actually has a range of possibilities rather than just choosing between two separate options, traditional FMS or traditional DCS. In reality, there are several options available for most acquisition scenarios. The range of options focuses on the degree of foreign purchaser participation in the overall procurement activities. In essence, the decision concerning procurement via FMS or DCS fundamentally involves a decision about the degree of procurement involvement the foreign purchaser desires to assume and what degree of procurement responsibility the foreign purchaser is willing to delegate to the DOD. Table 15-1 presents the range of options, each of which will be discussed further in the sections below.

Table 15-1
Customer Participation Options

Traditional FMS
FMS funded with FMFP
FMS with Sole Source designated
FMS with Customer Participation in Contracting
FMS with Industry Offsets
Hybrid FMS/DCS
DCS funded with FMFP
DCS with USG contract administration
DCS with Industry Offsets
Traditional DCS

Traditional Foreign Military Sales

Under traditional FMS, the foreign purchaser initiates the process by submitting an LOR to the USG. The IA will develop the necessary pricing and availability estimates to generate an LOA. Following any necessary technology transfer reviews, releasability reviews, and Congressional notifications, the IA will forward the LOA as an offer by the USG to sell the respective defense articles and/or services. If, upon review of the LOA, the foreign purchaser decides to accept the LOA, a foreign government representative will sign the LOA and forward the initial deposit to the Defense Finance and Accounting Service (DFAS) Security Cooperation Accounting (SCA). At this point, per the SAMM C5.4.16, the foreign purchaser and the USG have entered a formal sales agreement for the provision of defense articles and services.

The LOA standard terms and conditions define the nature of this sales relationship. Section 1.2 specifically defines the procurement responsibilities and states that the foreign purchaser has delegated the procurement process to the DOD. The DOD will conduct the procurement on behalf of the customer using the same regulations and procedures that DOD uses to procure for itself. Under traditional FMS, the foreign purchaser is not responsible for accomplishing any procurement actions following acceptance of the LOA. Under the provisions of the LOA, the DOD takes responsibility for:

- Conducting the entire procurement process to include contractor source selection and negotiating the contract terms and conditions

- Contract administration, quality control, inspection, acceptance, and audit functions

As a very broad generalization, the traditional FMS process can be characterized as a foreign purchaser, by means of the LOA, employing the DOD to conduct defense procurement on its behalf. As such, the foreign purchaser entrusts the DOD to make decisions and take actions on its behalf. The foreign purchaser relies on the good faith commitment that DOD makes to conduct FMS procurement business in essentially the same manner that it conducts procurement business for itself. In this relationship of trust, there is no need for direct participation of the foreign purchaser in the procurement. DOD will execute the procurement based on the content of the LOA. However, as discussed in chapter 9 of this text, "Foreign Military Sales Acquisition Policy and Process," both the SAMM and the *Defense Federal Acquisition Regulation Supplement* (DFARS) permit limited customer participation in the contracting process.

Sole Source Foreign Military Sales

Foreign purchasers often have an interest in reviewing various vendors' business proposals to fulfill a particular defense requirement. Depending on the country and type of purchase, there can be significant interest in source selection, i.e., deciding which vendor(s) will fulfill their contract. FMS procedures offer the foreign purchaser an important opportunity for direct involvement in that decision. Sole source procedures allow the foreign purchaser to request the DOD initiate a particular FMS procurement exclusively with a specific vendor of the foreign purchaser's choice. This process is referred to as sole source procurement. Details on the sole source process are presented in chapter 9 of this textbook, "Foreign Military Sales Acquisition Policy and Process."

Approved sole source requests are documented within the LOA notes and serve as the basis for the USG contracting officer to negotiate on a non-competitive basis with the specific company identified in the LOA. Under sole source, the foreign purchaser can be involved in source selection just as they would under DCS, while still benefiting from the FMS system's extensive expertise in contract negotiation, contract administration, quality control, inspection, acceptance, and audit functions.

Foreign Military Sales with Offsets

Offsets offer a mechanism for the foreign purchaser to leverage a major defense acquisition to obtain other domestic benefits for the foreign purchaser's nation. The concept of offsets is presented in detail in chapter 9 of this textbook, "Foreign Military Sales Acquisition Policy and Process." Many international customers have the misconception that offsets are only compatible with DCS procurements, but this is not true. Offset agreements can occur in conjunction with customer-funded FMS cases, but FMS cases financed with FMFP funds or other non-repayable credits are not permitted to include any offset costs.

Combination of Foreign Military Sales and Direct Commercial Sales

Another procurement option is to divide an overall procurement into both an FMS portion and a DCS portion. The SAMM permits FMS cases to be prepared to support elements of a DCS procurement. This is particularly applicable to sales that may include certain FMS-only items in the total system package. Additionally, FMS policy permits foreign purchasers to obtain follow-on logistics support by means of FMS for systems that were originally procured via DCS or by DCS for systems originally procured via FMS.

Direct Commercial Sales with Foreign Military Financing Program

Typically, countries that receive FMFP funds must use those funds via the FMS process. However, under law, ten countries are authorized, on a contract-by-contract basis, to use their FMFP funds in DCS contracts. This alternative was discussed earlier in this chapter under the section titled "Foreign Military Financing Program Funding."

There are very strict procedures governing the process for funding a DCS with FMFP, but this remains an option to be considered by these ten countries.

Direct Commercial Sales with United States Government Contract Administration

Countries with extensive international procurement expertise may prefer to independently conduct their own defense procurements directly with US industry. Typically, the only USG involvement in a DCS arrangement would relate to the export license approval decision. However, foreign purchasers should recognize they can purchase contract administration services (CAS) from the Defense Contract Management Agency (DCMA) to obtain CAS for their DCS.

While the foreign purchasers' government representatives may possess all the skills and abilities to negotiate a favorable contract with US industry, the subsequent process for DCS contract administration, quality control, inspection, acceptance, and audit functions may present both a logistical and financial barrier. The US contractor may perform work at multiple geographically dispersed locations. As such, it may be difficult and expensive for the foreign purchasers' representatives to conduct these functions throughout the US.

Acquiring CAS from DCMA for self-negotiated DCS may be a cost-effective option to support DCS. Under this approach, upon receipt of an LOR, DCMA would develop an LOA for the cost of its CAS in support of the particular DCS. Under the LOA, DCMA uses its existing contract administration infrastructure to perform CAS on behalf of the foreign purchaser.

Direct Commercial Sales with Offsets

Customers electing to conduct their defense procurement via DCS may also choose to require industry to provide an offset in association with the sale. The limitation is that DCS contracts funded by USG FMFP, or other nonrepayable funds, cannot include an offset agreement.

Traditional Direct Commercial Sales

Traditional DCS offers the foreign purchaser the greatest degree of direct involvement in their US-sourced defense procurement. In DCS, the foreign purchaser directly interfaces with the contractor on all elements of the contract without DOD being an intermediary. Traditional DCS provides a range of opportunities. However, the foreign purchaser must be prepared to accept a significant level of responsibility.

Under traditional DCS, the USG essentially has no direct involvement in the procurement process except for one essential element–the export license. For a DCS of defense articles or services, the US company that is preparing to enter a sales contract with the foreign purchaser must first obtain USG approval for the sale. This approval is indicated in the form of an approved export license. More detailed information on the export license process is contained in chapter 7.

Following export license approval, the USG does not participate in the DCS. This exclusion includes contract negotiation, contract administration, quality control, inspection, acceptance, and audit functions. In DCS, the old saying: "you get what you negotiate" applies. In general, US defense contractors will work diligently to deliver quality items and services in accordance with all of the contract provisions. They are in business for the long term and are very interested in maintaining a positive relationship with each of their customers, as well as maintaining a solid reputation in the international marketplace.

In spite of all the positive intentions, the performance of major acquisition contracts will inevitably generate a variety of issues that must be resolved. In the DCS scenario, the foreign purchaser must be prepared to address the contractor directly to resolve any issues that arise. The promptness and acceptability of the resolution will depend solely upon the country and the defense contractor. Although the DOD may concurrently be procuring the same or similar items with the same contractor, DOD is not a participant in the DCS contract and therefore has no legal authority to direct the contractor in any aspect of DCS contract performance.

Summary

The FMS and DCS systems are simply different procurement methods that a foreign government may employ for the purchase of US defense articles and services. In a commercial acquisition, a US contractor and a foreign government enter into a direct contract in accordance with US law and regulations and provisions of international commercial law. The USG is not a party to these commercial contractual transactions. The foreign government has the responsibility to select the source and manage the contract directly with the US contractor.

Under the FMS system, the USG and the foreign purchaser enter into an agreement, the FMS LOA, which specifies the terms and conditions of the sale. Except for items supplied directly from DOD inventory, the USG purchases the desired items or services from the US manufacturer on behalf of the foreign government. The DOD employs essentially the same procurement criteria as if the item/service was being purchased for US needs. The USG, not the foreign government, selects the source and manages the contract, consistent with the provisions of the FAR, DFARS, and the LOA.

Unless the USG has determined that a specific item or service will only be offered via FMS, there are few absolutes which dictate that all countries should select exclusively either FMS or commercial channels for a given purchase requirement. Rather, there are many considerations, unique both to the individual purchaser and to the items being procured, that are involved in such a choice. In fact, in comparing the FMS system to the DCS system, it is important to realize that the decision regarding a potential procurement actually has a range of possibilities rather than just choosing between two separate options, traditional FMS or traditional DCS. The question of whether to procure via FMS or DCS ultimately involves a decision by the customer about how much procurement responsibility they are willing to assume and how much they are willing to delegate to the DOD.

The final decision on purchasing channels varies from country to country, and even from purchase to purchase. Given the variety of factors involved, it is important that the purchasing government's decision encompass as many factual considerations as possible.

References

DSCA Manual 5105.38-M. *Security Assistance Management Manual* (SAMM). Chaps. 2, 4, 6, 9, and 11. http://www.samm.dsca.mil/.

Guidelines for Foreign Military Financing of Direct Commercial Contracts and Contractor's Certification and Agreement. www.dsca.mil/DSCA.memoranda/fmf_dec_2009/2009_Guidelines_for_FMF_of_DCS.pdf

Contractor's Certification and Agreement with DSCA August 2009. (www.dsca.mil/DSCA_memoranda/fmf_dcc_2009/Contractor_Certificationv4.pdf

Potential Advantages	Considerations
Total package approach based on US military experience	Purchaser must decide whether the total package approach may exceed its needs or financial capabilities
USG uses its own procurement procedures and acts as procurement agent for foreign countries	Sophisticated foreign purchasing staff may (or may not) be able to achieve better overall deal by negotiating directly with the contractor.
Proven and established logistics support for items common to DOD	Contractor may be able to offer a similar range of contractor logistics support.
Federal acquisition regulations, economic order quantity buys, use of GFE or GFM tends to reduce price	Compliance with DOD procedures may increase lead time
Facilitates establishment of design configuration and enhances potential for interoperability	Purchaser must decide on the degree of standardization required for a purchase.
Purchaser pays only the actual cost to DOD (including management expenses), with profits controlled by the FAR	While initial LOA estimates tend, in the aggregate, to be higher than final LOA costs, final costs fluctuate both up and down.
Cross-leveling in the FMS trust fund can maximize use of country funds	Firm fixed price contracts and fixed payment schedules can be obtained under direct commercial contracts.
Quality control to ensure item meets MILSPECs is done by USG personnel	This service can be purchased under FMS for certain commercial contracts.
Items may be available from DOD stocks in times of emergency	Availability is significantly dependent on DOD's own priorities and inventory positions
Government-to-government obligation, assuring involvement of DOD personnel in total package planning and sustainment concepts	Due to the political climate, the purchaser may prefer procuring from the US contractor rather than the USG.
Total package includes training at US military schools	Purchaser can procure hardware under commercial contract and generally obtain associated training at US military schools via FMS.
FMS customers can require offsets in FMS-related contracts	Dependent on the funding source. If non-repayable FMFP, offset cost cannot be included

ATTACHMENT 15-2
DIRECT COMMERCIAL SALES—POTENTIAL ADVANTAGES AND CONSIDERATIONS

Potential Advantages	Considerations
Potential for fixed delivery or fixed price, with penalty if contractor fails	Requires considerable experience and sophistication by country negotiators.
Business-to-business relationship allows country to negotiate cost and contract terms.	If closer military-to-military relationships are a purchaser's objective, FMS provides an avenue to achieve this objective.
Direct negotiations with contractor can result in a quicker response.	Requires considerable experience and sophistication by country negotiations.
Generally better support for nonstandard items.	Purchaser must decide upon desired degree of standardization with US forces.
More capability to tailor package to unique country needs.	Tailored package may detract from standardization desires.
Continuity of personal contacts with contractor technical personnel.	Value of continuity must be compared to the value of direct miltary-to-military contacts.
New equipment directly from production line.	Option exists to request only new and unused items via FMS.
Lower prices possible under certain circumstances.	Final price may be dependent on experience and sophistication of country contract negotiators.
Generally fixed payment schedule which eases budgeting problems.	Payment schedules may be more front-loaded than under FMS.
Purchaser can include offset provisions in one contract.	Purchaser can negotiate offsets (directly with contractor) and still procure under FMS.
FMS administrative surcharge and DOD management costs can be avoided.	Purchaser must consider entire cost of transaction, including its contracting staff costs and possibly increased contract administrative costs.
Commercial purchases of some types of items could help to create and develop a procurement capability.	Scarcity of resources and time may not allow for retaining procurement staff.

ATTACHMENT 15-3
COMMON MISPERCEPTIONS OF FOREIGN MILITARY SALES OR COMMERCIAL SALES

Misperceptions	Facts
FMS offers better assurance for approval of transfer of technology.	Technology release considerations are identical for FMS and commercial sales.
Commercial sales offer a better assurance for approval of transfer of technology.	Technology release considerations are identical for FMS and commercial sales.
FMS is unreliable during hostilities involving either the user or the USG.	Foreign policy or DOD military priority decisions affect the flow of supplies to a country and can be expected to relate to the resources involved. FMS orders may still be filled and may receive priority support depending on the nature of the hostilities.
Commercial sales are unreliable during hostilities involving either the user or the USG.	Foreign policy or DOD military priority decisions affect the flow of supplies to a country and can be expected to relate to the resources involved. FMS orders may still be filled and may receive priority support depending on the nature of the hostilities.
FMS provides slow delivery with frequent slippages.	The numerous built-in FMS system safeguards do sometimes slow the procurement process, but there are seldom slippages once delivery schedules are established. However, in a contingency, a potential exists to divert items from stocks and expedite delivery.
Nonrecurring cost recoupment charges for major defense equipment is always assessed on FMS.	Nonrecurring cost recoupment waivers may be authorized for FMS on a case-by-case basis. Recent history indicates a high probability of waiver approval.
A country cannot have an offset arrangement when they have an FMS case.	A country may negotiate a separate arrangement with the contractor in addition to an FMS agreement, but the USG will not be the enforcer of offset arrangements between the country and the commercial contractor.
No purchaser control or participation is permitted in FMS.	Selection of configuration, range and depth of spares, support equipment, etc., remains in control of purchaser. Program management review conferences are held as necessary to assure purchaser needs are met. Under certain circumstances, the purchaser may participate in selected contract discussions.
FMS system is characterized by a lack of continuity of personnel contact due to military personnel rotations.	While this may be true for some cases, there are many DOD civilians who do not rotate. Also, military tour is normally three to four years, about equal to commercial executive transfer patterns.

Misperceptions	Facts
Only FMS requires USG approval and Congressional notifications [section 36(b), AECA], if necessary	All items meeting AECA notification thresholds require notification under both sales systems. AECA, section 36(c), applies to commercial sale notifications to Congress.
USG reserves the right to terminate only FMS in the US national interest but not DCS.	Applies equally to both FMS and commercial sale systems.
Quality control is not assured for items bought commercially.	Contractor sales depend on product reputation. Also, USG quality control procedures may be purchased for standard items.
Contractor involvement stops once an end item is sold.	Contractor participation in follow-on support and maintenance programs is common under either commercial or FMS.
USG controls third country sales only for items sold under FMS	Criteria and policy are the same for items purchased through either commercial or FMS.

DEFENSE SECURITY COOPERATION AGENCY
201 12TH STREET SOUTH, STE 203
ARLINGTON, VA 22202-5408

AUG 0 4 2009

MEMORANDUM FOR SEE DISTRIBUTION

SUBJECT: Responses to Industry Requests for Foreign Military Sales (FMS) Support
Relating to Direct Commercial Sales (DCS), DSCA Policy 09-32
[SAMM E-Change 137]

Advance planning and coordination are essential in situations involving sales to
foreign partners that combine both FMS and DCS elements, particularly when those sales
originate through DCS channels. On occasion, industry has asked the United States
Government (USG) to provide FMS support (e.g., airworthiness certification, training in
U.S. military schools, ferrying aircraft, and the provision of equipment or components
available only through FMS channels) to fulfill terms of DCS contracts.

Whether or not there is a DCS contract, industry is not authorized to make
commitments on behalf of the USG and the USG cannot be held liable for industry's
inability to provide support in conjunction with DCS - even if requested by the FMS
purchaser. It is in industry's best interest to advise the foreign purchaser if FMS articles
or services are required to support DCS purchased equipment. In this case, the purchaser
must submit a Letter of Request (LOR) to obtain support and industry should inform
DSCA and the relevant Implementing Agency of the possibility of a requirement for
FMS support early in the process. Additionally, Security Cooperation Officers providing
support to U.S. companies in-country must be alert to the need for the purchaser to
submit a LOR and remind their foreign counterparts and industry representatives of this
requirement.

Chapters 4 and 5 of the Security Assistance Management Manual (SAMM) have
been updated to provide additional guidance on the importance of advance coordination
in circumstances involving FMS support in conjunction with DCS.

If you have any questions concerning this policy or the SAMM, please contact Ms.
Kathy Robinson, DSCA-STR/POL, at (703) 601-4368 or e-mail: kathy.robinson@dsca.mil.

Jeffrey A. Wieringa
Vice Admiral, USN
Director

Attachment:
As stated

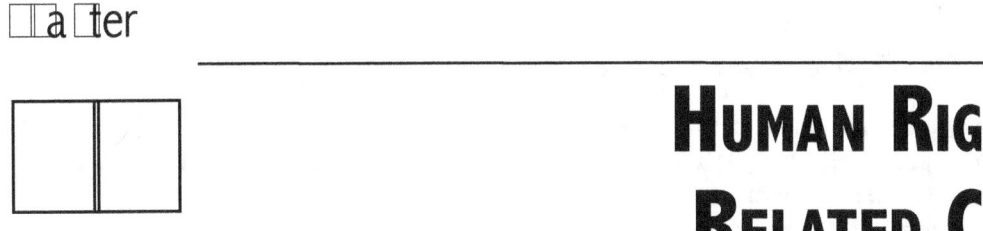

HUMAN RIGHTS AND RELATED CONCEPTS

INTRODUCTION

Human rights, which constitute a fundamental category of rights, may be defined as a relationship between individuals (citizens) and governments (states). The concept that legal systems should protect the rights of individuals from abuses by government is rooted in natural law. As reflected in his *Two Treatises of Government*, published in 1690, the English philosopher John Locke believed that human rights, not governments, came first in the natural order of things.

Civil and political rights are often referred to as fundamental or core human rights. Examples include the rights to life, liberty, security; freedom from enslavement, torture, and cruel, inhuman, or degrading punishment; freedom from arbitrary arrest, and presumption of innocence until found guilty by a competent and impartial tribunal. All citizens have the right to participate in their governments, either directly or through free elections of their representatives.

Governments have also created economic, social, and cultural rights or perhaps more accurately, entitlements, such as a minimum living standard, including food, clothing, housing, medical care, education, and social security.

Human rights considerations have been a long-standing element of the US foreign policy. Members of the security cooperation community, in particular, should understand and appreciate the importance accorded human rights and civilian control of the military in our relationships with other nations. This importance is reflected in a variety of ways. Countries suspected of gross human rights violations can be prohibited by Congress from participating in security assistance programs or have their programs suspended. International students attending US military schools under the International Military Education and Training (IMET) and Foreign Military Sales (FMS) programs are purposely exposed to human rights policies and issues as part of their studies. Foreign military members are frequently invited to attend fully funded regional seminars focused on human rights and civilian control of the military.

US personnel permanently assigned or temporarily deployed to foreign nations should be able to intelligently discuss the important human rights themes and policies of the US government (USG). The purpose of this chapter is to introduce and familiarize the reader with these key concepts and ideas.

HUMAN RIGHTS INSTRUMENTS AND AUTHORITY

Several nations have constitutions, fundamental or organic laws that establish the framework of the government of a state, assign the powers and duties of governmental agencies, and establish the relationship between the people and their government. Constitutions may be written, e.g., the US Constitution, or unwritten, as in the English model. Domestic guarantees concerning human rights may be embodied in such constitutions or in other statutes. In addition, international protection of recognized human rights is found in documents such as the Charter of the United Nations (UN Charter) and international conventions which have been accepted by the vast majority of the world's states. Regional declarations also recognize the existence of human rights.

United States Sources

The Constitution of the United States of America

Human rights have been an integral part of America as a nation from its inception. The Constitution of the United States specifically and deliberately embodies the principles of human rights. It does so generally by intoning the necessity of these principles in the opening Preamble. The basic Constitution outlines the plan of representative government and an electoral mechanism through which the people can express their will. It declares specific human rights principles in the text of the constitution's first ten amendments or, as they are more commonly referred to, the Bill of Rights. These amendments contain a listing of the rights that Americans enjoy that cannot be infringed upon by the government. Included are freedom of religion, freedom of speech, the right of the people to be secure in their persons and houses against unreasonable searches and seizures, and other rights commonly taken for granted by US citizens.

Although these principles were not definitively articulated in the body of the original text of the US Constitution, it is clear that a majority of the delegates present at the constitutional convention intended for a number of basic egalitarian principles or human rights to be incorporated within the constitutional scheme. The US Congress, in one of its first sessions, debated the inclusion of these principles through amendments, ultimately approving them. The original thirteen states, for their part, ratified ten of the original twelve proposed. Collectively, in many ways, the ten amendments compiled in the Bill of Rights represent and have come to symbolize the embodiment of the American character. It also is a tangible reminder of what America and Americans often hold most dear, their identity as a people, and their realization as individuals.

Declaration of Independence

The Declaration of Independence, adopted by the Second Continental Congress on July 4, 1776, also makes reference to certain self-evident truths such as the equality of all men, natural rights, government by consent, and so forth. Unlike the Bill of Rights, which is incorporated into the US Constitution, the Declaration does not have any legal effect today. Nonetheless, it is recognized throughout the world as the basic statement of the American creed.

International Sources

Charter of the United Nations

The UN Charter, which entered into force in 1945, specifically addresses human rights in its preamble and in two of its articles. Article 55 reads as follows:

With a view to the creation of conditions of stability and well-being which are necessary for peaceful and friendly relations among nations based on respect for the principle of equal rights and self-determination of peoples, the UN shall promote:

- Higher standards of living, full employment, and conditions of economic and social progress and development

- Solutions of international economic, social, health, and related problems, and international cultural and educational cooperation

- Universal respect for, and observance of, human rights and fundamental freedoms for all without distinction as to race, sex, language, or religion

Article 56 of the UN Charter states that all members pledge themselves to take joint and separate action in cooperation with the UN to achieve the purposes set forth in article 55.

United Nations Universal Declaration of Human Rights

Due to the general language of Article 55 of the UN Charter, member states quickly turned to efforts to specify its meaning. The first result was the often cited and widely heralded Universal Declaration of Human Rights (UDHR), which was adopted by the UN General Assembly in 1948. It is important to recognize that the Universal Declaration is not binding international law, but a UN recommendation to nations. Thus, the Declaration, in and of itself, offers no means of implementation other than through the good will of the member states.

Notwithstanding these technical deficiencies, the Declaration was, and still is, important because it is an attempt at authoritatively stating the meaning of Article 55, and parts of the Declaration reflect customary international law.

The Universal Declaration covers civil and political rights in articles 1 through 22 and social, economic and cultural rights in articles 23 through 28. Article 29, known as the derogation clause, permits limitations of rights when necessary for securing the rights of others or securing morality, order or general welfare in society. The text of the Universal Declaration is in attachment 16-1.

Human Rights Treaties

In addition to the UN Charter and Universal Declaration, there are a number of international human rights conventions which are often in the form of treaties or international agreements. These conventions are compiled in an appendix to the annual *Country Reports on Human Rights Practices*, produced by the Department of State (DOS). The US is shown in the 2012 report as a party to twelve agreements (having signed and ratified), and seven other agreements (having signed but not ratified). In addition, any nation that is a party or signatory to an agreement can attach specified reservations to such an agreement.

The following international conventions and agreements were selected from the Country Reports appendix:

Geneva Conventions. These refer to agreements among nations, reached in Geneva, Switzerland, relative to wartime situations and sometimes referred to as part of international humanitarian law or the law of armed conflict. Included are the *Geneva Convention Relative to the Treatment of Prisoners of War*, and the *Geneva Convention Relative to the Protection of Civilian Persons in Time of War*, both dated 12 August 1949. The US is listed as a party to both agreements. These are expansions of similar humanitarian conventions of 1906 and 1929. The rights protected by the Geneva Conventions may not be limited or abrogated. In an armed conflict situation, the Geneva Conventions and the customary law of armed conflict are the primary sources of law. Although listed in the appendix to the annual *Country Reports on Human Rights Practices*, produced by the DOS, these treaties are not part of international human rights law. Rather they are part of a separate and distinct category known as "international humanitarian law" that deals with the specific situation of armed conflict.

International Covenants. The US is listed as a party to the International Covenant on Civil and Political Rights of 16 December 1966. The Covenant, which is regarded by many to be the single most important human rights treaty, codifies the essential freedoms people must enjoy in an effective democratic society, such as the right to vote and participate in government, freedom of peaceful assembly, equal protection under the law, the right to liberty and security, and freedom of opinion and expression. Temporary limitations or "derogations" on Civil and Political Covenant rights are permissible during "times of public emergency." However, "derogation" is never allowed when there is an obligation to protect the right to life, to preserve the freedom of conscience, or to protect against the prohibition against torture and slavery. Subject to a few essential reservations, e.g., to reflect the requirements of the First Amendment of the US Constitution, the principles that the Covenant expresses are entirely consistent with the US Bill of Rights. The US is also listed as a signatory, but not a party, to a second related covenant, the International Covenant on Economic, Social, and Cultural Rights of 16 December 1966, which requires state parties to provide subsistence, education and medical care "to the maximum of its available resources."

Other Treaties. Additional agreements to which the US is listed as a party in the appendix to the Country Reports are:

- Convention to Suppress the Slave Trade and Slavery of 25 September 1926, as amended by the Protocol of 7 December 1953

- Convention on the Prevention and Punishment of the Crime of Genocide of 9 December 1948

- Convention on the Political Rights of Women of 31 March 1953

- Supplementary Convention on the Abolition of Slavery, the Slave Trade, and Institutions and Practices Similar to Slavery of 7 September 1956

- Convention Concerning the Abolition of Forced Labor of 25 June 1957

- International Convention on the Elimination of All Forms of Racial Discrimination of 21 December 1965

- Protocol Relating to the Status of Refugees of 31 January 1967

- Convention against Torture and Other Cruel, Inhuman or Degrading Treatment or Punishment of 10 December 1984

Customary International Law

The most fundamental human rights, such as the right to be free from extra-judicial killings, torture, arbitrary arrests, detentions and disappearances, genocide and slavery, are generally thought to be customary international law. A distinction is made between conventional international law and customary international law. With conventional international law, nations that are parties to a treaty or convention explicitly agree to be bound by certain rules. With customary international law, consent is implicit and founded in international practice. This would make these principles legally binding internationally on all nations even if they have not ratified the applicable human rights treaties. Customary international law arises when there exist long-standing and continuous practices by countries that are rooted in the belief that the practice is required by, or consistent with, international law. Customary law also exists when there is a general acceptance, not only of the practice, but of the belief of the practice by other states. The *US Army Operational Law Handbook* (2012) states, "Unfortunately, for the military practitioner there is no definitive 'source list' of those human rights considered by the United States to fall within this category of fundamental human rights. As a result, the Judge Advocate (JA) must rely on a variety of sources to answer this question. These sources may include, but are not limited to, the UDHR, Common Article III of the Geneva Conventions, the Restatement (Third) of The Foreign Relations Law of the United States, and authoritative pronouncements of US policy by ranking government officials."

Figure 16-1 provides human rights excerpts from various international sources, ranging from the UN Charter to regional agreements.

Figure 16-1
Illustrations of Human Rights Provisions

"We the peoples of the United Nations determined to reaffirm faith in fundamental human rights. . . ."   Preamble to the Charter of the United Nations, composed in San Francisco, June 26, 1945.
"All human beings are born free and equal in dignity and rights . . . "   Universal Declaration of Human Rights, adopted by the UN General Assembly, December 10, 1948.
"Everyone has the right to respect for private and family life, his home and his correspondence."   Article 8.1 European Convention for the Protection of Human Rights and Fundamental Freedoms, done in Rome November 4, 1950.
"All peoples have the right of self-determination. By virtue of that right they freely determine their political status and freely pursue their economic, social, and cultural development."   Article 1.1, International Convention on Civil and Political Rights, composed at New York, December 16, 1966.
"Every individual shall have the right to freedom of movement and residence within the borders of a State provided he abides by the law. Every individual shall have the right, when persecuted, to seek and obtain asylum in other countries in accordance with laws of those countries and international conventions."   Article 8, African Charter on Human and Peoples' Rights, done at Banjul, composed in Banjul, June 26, 1981.
"Congress shall make no law respecting an establishment of religion or prohibiting the free exercise thereof; or abridging the freedom of speech, or of the press; or the right of people to peacefully assemble, and to petition the Government for a redress of grievances."   First Amendment to the Constitution of the United States ratified December 15, 1791.

United States Foreign Policy Concerning Democracy and the Rule of Law

Several related themes and concepts are often introduced in USG policy statements and educational programs addressing human rights. Some of these concepts are democracy and the rule of law, civilian control of the military, and a legal system covering military personnel that equates to a country's legal protections for civilians, unless otherwise required by military necessity.

The Rule of Law

The DOS has offered the following meaning of rule of law:

> The rule of law is a fundamental component of democratic society and is defined broadly as the principle that all members of society—both citizens and rulers—are bound by a set of clearly defined and universally accepted laws. In a democracy, the rule of law is manifested in an independent judiciary, a free press and a system of checks and balances on leaders through free elections.

Civilian Control of the Military

Civilian control of the military is also seen as an important means of protecting human rights and democracy because of the belief that a military establishment, particularly a large standing army, potentially poses a threat to individual liberty and to popular control of the government. Civilian control generally requires that:

- The armed forces do not dominate government or impose their unique values upon civilian institutions and organizations

- The armed forces have no independent access to sources of military funding

- The armed forces' policies on the recruitment, pay, education, training, treatment, promotion, and use of personnel are not inconsistent with basic civil liberties and individual beliefs, with some compromises for military discipline and combat effectiveness

- The use of military force, either for or against military action, is not determined by the values of the military establishment itself

Military Justice

Military justice relates to legal systems within each nation which govern order and discipline of members of their armed forces. For example, US armed forces members are subject to the *Uniform Code of Military Justice* (UCMJ). The following military justice-related topics are especially complementary to the overall framework of human rights:

- The rights and responsibilities of military personnel

- The role of the military commander in military justice

- Effective military justice systems and how they ensure accountability for and deterrence from human rights abuses by military personnel

Section 541 of the Foreign Assistance Act of 1961 (FAA) stresses the importance of the IMET program as a means to improve military justice systems and procedures in accordance with internationally recognized human rights.

Increased attention concerning human rights and related themes can be traced to the 1991 changes to the FAA which established expanded IMET (E-IMET). The principal objectives of E-IMET are:

- Fostering greater respect for, and understanding of, the principle of civilian control of the military

- Improving military justice systems and procedures in accordance with internationally accepted standards of human rights

- Increasing professionalism and responsibility in defense management and resource allocation

- Contributing to cooperation between military and law enforcement personnel with respect to counter-narcotics law enforcement efforts [section 541, FAA]

These objectives, combined with the traditional purposes of the IMET program (to expose international students to the US professional military establishment and the American way of life, including US regard for democratic values, respect for individual and human rights, and belief in the rule of law) make human rights and related concepts high priorities in the conduct of the US security assistance program.

HUMAN RIGHTS AND THE FOREIGN ASSISTANCE PROGRAM

Foreign Policy Goal

Human rights are addressed in section 502B, FAA:

> The US shall, in accordance with its international obligations as set forth in the UN Charter and in keeping with the constitutional heritage and traditions of the US, promote and encourage increased respect for human rights and international freedoms throughout the world without distinction as to race, sex, language, or religion. Accordingly, a principal goal of US foreign policy shall be to promote the increased observance of internationally recognized human rights by all countries.

This section also provides that any nations receiving security assistance that engage in a consistent pattern of gross violations of internationally recognized human rights risk a combination of statutory and policy-based suspension or termination of US military and economic assistance, including FMS and direct commercial sales transfers of defense articles and services. The term "gross violations of internationally recognized human rights" as defined in section 116(a), FAA, includes torture or cruel, inhuman, or degrading treatment or punishment, prolonged detention without charges, causing the disappearance of persons by the abduction and clandestine detention of those persons, or other flagrant denial of the right to life, liberty, and the security of the person. Any exception to this policy requires a Presidential certification to Congress that extraordinary circumstances warrant such assistance. The goal of any such sanctions is not to punish the offending country but to change its behavior, bringing it back into compliance with international norms for human rights.

Role of the Department of State

Section 624(f), FAA, vests in the Assistant Secretary of State for Democracy, Human Rights and Labor Affairs overall policy responsibility for the creation of USG human rights policy. The assistant secretary is responsible for the following:

- Detailed information regarding humanitarian affairs and the observance of and respect for internationally recognized human rights

- Preparing the annual country reports, discussed below

- Making recommendations to the Secretary of State and the administrator of the US Agency for International Development (USAID) regarding compliance with sections 116 and 502B, FAA

- Performing other responsibilities which serve to promote increased observance of internationally recognized human rights by all countries.

In accordance with sections 116(d) and 502B(b) of the FAA, and section 505(c) of the Trade Act of 1974, as amended, the DOS submits an annual document regarding country reports on human rights practices to the US Congress. The reports cover the human rights practices of all nations that are members of the UN as well as a few that are not. They are submitted to assist members of Congress in the consideration of legislation, particularly foreign assistance legislation. Each country report follows a standard format, consisting of a brief introductory statement followed by a more detailed discussion of human rights practices and concerns under the headings listed in figure 16-2.

Figure 16-2
US Department of State Country Report Format

Section 1 Respect for the integrity of the person, including freedom from:

  a. Arbitrary or unlawful deprivation of life

  b. Disappearance

  c. Torture and other cruel, inhuman, or degrading treatment or punishment

  d. Arbitrary arrest or detention

  e. Denial of fair public trial

  f. Arbitrary interference with privacy, family, home, or correspondence

Section 2 Respect for civil liberties, including:

  a. Freedom of speech and press

  b. Freedom of peaceful assembly and association

  c. Freedom of religion

  d. Freedom of movement, internally displaced persons, protection of refugees, and stateless persons

Section 3 Respect for political rights: the right of citizens to change their government

Section 4 Governmental attitudes regarding international and nongovernmental investigation of alleged violations of human rights

Section 5 Discrimination, societal abuses, and trafficking in persons

Section 6 Worker rights

  a. The right of association

  b. The right to organize and bargain collectively

  c. Prohibition of forced or compulsory labor

  d. Prohibition of child labor and minimum age for employment

  e. Acceptance conditions of work

The DOS and USAID strategic plan on the DOS web site outlines the US commitment to advance the growth of democracy and good governance, including civil society, the rule of law, respect for human rights, and religious freedom in other countries.

Attachment 16-2 provides a suggested action and reporting guideline known as the "Five Rs" for use by the security cooperation officer (SCO) in the event of discovering or witnessing a possible human rights violation.

Role of International and Non-governmental Organizations

Section 502B(b)(1), FAA, recognizes the contributions of international organizations and nongovernmental organizations within the area of human rights. Accordingly, this statutory section mandates that consideration shall be given to the relevant findings of appropriate international organizations, including such non-governmental organizations as the International Committee of the Red Cross, in the preparation of statements and reports concerning human rights conditions in other countries.

Some non-governmental organizations, e.g., Amnesty International and Human Rights Watch, publish their own human rights reports. The DOS customarily acknowledges the inputs provided by non-governmental organizations as well as other sources, e.g., private citizens and officials of foreign governments, in the development of its annual country reports on human rights practices. Amnesty International, for instance, lists country reports on its web site at http://www.amnesty.org.

Expanded-International Military Education and Training

The E-IMET initiative was started in 1990 to educate US friends and allies in the proper management of their defense resources, to improve their systems of military justice in accordance with internationally recognized principles of human rights, and to foster a greater respect for, and understanding of, the principle of civilian control of the military. The program is based upon the premise that active promotion of democratic values is one of the most effective means available for achieving US national security and foreign policy objectives and fostering peaceful relationships among the nations of the world.

In response to a 2011 GAO report entitled "International Military Education and Training: Agencies Should Emphasize Human Rights Training and Improve Evaluations" (GAO-12-123), the answers to the following questions are now called for in Combined Education and Training Program Plans CETPP submitted annually by SCOs: (1) Does the country generally receive poor marks on human rights from internationally recognized organizations like Freedom House? (2) If "yes" to question 1 above, to what degree is the military part of the rationale for the poor marks? (3) If the country receives poor marks, how does IMET-provided training planned for this country address human rights, civil-military relations, etc.?

Vetting for US Assistance (Including Leahy Amendment Compliance)

Increased Congressional interest in human rights violations worldwide has resulted in more stringent statutory guidance and limitations on US foreign assistance, including (but not limited to) training programs for foreign individuals and military units. A key component of US human rights policy as it applies to security cooperation is the vetting of those individuals and units, which serves as a background check to determine if they were previously involved in human rights abuses or related abuse of authority such as corruption.

Congress distinguishes in law between assistance provided by State Department oversight under the FAA and the Arms Export Control Act (AECA) and DOD-funded assistance such as counter-drug programs (1004 and 1033) and humanitarian demining. For State Department programs, including FMS, DCS, FMF, and IMET, new legislative provisions were created in the State/Foreign Operations Appropriations Act (S/FOAA) for FY 2012 (PL 112-74). This law amends the FAA with a new section 620M, "Limitation on Assistance to Security Forces." The key provision states that "no assistance shall be furnished under this Act (FAA) or the AECA to any unit of the security forces of a foreign country if the Secretary of State has credible information that such unit has committed a gross violation of human rights." The new section 620M is considered the latest version of the so-called "Leahy Amendment," requiring the vetting of individuals or units for possible human rights violations prior to receiving US assistance. Such assistance includes not only military training but also the transfer of defense articles and the providing of defense services.

For DOD-funded training, Congress enacted a similar provision in the DOD Appropriations Act for FY 2012 (also in PL 112-74). Section 8058 of the act states, "no FY 2012 DOD funds may be used to support any training program involving a unit of the security forces of a country if the Secretary of Defense has received credible information from the DOS that the unit has committed a gross violation of human rights, unless all necessary corrective steps have been taken." This provision of the law has the same effect as the Leahy Amendment. In either case, it is the responsibility of the SCO coordinating the training program to initiate the vetting process as determined by its embassy and CCMD.

Attachment 16-3 provides a suggested checklist for the vetting process to be performed by the SCO.

SUMMARY

A solid understanding of internationally recognized human rights policies is of key importance to members of the US security cooperation community, particularly those who conduct education and training programs for international students as well as SCO personnel who interface on a day-to-day basis with partner country personnel. Human rights are not just a matter of US emphasis; rather, human rights policies are grounded in multiple international conventions, including the UN Charter.

The human rights conditions within each country are documented in an annual report prepared by the DOS. SCO personnel and US military personnel deployed to unified command theaters need to be aware of their responsibilities for reporting human rights violations. To provide further focus on the importance of human rights, military justice, and civilian control of the military, the DOD education and training establishment is tasked with providing appropriate instruction on these topics to international students.

REFERENCES

Buergenthal, Thomas. *International Human Rights in a Nutshell*. St. Paul: West, 1995.

Burns H. Weston, Richard A. Falk, and Anthony D'Amato. *Basic Documents in International Law and World Order*. St. Paul: West, 1990.

Country Reports on Human Rights Practices for (Year). US Government Printing Office. http://www.state.gov/j/drl/rls/hrrpt/index.htm.

Janis, Mark W. *An Introduction to International Law*. Boston: Little, Brown, 1993.

Lawson, Edward. *Encyclopedia of Human Rights*. New York: Taylor & Francis, 1991.

The Judge Advocate General's School. Operational Law Handbook (updated annually).

US Congress. Joint Committee Print. Report to the Committee on Foreign Relations, US Senate, and the Committee on Foreign Affairs, US House of Representatives, by the DOS.

US DOS and USAID Strategic Plan for Fiscal Years 2007–2012. http://www.state.gov/s/d/rm/rls/dosstrat/2007/.

USDOS and USAID Strategic Plan and Addendum for Fiscal Years 2011–2016. http://www.usaid.gov/sites/default/files/documents/1868/qddraddendum201120116.pdf.

International Military Education and Training: Agencies Should Emphasize Human Rights Training and Improve Evaluations, GAO 12-123 October 2011.

Preamble: Whereas recognition of the inherent dignity and of the equal and inalienable rights of all members of the human family is the foundation of freedom, justice, and peace in the world,

Whereas disregard and contempt for human rights have resulted in barbarous acts which have outraged the conscience of mankind, and the advent of a world in which human beings shall enjoy freedom of speech and belief and freedom from fear and want has been proclaimed as the highest aspiration of the common people,

Whereas it is essential, if man is not be compelled to have recourse, as a last resort, to rebellion against tyranny and oppression, that human rights should be protected by the rule of law,

Whereas it is essential to promote the development of friendly relations between nations,

Whereas the peoples of the United Nations have in the Charter reaffirmed their faith in fundamental and human rights, in the dignity and worth of the human person and in the equal rights of men and women and have determined to promote social progress and better standards of life in larger freedom,

Whereas Member States have pledged themselves to achieve, in cooperation with the United Nations, the promotion of universal respect for and observance of human rights and fundamental freedoms,

Whereas a common understanding of these rights and freedoms is of the greatest importance for the full realization of this pledge,

Now, Therefore,

The General Assembly,

Proclaims this Universal Declaration of Human Rights as a common standard of achievement for all peoples and all nations, to the end that every individual and every organ of society, keeping this Declaration constantly in mind, shall strive by teaching and education to promote respect for these rights and freedoms and by progressive measures, national and international; to secure their universal and effective recognition and observance, both among the peoples of Member States themselves and among the peoples and territories under their jurisdiction.

Article 1. All human beings are born free and equal in dignity and rights. They are endowed with reason and conscience and should act towards one another in spirit of brotherhood.

Article 2. Everyone is entitled to all the rights and freedoms set forth in this Declaration, without distinction of any kind, such as race, color, sex, language, religion, political or other opinion, national or social origin, property, birth or other status. Furthermore, no distinction shall be made on the basis of the political, jurisdictional, or international status of the country or territory to which a person belongs, whether it be independent, trust, non-self-governing or under any other limitation of sovereignty.

Article 3. Everyone has the right to life, liberty, and security of person.

Article 4. No one shall be held in slavery or servitude; slavery and the slave trade shall be prohibited in all their forms.

Article 5. No one shall be subjected to torture or to cruel, inhuman, or degrading treatment or punishment.

Article 6. Everyone has the right to recognition everywhere as a person before the law.

Article 7. All are equal before the law and are entitled without any discrimination to equal protection of the law. All are entitled to equal protection against any discrimination in violation of this Declaration and against any incitement to such discrimination.

Article 8. Everyone has the right to an effective remedy by the competent national tribunals for acts violating the fundamental rights granted him by the constitution or by law.

Article 9. No one shall be subjected to arbitrary arrest, detention, or exile.

Article 10. Everyone is entitled in full equality to a fair and public hearing by an independent and impartial tribunal, in the determination of his rights and obligations and of any criminal charge against him.

Article 11. (1) Everyone charged with a penal offense has the right to be presumed innocent until proven guilty according to law in a public trial at which he has had all the guarantees necessary for his defense. (2) No one shall be held guilty of any penal offense on account of any act or omission which did not constitute a penal offense, under national or international law, at the time when it was committed. Nor shall a heavier penalty be imposed than the one that was applicable at the time the penal offense was committed.

Article 12. No one shall be subjected to arbitrary interference with his privacy, family, home or correspondence, nor to attacks upon his honor and reputation. Everyone has the right to the protection of the law against such interference or attacks.

Article 13. (1) Everyone has the right to freedom of movement and residence within the borders of each state. (2) Everyone has the right to leave any country, including his own, and to return to his country.

Article 14. (1) Everyone has the right to seek and to enjoy in other countries asylum from persecution. (2) This right may not be invoked in the case of prosecutions genuinely arising from non-political crimes or from acts contrary to the purposes and principles of the United Nations.

Article 15. (1) Everyone has the right to a nationality. (2) No one shall be arbitrarily deprived of his nationality nor denied the right to change his nationality.

Article 16. (1) Men and women of full age, without any limitation due to race, nationality or religion, have the right to marry and to found a family. They are entitled to equal rights as to marriage, during marriage, and its dissolution. (2) Marriage shall be entered into only with the free and full consent of the intending spouses. (3) The family is the natural and fundamental group unit of society and is entitled to protection by society and the State.

Article 17. (1) Everyone has the right to own property alone as well as in association with others. (2) No one shall be arbitrarily deprived of his property.

Article 18. Everyone has the right of freedom of thought, conscience and religion, this right includes freedom to change his religion or belief, and freedom, either alone in community with others, and in public or private, to manifest his religion or belief in teaching, practice, worship and observance.

Article 19. Everyone has the right to freedom of opinion and expression; this right includes freedom to hold opinions without interference and to seek, receive, and impart information and ideas through any media and regardless of frontiers.

Article 20. (1) Everyone has the right to freedom of peaceful assembly and association. (2) No one may be compelled to belong to an association.

Article 21. (1) Everyone has the right to take part in the Government of his country, directly or indirectly or through freely chosen representatives. (2) Everyone has the right of equal access to public service in his country. (3) The will of the people shall be the basis of the authority of government, this will shall be expressed in periodic and genuine elections which shall be by universal and equal suffrage and shall be held by secret vote or by equivalent free voting procedures.

Article 22. Everyone, as a member of society, has the right to social security and is entitled to realization, through national effort and international cooperation and in accordance with the organization and resources of each State, of the economic, social, and cultural rights indispensable for his dignity and the free development of his personality.

Article 23. (1) Everyone has the right to work, to free choice of employment, to just and favorable conditions of work and to protection against unemployment. (2) Everyone, without any discrimination, has the right to equal pay for equal work. (3) Everyone who works has the right to just and favorable remuneration ensuring for himself and his family an existence worthy of human dignity, and supplemented, if necessary, by other means of social protection. (4) Everyone has the right to form and to join trade unions for the protection of his interests.

Article 24. Everyone has the right to rest and leisure, including reasonable limitation of working hours and periodic holidays with pay.

Article 25. (1) Everyone has the right to a standard of living adequate for the health and well-being of himself and of his family, including food, clothing, housing, and medical care and necessary social services, and the right to security in the event of unemployment, sickness, disability, widowhood, old age or other lack of livelihood in circumstances beyond his control. (2) Motherhood and childhood are entitled to special care and assistance. All children, whether born in or out of wedlock, shall enjoy the same social protection.

Article 26. (1) Everyone has the right to education. Education shall be free, at least in the elementary and fundamental stages. Elementary education shall be compulsory. Technical and professional education shall be made generally available and higher education shall be equally accessible to all on the basis of merit.

(2) Education shall be directed to the full development of the human personality and to the strengthening of respect for human rights and fundamental freedoms. It shall promote understanding, tolerance, and friendship among all nations, racial or religious groups, and shall further the activities of the United Nations for the maintenance of peace. (3) Parents have a prior right to choose the kind of education that shall be given to their children.

Article 27. (1) Everyone has the right freely to participate in the cultural life of the community, to enjoy the arts and to share in scientific advancements and its benefits. (2) Everyone has the right to the protection of the moral and material interests resulting from any scientific, literary, or artistic production of which he is the author.

Article 28. Everyone is entitled to a social and international order in which the rights and freedoms set forth in this Declaration can be fully realized.

Article 29. (1) Everyone has duties to the community in which alone the free and full development of his personality is possible. (2) In the exercise of his rights and freedoms, everyone shall be subject only to such limitations as are determined by law solely for purpose of securing due recognition and respect for the rights and freedoms of others and of meeting the just requirements of morality, public order, and the general welfare in a democratic society. (3) These rights and freedoms may in no case be exercised contrary to the purposes and principles of the United Nations.

Article 30. Nothing in this Declaration may be interpreted as implying for any State, group or person any right to engage in any activity or to perform any act aimed at the destruction of any of the rights and freedoms set forth herein

ATTACHMENT 16-2
THE "FIVE RS"

The responsibilities of US military members, particularly those permanently assigned or temporarily deployed to a foreign country, with respect to human rights can be summarized by the "Five Rs," which are the following guidelines extracted from educational materials developed by the US Army Judge Advocate School.

- Recognize human rights violations. This involves recognizing unlawful action by a government official, or someone acting under the color of government authority, and distinguishing gross violations of human rights from other violations. One must also be mindful that not all "bad" conduct constitutes a human rights violation.

- Refrain from committing human rights violations. Each military member is a government official, and government officials must not commit or aid in the commission of violations. Moreover, military members may be responsible for the acts of subordinates and possibly the acts of fellow soldiers. Upon encountering apparent violations in foreign countries, visiting military members should generally disengage from activity and leave the area, provided they can disengage without impairing their mission.

- React to human rights violations. If observed conduct of a government official involves a gross violation, intervention to protect a victim may be appropriate in certain limited cases:

  ◊ The threat to life or limb is clear and compelling, e.g., without the soldier's intervention, a death, dismemberment, or rape will almost certainly occur.

  ◊ No other government officials or military personnel are able to intervene.

  ◊ Intervention is possible without serious threat to the US soldier's safety, unit security, or mission.

  ◊ Intervention involves no force or absolute minimum force to protect the victim, for example, shouting, not shooting at, the perpetrator. The objective is to restore the status quo, not to punish the perpetrator. If an official's conduct does not involve a gross violation, the soldier follows the report procedures outlined below and secures the consent of higher authority before intervening or notifying others of the apparent violation.

- Report human rights violations.

  ◊ Report all instances of suspected human rights violations immediately to higher authority; use the most secure communications means available.

  ◊ Indicate what official appears to be committing an offense, describe victim(s), and state whether any US military or civilian personnel were involved in any way.

  ◊ As appropriate, provide recommendations as to what the commander should do to protect the victim(s), restore the status quo, and preserve evidence of these events.

- Record human rights violations.

  ◊ In line with personnel or unit safety and mission requirements, use available means to preserve evidence and record other details of any apparent violation of human rights. Such means may include photography and tape recordings as well as written notes and diagrams.

  ◊ As the location may be later examined by professional investigators from the proper host nation authorities or by other international investigators from the United Nations, regional organizations or perhaps the US, be cautious about entering the area where events took place and collecting items of evidence without clearance from a higher authority.

ATTACHMENT 16-3
GUIDANCE FOR SCREENING CANDIDATES OF US-SPONSORED TRAINING PROGRAMS

The Leahy Amendment requires that candidates for training, individuals or members of units, must be vetted by the US country team, for involvement in gross human rights abuses or criminal acts prior to attending or participating in any US-sponsored training. Per Joint Staff document dated 01 November 1998, a gross human rights abuse is defined as torture or cruel, inhuman, or degrading treatment or punishment, prolonged detention without charges and trial, causing the disappearance of persons by the abduction and clandestine detention of those persons, and other flagrant denial of the right to life, liberty, or the security of person.

The following checklist is designed to assist in the process of screening:

- SCO requests the partner nation to provide student nomination for US training programs.

- SCO specifies to the partner country the type of local record and background checks to be completed.

- SCO informs host country that the provision of student names, in writing, constitutes certification that checks have been completed satisfactorily.

- Training includes all DOD-sponsored training, IMET, FMS purchased training at DOD educational institutions, police training, counter-terrorism and counter-narcotics training, and personnel exchange programs.

- The partner nation conducts local record/background checks and provides, in writing, student nomination to SCO. As indicated above, provision of student nomination constitutes host country certification that requested checks have been completed satisfactorily.

- American embassy personnel, including all relevant members of the country team including human rights officers, Regional Security Officer, Drug Enforcement Agency, Defense Attaché, consular section, and other offices, as appropriate, check and screen the nominees thoroughly.

- SCO interviews the nominees for suitability.

- SCO maintains documentation of local record and background checks.

DOD directs that SCOs develop a checklist that encompasses the guidelines above. This checklist should be included with other documentation related to potential nominees and maintained for a minimum of ten years. Each SCO may adjust the guidelines above as necessary to accommodate the local situation.

RESOURCE MANAGEMENT FOR THE SECURITY COOPERATION ORGANIZATION

INTRODUCTION

Security cooperation organization (SCO) personnel are responsible for managing all the resources that are made available to the SCO. The majority of military and Department of Defense (DOD) civilians are familiar with annually appropriated DOD Operations and Maintenance (O&M) funds as the common source of funds for their activities; at the SCO, however, there may be a variety of programs, each with its own funding and requirements for implementation. These disparate, complex programs, combined with a certain level of autonomy at a SCO, make it relatively easy for those responsible to lose accountability of resources. This chapter addresses the realities and requirements of resource management in the SCO, especially for the SDO/DATT position. The processes and procedures outlined within this chapter support the SCO's internal management controls program.

INTERNAL MANAGEMENT CONTROLS

The Federal Managers' Financial Integrity Act of 1982 requires an internal management control program to prevent fraud, waste, abuse, and mismanagement. The SCO implementation of management controls should consist of the following four elements:

1. Documentation—The SCO should document the procedures of the internal control program.

2. Instruction—The SDO/DATT should instruct all SCO members about the program's requirements.

3. Review—The SCO should conduct periodic internal reviews, with one element/sub-element within the SCO performing independent checks of records and procedures on another. Records should be periodically reconciled to ensure accuracy. Periodic physical inventories should also be made of all SCO property.

4. Inspection—Periodic external audits, such as those from the Combatant Command (CCMD) Inspector General, should be conducted approximately every 18 months.

These four elements should minimize loss of resources due to fraud, waste, and abuse.

HUMAN RESOURCES

One of the key resource areas in a SCO is human resources. Section 515 of the Foreign Assistance Act (FAA) contains a variety of provisions dealing with the organization and roles of SCOs. These provisions limit the number of members of the armed forces permanently assigned to a SCO for the management of the United States (US) security assistance (SA) to six, unless specifically authorized by the Congress. This provision does not apply to civilian billets or to CCMD SC billets within the SCO. This limitation for SA related staffing may be waived if the President determines that US national interests require more than six such personnel. Changes to the SCO's authorized staffing must follow the procedures outlined in attachment 17-2, *Guidelines to Implement National Security Decision Directive Number 38* (NSDD 38). Operational and overhead support for the SA billets comes from the Security Assistance Administrative Trust Fund. All SC billets are supported by O&M funds or funds from the program that authorizes their presence.

Security Cooperation Office Personnel Authorizations

SCO staffing varies according to the SA and SC program workload, as determined by joint Defense Security Cooperation Agency (DSCA) and CCMD manpower surveys. The workload includes the volume of active Foreign Military Sales (FMS) cases, the number of students programmed for training, the volume of SC programs being managed, and other factors. As a general rule, more than 50 percent of an individual's workload must be performing SA functions in order to be funded from the Security Assistance Administrative Trust Fund. Billets primarily supporting SC programs not to include SA, are normally funded through the CCMD O&M program objective memorandum (POM) process. Once the authorized staffing is approved by DSCA and the Joint Chiefs of Staff (JCS), it is published to the CCMD's Joint Manpower Program (JMP). This document is maintained by the CCMD. There are a finite number of billets available world-wide and, as new requirements arise for a SCO, the CCMD and/or DSCA may require the billets be shifted from one SCO to another or from one CCMD to another. The following categories of billets, authorized for the SA workload of the SCO, may be reflected on a JMP:

- US military personnel. As indicated above, the number of those performing security assistance duties is reported annually to Congress and is subject to Congressional limitation.

- US civilian direct-hires. These DOD civilians are hired through the civilian personnel agency associated with the CCMD.

- Locally Employed Staff (LE Staff). A general term used for Foreign Service Nationals (FSNs) and resident US citizens who are employed at a post by a USG agency that is under Chief of Mission (COM) authority. They are employed under a direct-hire appointment, a personal services contract, or a personal services agreement. Typical jobs for LE Staff within a SCO include budget analyst, SA training manager, FMS case technician, administrative assistant, translator, and vehicle driver.

The following categories of billets may be present in a SCO but will not be reflected on the JMP:

- Personal Services Agreement (PSA). Personnel (local national personnel, US family members, or local non-official US personnel) hired under a limited-term (one year, extendable to ten years) contract to fill bona fide requirements in a SCO. PSAs can fill positions as noted above for LE Staff; however, PSA personnel cannot be contracted to perform duties that are required to be performed by a USG employee, such as certifying funds. The primary advantage in hiring a PSA is that it does not require NSDD 38 approval, whereas hiring LE Staff does.

- Assistance-in-Kind (AIK). The partner nation government may, by way of a bilateral agreement, assign local Ministry of Defense (MOD) personnel to the SCO. These personnel perform administrative or management functions on the country's SA programs and work under the direction of the SCO. The partner nation may also have liaison officers assigned in the SCO.

- Case-funded personnel. In a few countries, the SCO includes personnel (US and non-US) whose services are paid for under an FMS case. These billets are on a relatively permanent basis, but the individuals may change based on the length-of-tour rules included in the case.

US military and civilian direct-hire personnel are compensated in accordance with relevant US laws and regulations. Locally employed staff are compensated in accordance with the local compensation plan (LCP), the embassy's official system of compensation. LCPs are established in accordance with section 408 of the Foreign Service Act of 1980, as amended *United States Code 22* (22 U.S.C.), 3968. Each LCP consists of the salary schedule and rates, statements authorizing various types of benefit payments and premium pay rates, and other pertinent facets of local compensation

Changes in Security Cooperation Organization Manpower

The SCOs and CCMDs should review JMPs at least annually to ensure that SCO manning conforms to established policy for effectively managing SA and SC programs. When changes are required for SCO JMPs (or when JMPs are required for new SCOs), the requests, with detailed justification in accordance with DOD Instruction 5132.13, *Staffing of Security Cooperation Organizations (SCOs) and the Selection and Training of Security Cooperation Personnel*, must be submitted to the JCS and DSCA through the CCMD.

Additionally, the COM must concur with any changes affecting the size, composition, or mission of the SCO. The NSDD 38 (See attachment 17-1), assigns primary responsibility for approval of changes in the size, composition, or mandate of any agency at a US embassy to the applicable COM, in consultation with the DOS. In reviewing his JMP, the SDO/DATT has the ability to narrow or broaden the required or preferred background, skills, and prior training specified for any given billet. This often requires striking a balance between the needs of the SCO and the available pool of manpower. Making a requirement too specific may ensure an ideal candidate for any given position but at the cost of a gapped billet. Conversely, too general a requirement may help ensure timely personnel fills but with personnel who do not have the best qualifications for the job.

Security Cooperation Organization Selection

Personnel are nominated to SCO positions in accordance with DODI 5123.13. Requirements for nomination to a SCO may entail slightly different criteria from the norm with respect to:

- Civilian education
- Training
- Language qualifications
- Military schooling
- Experience
- Area familiarity
- Health
- Family considerations

However, a nomination does not assure the job, because the area CCMD, the ambassador, and the SDO/DATT retain final selection rights.

FUNDING RESOURCES

There are several types of funds and assets that a SCO may manage. They come primarily from the Security Assistance Administrative Trust Fund and from operations and maintenance funds. In this section, we will discuss these sources of funds. Typical expenditures of funds would be for:

- Operational and overhead expenses
- Utilities
- Rent
- Temporary duty (TDY)
- Office equipment
- Civilian salaries
- Selected entitlements

Security Assistance Administrative Trust Fund

The Security Assistance Administrative Trust Fund is primarily sourced from the mandated administrative surcharge added to FMS cases. The other portion of this trust fund is sourced through Congressional appropriations under the Foreign Operations Authority U.S.C. Title 22. These appropriated funds generally account for about half of the total SA administrative budget. For SCO purposes, the Defense Finance and Accounting Service–Security Cooperation Accounting (DFAS–SCA) in Indianapolis, IN consolidates these funds into a single funding source for the SCOs, the CCMD headquarters, and other DOD activities.

A portion of the Security Assistance Administrative Trust Fund is allocated to the SCO and is officially referred to as SA Admin funds. They are colloquially referred to as "T-20" funds. These funds pay for the SA mission requirements of the SCO. They cover the typical expenditures listed above and any other requirements that directly support the authorized members of the SCO who are conducting SA activities.

SA Admin funds allocated to the CCMD headquarters to manage SA programs are referred to as "HQ T-20" funds. The HQ T-20 funds pay for the SA operational requirements of the CCMDs.

Operations and Maintenance Funds

The CCMD provides O&M funds for support of the DOD or CCMD security cooperation programs other than SA in the country. These funds are used for the same types of expenses as T-20 funds, but in support of non-SA programs. They are known as:

- O&M funds in the Air Force

- O&M Army (OMA) funds in the Army

- O&M Navy (O&MN) funds in the Navy

Congress authorizes and appropriates O&M funds for the support of US forces under U.S.C. Title 10. The SCO uses these O&M funds for SC Other Than SA requirements of the SCO. These funds are managed by the CCMDs, MILDEPs, DOD agencies and components, and are identified with the specific programs that authorize the funds. Each of these O&M funding programs will have its own rules and procedures to be followed. The SCOs who have security cooperation billets on their JMP are required to prepare and execute a separate budget for each of the authorized programs.

Partnership for Peace

The Partnership for Peace (PfP) fund is annually appropriated for DOD by Congress, in support of US efforts with countries participating in the North Atlantic Treaty Organization's (NATO's) PfP program. The program directly supports partner countries becoming more operationally compatible with NATO forces. The funds are provided by the CCMD to component commands, the Defense Attaché Offices (DAOs), and SCOs for implementation of the program.

Traditional Combatant Commander Activities

The Traditional Combatant Commander Activities (TCA) funds are used to conduct military-to-military contact and comparable activities designed to encourage a more democratic orientation by defense establishments and military forces in other countries. The SCO submits proposed projects and their estimated cost to the CCMD. The CCMD approves projects and then, when funding is available, provides the funding to the SCO to execute the project.

Traditional Combatant Commander Initiative Fund

The Combatant Commander Initiative Fund (CCIF) is controlled in accordance with DODD 7280.4 by the Chairman of the JCS. A CCMD may request this funding in support of a myriad of projects to include:

- Force training

- Contingencies

- Selected operations

- Command and control

- Joint and combined exercises

- Military education and training to military and civilian personnel of foreign countries

- For personal expenses of defense personnel for bilateral and regional cooperation programs

These funds are used for a single project and are not a source of funding for a continuing project. Once the funding authority is granted, the funds are managed by the CCMD in the same manner as other O&M funds.

Counternarcotics

The counternarcotics (CN) funds are appropriated to DOD for the support of US and partner nations in fighting the war on drugs. This funding is managed by the Assistant Secretary of Defense for Special Operations and Low Intensity Conflict (ASD/SOLIC). These funds may be allocated to use via the FMS process to fund a country's training, support, and equipment needs, or for in support of US forces/activities engaged in CN operations. Normally, however, these funds are allocated to the military service and managed like O&M funds. The International Narcotics Control Act (INCA) provides funds managed by the DOS which are used to pay for DOD-provided material, services, or training via the FMS process or direct commercial sales (DCS).

International Armaments Cooperation (IAC)

The IAC program provides O&M funds in support of the US personnel authorized under the JMP of the CCMD for IAC activities. The term Defense Cooperation in Armaments (DCA) is used in the law that originally authorized this program managed by the Under Secretary of Defense for Acquisition, Technology and Logistics (USD [AT&L]). These funds are allocated to the CCMD and are managed like other O&M funds. The SCOs with IAC billets on their JMP are required to maintain a separate budget and separate budget execution procedures for these funds.

Demining

Demining funds may be allocated for use via the FMS process. These funds are made available to aid a country in the removal of landmines. The SCO will be involved in the management of this program and overseeing the use of these funds. The SCO does not budget for these funds; rather, yearly targets are directed from higher headquarters.

Humanitarian Assistance

Humanitarian Assistance funds may be allocated for use to assist the partner nation in construction of needed infrastructure, schools, and hospitals. The SCO will be involved in the management of this program and overseeing the use of these funds. The SCO submits the proposed projects and estimated cost to the CCMD. The CCMD approves the projects and when funding is available, provides the funding to the SCO to execute the project.

United States Code Title 10 Programs

The CCMD centrally manages a special category of funding known as the Title 10 programs, with which the SCO may be involved. These special programs get their name from the same authorizing legislation that Congress provides for Armed Forces activities; they should not be confused with U.S.C. Title 10 O&M funds. Title 10 provides funds to support cooperative engagement. It funds material support for the following:

- Humanitarian and civic assistance projects

- Participation in exercises

- Attendance at conferences, seminars or exchanges

The SCO does not budget for these funds; they are provided by the owning organization as needed.

Assistance-in-Kind

Assistance-in-Kind (AIK) is generally non-monetary support of SCO operational requirements, typically including office space, transportation, utilities, or personnel. AIK support is provided for operational requirements that would normally be funded using SA administrative, FMS case, or O&M funds. The range of support to be provided under AIK is decided by a bilateral agreement signed between the US and the partner nation.

Antiterrorism and Force Protection Funding

Antiterrorism and force protection (ATFP) funding is an area of great concern and confusion. The DOS is responsible for funding ATFP for most of the SA authorized billets, with the CCMD, by agreement, being responsible for ATFP at selected SCOs and all personnel assigned there, i.e., the DCA officer. DOS will, therefore, be the first place to look for funding of ATFP requirements. If sufficient funds are not available in from the DOS, then the SCO should submit an unfunded requirement (UFR) to the CCMD to pay for the deficiency. The embassy Regional Security Officer (RSO) should include a statement that the security requirement is valid and that DOS does not have funding.

Other Sources of Funding

Morale, welfare and recreation (MWR), overseas housing allowance (OHA), basic allowance for housing (BAH), and military pay are some of the other sources of funding.

MWR funds are available on a limited basis through the MILDEPs, in accordance with DODI 1015.10, to support US military personnel at a SCO. These funds are often used for such items as weight-lifting and exercise equipment. The SCO does not budget for these funds; they request them on an as-needed basis.

Housing is typically provided or funded for members of the SCO in one of four ways. The first method is a private lease obtained by the SCO member. In this case, OHA in conjunction with BAH will be used to pay for housing costs for US military personnel. The second method is provided through a government lease and paid directly by the SCO. The lease can be through the embassy housing pool or handled separately by the SCO. These SCO–funded leases are generally used only when housing is in limited supply or for security reasons. The third method of providing housing is DOS housing. This is a residence either purchased or on a long-term lease by DOS. This type of housing is rarely available, but when it is, it is funded by DOS. The fourth method of housing, DOD military quarters, is even rarer. These are quarters on a military installation funded by the applicable installation MILDEP.

Military pay is not budgeted by the SCO but paid directly by each member's military service. DSCA centrally funds for all US Coast Guard (USCG) personnel.

PRACTICAL APPLICATION OF DIFFERENT FUND TYPES

The following example, using the mythical country of Bandaria, shows the sometimes confusing use of various types of funds. This example only identifies a few of the funding sources that a SCO might have and should not be considered an all-inclusive list. Table 17-1 shows the makeup of SCO Bandaria by position.

Table 17-1
Security Cooperation Office Bandaria
Make Up and Funding Source

JMP Position	Name	Grade	Type Funds
ODC Chief	COL Dave Encharge, USA	06	SA Admin
Secretary (US Civlilian)	Ms. Mary Noit	GS	SA Admin
Budget Analyst (LE Staff)	Ms. She Counts	LES	SA Admin
Training Assistant (LE Staff)	Mr. Kan Sendum	LES	SA Admin
Armaments Cooperation	Lt Col Terry Helper, USAF	05	O&M (DCA)
Logistics-Plans Coordination	MAJ Don Supli, USA	04	O&M (CCMD)

This office has six people funded by three different types of funds. The following provides the funding background for each of the office members.

Colonel Dave Encharge is married, with two teenage children, for a total of three sponsored dependents. His house is rented, not provided through a government lease, so he uses service-provided BAH and OHA to pay the rent on his house in Bandaria. SA Admin pays the cost of his children's private school; pays for the purchase of office supplies and equipment; and funds his SA-related travel. He and his dependents are also authorized funded environmental morale leave (FEML), since they are assigned to an austere location. Colonel Encharge can decide to go to the designated location or another location, but will receive funds up to the constructed cost of traveling to the designated location. The US Army pays his salary.

Ms. Mary Noit, the secretary, has no dependents. Because she was hired locally, she does not receive any housing, dependent education, or transportation entitlements. There are a few US civilians that receive these entitlements, but only if they have a transportation agreement. SA Admin funds pay her salary, for her office supplies and equipment, and any SA-related travel costs she may have.

Ms. She Counts and Mr. Kan Sendum are local nationals. As LE Staff, housing and dependent education are not paid for using any type of SCO funds. SA Admin funds pay their salaries, for the purchase of their office supplies and equipment, and any SA-related travel.

Lieutenant Colonel Terry Helper has no dependents. The US Air Force pays her salary and the BAH and OHA to rent her house in Bandaria. DCA funding pays for the purchase of her office supplies and equipment, and for any DCA–related travel. T-20 pays for any SA-related travel.

Major Don Supli has one sponsored dependent and the US Army pays his salary. He uses BAH and OHA to pay the rent on his house in Bandaria. CCMD O&M funds pay for the purchase of his office supplies and equipment, and funds CCMD-related travel.

The Bandarians have decided to provide vehicles for SCO use under an FMS case. A case was written to lease four Jeep Grand Cherokees, including their maintenance. The SCO only pays for the fuel for these vehicles.

The SCO does not use office space in the embassy, but has an office next to the MOD. Although Bandaria provides this office to the SCO as no-cost AIK, the SCO must pay for all utilities. The electric bill for the entire SCO office is for one lump sum of 2,600bd ($1,300.00), yet each funding source must pay for its own requirements. Various cost accounting methods can be employed; one method would take the square footage allocated to each person and use that to determine how much each owes. In this example, the SA Admin-funded personnel occupy 64 percent of the office, the DCA billet occupies 18 percent, and the CCMD-funded billet occupies the other 18 percent. The correct method of funding is for T-20 funds to pay 64 percent, DCA funds to pay 18 percent, and CCMD funds to pay 18 percent.

Now, examine one of the more interesting items that come up on a daily basis in the SCO.

Colonel Encharge will not be able to attend the next CCMD SA conference and decides to send Lieutenant Colonel Helper in his place. In this case, although Lieutenant Colonel Helper is mainly funded using DCA funds, she will be performing an SA mission and therefore is authorized to use T-20 funds to pay the cost of her TDY. Any time the funding source or the legality of expending funds for an item is unclear, the SCO should check with the CCMD resource manager and/or legal office.

FLOW OF FUNDING AUTHORITY FOR THE SECURITY COOPERATION OFFICE

The flow of funding authority to the SCO is complicated, due to the number of funds, the types of activities, and the number of organizations involved. This process can, however, be broken down into some key basic concepts.

Figure 17-1 depicts the flow of funding authority from the sources of funding to the SCO. Starting at the top, the primary fund the SCO uses is the Security Assistance Administrative Trust Fund. The top left shows the flow of funding authority provided by Congress for Security Assistance administration–related requirements for grant programs. The top right shows the flow of funds from the FMS administrative surcharge on FMS cases. Both sources of funds are accounted for in the Security Assistance Administrative Trust Fund account

Funding authority for the SA administrative functions of the CCMD is sent to the CCMD and referred to as HQ SA Admin funds. Funding authority for the SCO SA funding requirements is sent to the CCMD for further distribution to the SCOs. From the Trust Fund, funds are sent to DOS to pay for indirect costs that are centrally-funded by DSCA, such as International Cooperative Administrative Support Services (ICASS).

The bottom left of the chart shows the flow of Congressionally-appropriated O&M funds to the CCMD and MILDEPs. The MILDEPs also distribute these O&M funds to the other SC organizations that require O&M funds. The CCMDs then provide the necessary O&M funds to the SCO.

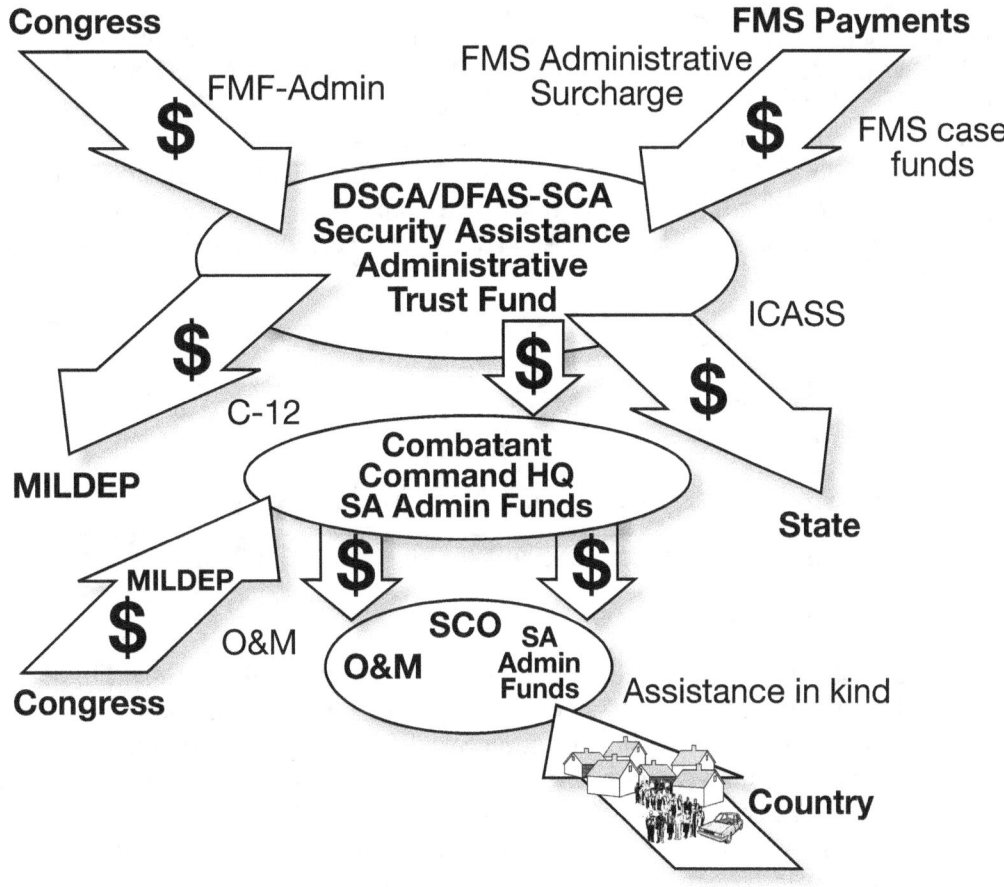

Figure 17-1
Flow of Funds

SECURITY COOPERATION OFFICE BUDGET ORGANIZATIONS

An understanding of the various players in the budget process is required before looking at the process itself. There are nine major players involved with the SCO budget process:

- Congress

- DOS

- DSCA

- MILDEPs

- CCMD

- SCO

- Embassy

- Global Financial Service Center (GFSC)

- DFAS–SCA

Congress legislates the appropriated funds portion of the SA FMFP funding and the O&M funding to be used by the SCO. Congress separately legislates an annual dollar ceiling authority for expenditure of SA administration funds out of the trust fund at DFAS–SCA.

The DOS submits the budget request to Congress for the appropriated funds portion of the SA fund requirement in the annual Congressional budget justification for foreign operations.

DSCA administers the Security Assistance Administrative Trust Fund and provides budget policy and guidance on the use of SA funds. DSCA also provides budget target levels to the CCMDs and reviews and approves their SA-related budgets. The budgets are approved based on the country submissions but the funding levels are issued to the CCMDs as a lump-sum dollar value. This allows the CCMDs to adjust country funding levels as changes in requirements occur. DSCA works with the DOS in preparing the budget request to Congress for the appropriated portion of the SA funds and disburses funds to the DOS for SCO ICASS costs. DSCA also centrally funds USCG salaries and the C-12 aircraft program.

The MILDEPs, as executive agents to the CCMDs, provide budget policy and guidance on the use of O&M funds. They review and approve the O&M budgets for the CCMDs. They also prepare the annual Program Objective Memorandum (POM) submission for the DOD to obtain the funds required. The executive agents for the CCMDs are as follows:

- The Air Force for Central Command and Northern Command

- The Army for European Command, Southern Command, and Africa Command

- The Navy for the Pacific Command

The CCMDs issue policies and procedures that expand and clarify those issued by DSCA and the executive agents. They issue funding targets for the SCOs to use as a starting point in developing their budgets. The CCMDs review and modify the individual SCO budgets as required and then submit consolidated budgets to DSCA for SA requirements and to the executive agent for O&M requirements. The CCMDs then issue the obligation authority/fund certification authorization (OA/FCA) to the SCO as funding becomes available. This gives the SCO authority to obligate the USG to expend dollars. At the same time the OA/FCA is issued to the SCO, the CCMDs notify DFAS–SCA, so they can record the OA/FCA values in the official accounting system. This is the formal commitment of a portion of the trust fund to pay for the obligations generated by the SCO. The CCMDs are also responsible for overseeing SCO funds management and implementation.

The SCOs prepare their proposed budgets and submit them to the CCMDs. If the budget request exceeds the target level provided by the CCMD, then the SCO will submit an unfunded requirement (UFR) for each item above the target level. The SCO, upon receipt of the OA/FCA, will execute the day-to-day budget requirements in accordance with the DFAS Memorandum, *SAO Accounting Pamphlet*, 28 September 2003. The SCO will enter all accounting records into the Security Assistance Automated Resource Management Suite (SAARMS) Budget Execution program for all transactions. This information is transferred to DFAS–SCA and entered into the official DFAS accounting records. This information, plus payment information submitted through the DOS accounting system (Momentum) and received by DFAS–SCA, will be used for reconciliation with records in the SAARMS system.

The embassy will provide contracting support to most SCOs. Generally, DOS has the only bonded contracting officer available in-country so they provide this service to the other organizations. It is the exception for a SCO to have its own contracting officer. The embassy also provides certain administrative support services specified in the ICASS agreement. These services generally include fund disbursement for the SCO by the embassy and the Global Financial Service Center (GFSC). Again, a few SCOs perform this service in-house, but this too is the exception. Financial reports will also be provided to the SCO that show what financial functions the embassy performed for the SCO.

The GFSC is the DOS regional finance center for disbursing funds for the embassies assigned to it. The GFSC reports these disbursements to the embassy that requested them. The disbursements are also reported to DFAS–SCA for all SA disbursements. There are currently two GFSCs, located in Bangkok, Thailand, and Charleston, South Carolina.

DFAS–SCA is the financial and accounting activity for all SA funds. DFAS issues general accounting policy and procedures. At the direction of DSCA, they issue fund allotments to the CCMDs for dissemination to the various SCOs. DFAS–SCA maintains the official accounting records. They post all obligations provided by the SCOs and disbursements provided by DOS and others. Status reports are then supplied to each SCO via SAARMS. DFAS–SCA, in conjunction with the SCO, reconciles the records posted from DOS with those posted from the SCO. DFAS–SCA is also required to perform departmental reporting to the Office of Management and Budget (OMB).

REPRESENTATION FUNDS

Representation funds are used to maintain the standing and prestige of the US by extending official courtesies to authorized host nation personnel. The SCO will receive these funds from both T-20 and O&M funding. The SCO representation fund budget is small, generally only a few hundred dollars, but it receives a great deal of management attention. Rules for SA representation funds will differ from those of CCMD O&M and those for use by the DAO. To assist in the funding of representational activities during VIP visits (senior flag officers, DOD civilians and others), SCOs are encouraged to request funds from the person coordinating the VIP visit to offset the costs of the activities.

Representation Fund Uses and Limitations

Representation funds can be used to cover the cost of luncheons, dinners, and receptions for authorized personnel, to include gratuities up to 15 percent of the cost of the services. Mementos can be purchased at a cost not to exceed $350.00 per person for honored guests and their spouses. These mementos should only be presented to non-USG officials. Non-personal invitations, such as an invitation from SCO Bandaria, rather than from Colonel Encharge, can be bought with these funds. The SCO should refer to DODI 7250.13 for additional guidance, including a list of prohibited items.

Representation Fund Event Attendance Limitations

Invited guests should be limited to the minimum number required to meet the representational mission. However, the number of distinguished guests must be at least 20 percent of the attendees when the number of attendees is no more than thirty people and at least 50 percent when the number of attendees is more than thirty people. The SCO should refer to the CCMD regulations for additional limitations.

Representation Fund Records

Detailed records of all expenditures of representation funds must be maintained. Guest lists indicating invitees and attendees will be recorded for each event. The distinguished guests and party will be indicated and the ratio of distinguished guests to US personnel annotated. Financial records of all expenditures must be recorded as well as perpetual inventories of mementos and expendable items, to include documenting the date of presentation, the memento that was given, to whom it was given, and the reason for presentation.

International Cooperative Administrative Support Services

The International Cooperative Administrative Support Services (ICASS) program is a system for reimbursing the DOS for providing administrative services to the various organizations comprising the US mission in a partner nation. Key elements of ICASS include customer participation, local empowerment, and transparency.

The customer is defined as any organization using the various services available in the embassy. Although customers are involved in the selection of service providers, they can select a provider other than the one selected through ICASS; however, this should be done only after careful consideration of the total impact on the USG and future availability of the alternate source. Although service providers can be either USG agencies or local vendors, the DOS or US Agency for International Development (USAID) will provide the majority of the services.

The ICASS budget is locally generated and managed. Each embassy determines how much money will be required and how those funds will be spent. They identify what services will be provided, how they will be managed, and how much will be charged for those services.

Another element of ICASS is the total visibility of administrative services and cost elements. The customers help to establish performance standards for services provided. For example, it could be determined that vouchers should be processed within fifteen days. These standards would then be used to rate the effectiveness of the service providers.

ICASS is managed as a modified working capital fund. This fund is no-year funds to allow for unobligated funds to be carried over from one year to the next. These unobligated funds could be returned to all the participating agencies, reprogrammed for other ICASS needs, or retained to reduce the bills of all agencies for the next fiscal year (FY).

Each agency representative signs an ICASS memorandum of understanding (MOU), which defines the services that will be provided and identifies the customers and service providers. The MOU spells out the objectives and service standards established by the ICASS council and details the program evaluation and review procedures. Each customer completes an ICASS agreement for those services to be provided by the ICASS service provider for each type of fund.

The ICASS Council is the formal body of each embassy that develops the charter and approves the MOUs for the embassy. It is authorized to adopt by-laws suitable for local conditions. The council is composed of one senior manager from each Cabinet-level agency and each service provider, with the SDO/DATT representing all DOD agencies on the ICASS Council. The council develops and approves the annual ICASS budget and has the authority to manage all services. The council decides what services are to be provided, which organization will provide those services, and how the services will be provided. It establishes performance standards with each service provider and then evaluates the performance and costs of each service provider. The council will also resolve most disputes among participating agencies.

The Deputy Chief of Mission (DCOM) is an ex-officio member of the ICASS council, providing policy perspective to aid in resourcing decisions but is not a voting member. The DCOM keeps the COM informed on ICASS issues.

The primary role of the COM is in resolving disputes between agencies. An agency can bring a dispute to the COM that could not be resolved in the ICASS Council or a dispute that was decided by the ICASS Council that a participating agency does not agree with.

The ICASS Executive Board in Washington, DC provides the highest level of ICASS policy and is chaired by the Assistant Secretary of State for Administration. Participating agency representatives are at the assistant secretary level. The Executive Board meets quarterly to review and make policy.

Disputes that could not be resolved to the satisfaction of the COM can be sent to the ICASS Executive Board for resolution. This avenue should be pursued only for major items and then only after all other avenues of grievance have been exhausted.

The ICASS Interagency Working Group provides policy on items delegated by the ICASS Executive Board. It is made up of working-level representatives from each agency involved with ICASS and meets twice a month. It communicates policy developed within and from the Executive Board to ICASS member agencies and the field. It reviews and approves non-post costs and factors and resolves issues raised by embassy councils.

The ICASS Service Center is a full-time service organization that serves as the secretariat for the ICASS Executive Board and the ICASS Interagency Working Group. It is a permanent office consisting of interagency staff. It provides budget and financial services to the various ICASS Councils. It provides implementation guidance on ICASS budgets and procedures. It manages a cost distribution computer system and coordinates training on all ICASS issues. It provides customer assistance for post operations.

Capital Security Cost Sharing

Capital Security Cost Sharing (CSCS) is the DOS program designed to fund the construction of 150 new embassies and consulates worldwide. It authorizes the Secretary of State to determine the allowable cost share for each tenant agency under COM authority and is designed to generate $17.5 billion over a fourteen-year period. It is authorized by Section 604 of the Secure Embassy Construction and Counterterrorism Act of 1999, as amended by the FY 2005 Consolidated Appropriations Act (P.L. 108-447). CSCS is also designed as an incentive for all tenant agencies to right-size their overseas staffs to the numbers essential for mission accomplishment.

The DOD is one of the largest tenant agencies; rightsizing is the mechanism by which DOD can minimize its footprint in the embassies and thereby reduce overall CSCS costs. For FY 2014 through FY 2016, DOS will be paid by its tenant agencies for billets at the following rates:

- Controlled Access Area (CAA) Office—$76,017

- Non-CAA Office—$ 11,429

- Non-Office (warehouse)—$2,893

- Non-embassy space—$0

Based on these rates, every effort must be taken to minimize the number of billets within the CAA. DOS may grant a waiver for some work spaces to be located apart from the embassy, if the host nation facility provides safety and security equal to or greater than that which would be afforded within the embassy.

Annually, DOS sends a report to the Office of the Secretary of Defense (Comptroller) requesting verification of DOD staffing levels at all embassies. A copy of this report and request for verification is sent to DSCA and forwarded through the respective CCMDs to the SCOs for action. Each SDO/DATT or his/her designated representative must review this document with the SCO joint manning document provided by the CCMD and verify that each entry in the DOS Post Administrative Support System (PASS), maintained by the Administration Section or Human Resources Office, is correct. SDO/DATTs should also check organization title, job titles, numbers of personnel, location within the embassy (CAA, non-CAA, etc.), or external non-embassy space. The accuracy of this review is critical, since DOD pays DOS based upon what tenant agency data is in PASS. Corrections in PASS can only be made at each respective embassy; they cannot be made at the CCMDs or by DSCA.

For DSCA, the purpose of the review is to ensure that DOD pays DOS for the correct number of DOD personnel assigned to the SCO and that within the SCO, DOD is able to verify the correct numbers of personnel assigned to each represented fund source. Within each SCO, there are typically two types of funded positions, as noted above: SA (T-20) and O&M. DSCA is responsible for the SA positions; the CCMDs or military services are responsible for the O&M billets. Additionally, personnel assigned to a specialized training activity may be reflected in PASS as members of a SCO. In reality, they are not SA personnel but are funded by a military service, which would also be responsible for CSCS.

Upon completion of the review and verification by the SDO/DATT, the DSCA Comptroller is notified through the respective CCMD. If any discrepancies arise that cannot be resolved at the embassies, the SDO/DATT should immediately forward them through the CCMD to the DSCA Comptroller for resolution.

Although this CSCS review is done annually, it is in the best interests of the SCO to periodically review the SCO staffing in PASS to ensure that all corrections are made and that any changes in personnel (increases and decreases due to NSDD-38 and Personal Services Agreement actions) are properly reflected. Any questions should be addressed to DSCA, Directorate of Business Operations, Comptroller.

SECURITY ASSISTANCE AUTOMATED RESOURCE MANAGEMENT SUITE

The SAARMS is a suite of software applications that assist the SCO in managing its resources. SAARMS currently consists of three computer applications:

- Budget Execution application

- Budget Preparation application

- Property application

The Budget Preparation application automates the SA Admin budget preparation for the SCOs and CCMDs. It is a web-based application that provides the capability for the SCO to develop and modify their budget. The CCMD and DSCA can view the countries individually or view them rolled up into one budget. All required budget submission data is included in the program and all pertinent reports can be generated. The program is also designed so that it could be used for other than SA Admin fund budget submissions, if so desired.

The Budget Execution application serves as the web-based SA funds management system. The application provides the SCO with recording and reporting capability and meets generally accepted accounting standards. The application has built in controls to preclude over-obligation of the OA/FCA amount and provides fund control by management categories as specified by the CCMD. Obligations are created, disbursements are recorded, and required reports can be generated by the application. The application also transfers data to DFAS–SCA for entry into the official accounting system. The Budget Execution application is used to manage SA Admin funds and expenditures but can be used for the SCO's other types of funds as well.

The Property application serves as the SA property management system. A stand-alone application, it standardizes property management throughout a CCMD. The application creates and stores the required information on property records and provides the requisite reports.

SECURITY COOPERATION OFFICE SECURITY ASSISTANCE BUDGET PREPARATION PROCESS

The budget preparation process starts with the annual budget call. For SA Admin funds, DSCA provides a target ceiling level for each CCMD and notifies them of what information is required, when it is required, and with what details. The Executive Agent service performs this same role for O&M funds. The CCMDs then provide a target ceiling level for each SCO and notify them of what to provide to the CCMD and the due date. Typically, this process begins around May, with the publication of the DSCA budget call. However, many of the CCMDs will start their budget preparation process by early March.

The budget is created and submitted via the web-based SAARMS Budget Preparation application and consists of the SDO/DATT's narrative, detailed descriptions, and financial requirements summarized by object class. The SDO/DATT's narrative is the single most important item in the budget, as it provides the overall perspective on the SCO's program and why the requested budget is needed. The SA budget submission includes nine fiscal years of data, to include:

- Past FY (actual costs)

- Current FY (actual costs plus estimations for the remainder of the year)

- The next FY (taking last year's projected requirements and revising them)

- One out-year (projected requirements two years from now)

- Five POM years

Direct costs (LE Staff Pay, TDY costs, supplies, leases, etc.) are itemized in the budget and include total estimated expenses that will require distribution of funding authority to the SCO.

Indirect costs (ICASS, USCG, and FSN severance pay) are included in the budget as special exhibits, even though they are not obligated or paid by the SCO. DSCA has responsibility for budgeting for these items, but the SCO provides information on them and monitors them throughout the year.

For management and reimbursement purposes, there will be a special exhibit for each of the following items that apply to the SCO. These items are fully defined in the *SAARMS Budget Preparation User's Handbook*, found in the Budget Library on the SAN Web:

- C-12 flying hours

- Resource Allocation (workload distribution)

- Unfunded requirements

The budget will be prioritized with "must pay" items first and then discretionary items. A "must pay" is an item that is required by law or regulation, e.g., entitlements, leases, or utilities. A discretionary item can be either mission-essential or non-mission-essential but does not fit the "must pay" requirement, e.g., most TDYs, supplies, and equipment. Any mission requirement that cannot be included within the budget target ceiling may be submitted as an unfunded requirement. The CCMD reviews and modifies the budgets submitted by each SCO. When the CCMDs are satisfied with their budgets, DSCA reviews the overall budget and prepares it for submission to DOS and Congress.

The budget approval and execution process works in reverse of the budget submission process. Congress provides the funding appropriation and authority to DOS, which in turn provides the allocation of appropriated funding to DSCA. DSCA takes this allocated funding, along with the authorized funds from the administrative trust fund account, to provide the CCMDs with their approved allotment on a quarterly basis. CCMDs issue OA/FCA amounts to the SCOs, authorizing them to obligate the USG to expend funds.

Security Cooperation Office Security Assistance Budget Execution Process

Receipt of the OA/FCA ends the budget preparation process and begins the budget execution process. This phase consists of day-to-day operations, and the SAARMS Budget Execution program is used to record the following transactions and to aid the SCO in managing its resources wisely:

- Obligating funds

- Recording payments

- Reconciling records with DFAS–SCA

The SCOs can only procure those items that are authorized and required to perform their mission. These requirements will include everything from pens and pencils to dependent student education and TDY. For each requirement, the SCO will obligate funds to reserve them in the budget for the planned payment.

Once the SCO has established an obligation, the appropriate paperwork must be processed. This could be a TDY form, purchase request, miscellaneous obligation document, supply order, contract, purchase order, work order, or a requisition.

The vendor will usually be paid in one of five ways:

- The embassy budget and finance (B&F) office can pay the vendor by check or electronic funds transfer (EFT)

- The DOS GFSC can pay the vendor by check or EFT

- DFAS can pay the vendor by EFT

- The embassy B&F office could provide the SCO with cash to pay the vendor

- The vendor is paid using USG purchase card

Payment will be recorded by the SCO in SAARMS, regardless of how the payment is made. At regular intervals based on the size of the SCO, and at the end of each fiscal year, the SCO reconciles its records of obligations and payments to ensure that recorded payments agree with actual expenditures, that the budget has sufficient funds to pay all the bills, and that excess funds have been freed up for other obligations.

Security Assistance Automated Resource Management Suite Budget Execution Reports

The SAARMS Budget Execution application provides three kinds of reports: budget operation reports, including document history, open/closed documents, and reconciliation; record submission reports, including transaction summary and miscellaneous obligation document; and management reports, including status of funds and obligation plan.

The SDO/DATT is responsible for ensuring that the budget program consistently reflects assigned missions and priorities. At the beginning of each FY, the SCO will submit to the CCMD an annual funding plan, laying out how the SCO will fund its mission. This plan should be entered into the SAARMS Budget Execution application as an obligation plan.

The status of funds report uses the obligation plan, along with actual obligations and payments, to give an accurate accounting of funds. The SDO/DATT and CCMD should review this report periodically to ensure that actual expenditures are proceeding as originally planned.

The document history report, when sorted by management category, shows how funds are being obligated and expended in each category. This allows the SDO/DATT to see every transaction that was made in each category, making it a good internal management control tool.

The obligation and payment summary sorted by the management category, makes it possible for the SDO/DATT to quickly see how money has been obligated for each management category, how much has been paid, and how much is still unpaid. These are all available on the status of funds report but are shown in this report in greater detail.

The reconciliation report is used to reconcile SAARMS and DFAS records. This is arguably the most important report in SAARMS.

SECURITY COOPERATION OFFICE SECURITY ASSISTANCE BUDGET CAUTIONS AND PROBLEMS

There are several items that have consistently caused problems for SCOs. Government-leased housing is a prime example, because CCMD approval is required for any lease (plus annual utilities) over $50,000 of the SA Admin funds. The CCMD can approve new and replacement leases for less than $50,000 or delegate this approval to the SDO/DATT; however, the SDO/DATT may not approve the lease for his or her own quarters.

DSCA approves the purchase of all foreign-made vehicles to ensure the Buy-American Act is adhered to; all other vehicles are approved by the CCMDs. Vehicles may be armored only by sources approved by the General Services Administration (GSA).

Only the CCMD can grant authority for domicile-to-duty transportation, the use of a government vehicle for transportation between home and the office. Domicile-to-duty use of government vehicles requires all members of the SCO to be aware of the limitations of domicile-to-duty. It is based on the threat in a country, is approved by the Secretary of Defense, and is reviewed every six months. It also is deemed a fringe benefit by the Internal Revenue Service and may be noted on a person's W-2 form each year it is authorized.

The SCO will be involved with supporting a host of individuals that are not assigned to the SCO. It is incumbent on the SCO to ensure that funding is provided by the individuals' parent organization to cover the additional expenditures required for these personnel.

SUMMARY

The SCO is faced with a daunting task in managing its resources. Through prudent management and oversight, the SCO can avoid major pitfalls. The SCO is not alone; they are supported by many different organizations. They also must report to many different organizations, determined by the source of funding and services provided.

The SCO will generally receive SA administrative funds for most of their SA budget requirements but will also receive some O&M funds for their non-SA programs. The SCO might also use FMS case funding or have support provided to them by the partner nation through AIK. The SCO has several options available to them to fund ATFP but will start by requesting funds from DOS, then the T-20 or O&M budget, and finally, the CCMD.

The various types of funds do not flow directly to the SCO. The SCO has funding authority for these funds, sent by DSCA or the MILDEPs via the CCMDs, depending on what service or item is being funded. The actual SA funds will be accounted for and disbursed by DFAS–SCA.

There are many players in the SCO budget process. Congress appropriates some funds for the SCO. DOS will submit the appropriated portion of the SCO's budget to Congress annually. DSCA provides budget targets and fiscal oversight for SA funds. The MILDEPs provide budget targets and fiscal oversight for O&M funds. The CCMDs provide intermediary support and fiscal oversight for all types of funds. The embassy provides accounting and finance support as required to the SCO. The GFSC provides accounting support for DOS-processed transactions, and DFAS–SCA provides accounting support for all SA transactions. The SCO is responsible for developing its own budget and for effectively managing its funds. SAARMS is the software suite that provides budget preparation, budget execution, and property accounting support.

The SCO will receive representation funds to maintain the standing and prestige of the US by extending official courtesies to authorized personnel. There are many rules and regulations that govern the use, record keeping, and limitations of these funds, and they are likely to receive more attention than any other single category of funds.

ICASS is a system for providing administrative services to the various organizations in a US embassy. ICASS can be an effective tool for the SCO, and other US agencies within an embassy, to control costs and manage the quality of services. Participation of service providers and customers is essential to the effective implementation of the ICASS program. There are various levels of groups that oversee the ICASS program and provide for conflict resolution.

There are several areas that typically cause problems that the SCO must be vigilant in preventing. An internal management control program will help prevent difficulties from negatively affecting the mission of the SCO. The SCO is faced with a daunting task in managing its resources but, through understanding, vigilance, and asking the right people the right questions, it can maintain a good resource management program.

REFERENCES

Foreign Assistance Act of 1961, as amended.

DSCA Manual 5105.38-M, *Security Assistance Management Manual*. http://www.samm.dsca.mil/.

DODD 5105.75, *Department of Defense Operations at US Embassies*.

DODD C-5101.81 5105.81, *Implementing Instructions for Department of Defense Operations at US Embassies*.

DODI 5132.13, *Staffing of Security Cooperation Organizations and the Selection and Training of Security Cooperation Personnel*.

DOD 7000.14-R, *Financial Management Regulation*, Volume 15, "Security Cooperation Policy."

DFAS–SCA 7200.1-R, "Administrative Control of Appropriations and Financing of Requirements."

AR 1-75, AFR 400-45, and OPNAVINST 4900.31G, *Administrative and Logistical Support of Overseas Security Assistance Organizations*.

Code of Federal Regulations, Title 41, Public Contracts and Property Management.

DODD 7280.4, *Commander in Chief's* (CINC's) *Initiative Fund* (CIF).

DODD 1015.10, *Military Morale, Welfare, and Recreation (MWR) Programs*.

DODI 5010.40, *Managers' Internal Control Program* (MICP) *Procedures*.

DODI 7250.13, *Use of Appropriated Funds for Official Representation Purposes*.

CJCSI 7201.01A, *Combatant Commanders' Official Representation Funds*.

AF65-603, *Official Representation Funds*.

AR 37-47, *Representation Funds of the Secretary of the Army.*

NAVSEAINST 7042.1A, *Official Representation Funds.*

6 FAH-5, *ICASS Handbook.*

CENTCOM REGULATIONS

CCR 12-2, *Security Assistance Policy Administrative and Management.*

CCR 37-1, *Resource Management System.*

CCR 37-7, *Official Representation Funds.*

CCR 37-13, *Management Control Program.*

CCR 37-15, *Administration of Security Assistance Organization Operating Funds.*

CCR 37-16, *Security Assistance Program Representation Funds.*

CCR 310-2, *Military Publication Travel.*

ATTACHMENT 17-1

NATIONAL SECURITY DECISION DIRECTIVE NUMBER 38

The White House
Washington, DC
June 2, 1982
National Security Decision Directive Number 38

Subject: Staffing at Diplomatic Missions and Their Constituent Posts

This directive supersedes the directive of October 14, 1974 and subsequent directives governing the Monitoring Overseas Direct Employment (MODE) system.

In accordance with my letter to Chiefs of Mission, and the memorandum of September 22, 1981, conveying it to heads of Executive Departments and Agencies, all agencies with staffs operating under the authority of Chiefs of Mission will ensure that, in coordination with the DoS, the Chiefs of Mission's approval is sought on any proposed changes in the size, composition, or mandate of such staff elements. Departments and agencies wishing to initiate changes should transmit their proposals to Chiefs of Missions in consultation with the DoS. In the event the Secretary of State or his designee is unable promptly to resolve to the satisfaction of the parties concerned any disputes which may arise between Chiefs of Mission and Agency Heads or his designee, the Secretary of State and the other Agency Head concerned will present the differing views to me for decision through the Assistant to the President for National Security Affairs. Formal acknowledgement of changes approved by Chiefs of Mission or determined by me shall be transmitted to diplomatic missions by the DoS.

Overseas staffing of elements with US diplomatic missions abroad shall conform to decisions reached in accordance with the above procedures and decisions made through the budgetary process.

Departments and agencies will keep the DoS informed as to current and projected overseas staffing authorizations for each diplomatic post, differentiating between the number of US personnel and the number of foreign national personnel authorized for each post. The DoS shall maintain a current record of staffing authorizations for each overseas post. Agencies will cooperate with the DoS in providing data including any data needed to meet special reporting requirements.

The DOS, in consultation with concerned agencies, will develop guidelines by July 1, 1982 for my approval to implement this directive.

//SIGNED//

RONALD REAGAN

Attachment 17-2
Guidelines to Implement National Security Decision Directive (NSDD) Number 38
July 13, 1982

These guidelines are issued pursuant to the Presidential Directive of 2 June 1982 on Staffing at Diplomatic Missions and Constituent Posts. These guidelines replace all guidelines and other agreements previously in effect under the Monitoring Overseas Direct employment (MODE) system.

The purpose of the Directive and these guidelines is to allow the flexible, systematic and expeditious deployment and management of personnel of all USG agencies operating under the authority of Chiefs of Mission in support of US foreign policy objectives.

These guidelines will ensure that the approval of Chiefs of Mission is sought by USG agencies on proposed staffing changes for activities operating under the authority of Chiefs of Mission. The Chiefs of Mission will transmit their views on overseas presence to the DoS, as department and agency representatives will communicate with their respective department/agency headquarters in this regard.

These guidelines also provide for the resolution of disagreements, should such arise between the Chiefs of Mission and department/agency representatives and between the DoS and department/agency heads.

A. Requests for Changes in Staffing

1. Preliminary or exploratory consultation by the requesting agency with the Chief of Mission regarding staffing changes is encouraged. Such informal proposals may be initiated in Washington or by agency overseas representatives.

2. Formal requests for approval of staffing changes as required by the Directive must be made by the cognizant agency to the Chief of Mission in consultation with the DoS. Copies of such requests will be provided to the DoS.

3. The Chief of Mission will convey his views on formal requests to the Department of State. The point of contact in the DoS for such matters is the Office of Management Operations (M/MO), Room 7427, (Since changed to the Office of Management Policy and Planning, M/P, Room 5214), Attention: Assistant for Overseas Positions. The Chief of Mission's response to the formal request should be addressed to that office for action. Copies of requests and responses will be given to the appropriate regional and functional bureaus in the DoS and the requesting agency.

B. Resolution of Disagreements

1. If there are disagreements over staffing levels between Chiefs of Mission and agency heads, the views of both parties will be forwarded to M/MO (M/P) for immediate presentation to the Secretary of State for decision within 15 working days of receipt from M/MO.

2. If the Secretary of State is unable to resolve the issue to the satisfaction of the parties concerned, the Secretary and the Agency head concerned will present their respective views to the President for decision through the Assistant to the President for National Security Affairs.

C. Formal Acknowledgement of Changes

1. Changes in staffing levels at individual posts reached in accordance with the above procedures will be provided by telegram from the DoS to the Chief of Mission, and the agencies concerned

D. Staffing Authorization Records

1. The DoS shall maintain a current record of staffing authorization for each overseas post. Staffing authorization is defined as all full-time, permanent, direct hire, United States government employees, including foreign nationals, and United States Military Personnel under the authority of a Mission Chief.

2. Departments and agencies will provide the current and projected overseas staffing authorization information, required by the directive, to the DoS, Office of Management Operations (M/MO), Room 7427, (Since changed to the office of Management Policy and Planning (M/P), Room 5214), Attention: Assistant for Overseas Positions. That official will solicit additional information from departments and agencies when necessary to meet special reporting requirements as established by statute or as levied by the NSC, OMB, or the Congress.

END-USE MONITORING AND THIRD-PARTY TRANSFERS

INTRODUCTION

Sources for the policies and procedures for the end-use monitoring (EUM) and third-party transfer of US-origin defense articles, technical data, services, and training are the Arms Export Control Act (AECA), the Foreign Assistance Act of 1961 (FAA), as amended, various specific legislative initiatives, and the applicable regulations of the Department of State (DOS) and the Department of Defense (DOD). Restrictions and procedures for transfer or disposal under these individual security cooperation (SC) programs may vary significantly due the source of funding, specific legislation and other unique aspects of the various programs. This chapter is designed to augment chapter 8 of the *Security Assistance Management Manual* (SAMM) and serve as a guide to assist the defense community and the recipient foreign governments in fulfilling the obligations for EUM and third party transfer of US origin defense articles and services primarily provided through various DOD and DOS programs.

Section 40A of the AECA enacted in 1996 (Public Law 104-164) states, "The President shall establish a program that provides for End-Use Monitoring in order to improve accountability with respect to defense articles sold, leased, or exported under the AECA or FAA."

The DOD has made a determination that this requires, to the extent practicable, monitoring of US arms transfers by providing "reasonable assurance" that recipients comply with US government (USG) export control requirements regarding the use, transfer, and security of defense articles and services. It was also determined that this requirement applies to all US origin defense articles and services transferred under any government program.

The US policy goal for the EUM programs is to preserve the technological advantages enjoyed by US military forces over potential adversaries by impeding access to militarily significant items and technologies. As defined in the SAMM, EUM is a program designed to verify that defense articles or services transferred by the USG to foreign recipients are being used in accordance with the terms and conditions of the transfer agreement or other applicable agreement. A country receiving weapon systems and weapons systems technology from the US must agree to a variety of controls. The release of defense articles or data to a non-USG entity must be properly cleared within the DOS and DOD coordination processes. The recipient country or organization must provide substantially the same degree of security protection the USG would provide for the same article or information received. The recipient agrees that it will use the articles or information for the intended purpose and will not transfer or change the end-use (including disposal of the articles without prior consent of the USG). In addition, the recipient must permit verification of the security measures and end-use by representatives of the US.

These requirements are specified in the SAMM, chapters 5 and 8, and will be included in any of the documents authorizing the transfer of US-origin defense articles and services. For items transferred under the Foreign Military Sales (FMS) system, this normally is the letter of offer and acceptance (LOA) with the standard terms and conditions and any specific notes related to protection and verification. For direct commercial sales, the purchasing nation must sign either a Non-transfer Use Certificate (DSP-83) or a Statement by Ultimate Consignee and Purchaser (BIS-711 or BXA-711), and a security assurance agreement. Transfers of materiel and services through other grant programs (which are not documented on an LOA) are normally executed after the recipient has signed a bilateral agreement subject to the terms of the FAA, section 505 (i.e., sometimes referred to as a Section 505 Agreement).

DOD END-USE MONITORING

The Department of Defense's Golden Sentry Program

The AECA requires a comprehensive end-use monitoring program for arms sales and transfers authorized by the AECA and the FAA to verify with reasonable assurance that a recipient is in compliance with USG export controls. The DOS actively monitors, reports, and addresses unauthorized arms transfers and diversions in accordance with section 3 of the AECA through its Blue Lantern EUM program. Some of the procedures and considerations used in the DOS Blue Lantern program are incorporated into the framework of the DOD Golden Sentry EUM program. The Defense Security Cooperation Agency (DSCA) is responsible for reviewing requests for government-to-government exports of defense articles, defense services, and related technical data. DSCA provides significant details for the EUM program in chapter 8 of the SAMM. Titles to articles that are leased or loaned remain with the USG as detailed in the terms of the lease; however, EUM requirements still apply. All potential end-use violations must be reported to the Bureau of Political Military Affairs' Regional Security and Arms Transfers (PM/RSAT) Division at the DOS. Information regarding any potential violations should also be forwarded to the Golden Sentry program team, Weapons Division, Directorate for Programs at the DSCA. DOS PM/RSAT will determine if an investigation and a report to Congress is required in accordance with section 3 of the AECA.

Responsibilities for the Golden Sentry End-Use Monitoring Programs

The responsibilities for the conduct of the Golden Sentry EUM program are found in the SAMM, chapter 8, paragraph C8.2.3 and table C8.T2. The security cooperation office (SCO) is normally assigned the responsibility for in-country EUM requirements of the Golden Sentry program. There are two levels of EUM to be conducted by the SCO and the recipient nation: routine and enhanced.

Routine EUM

The SCO is required to conduct routine EUM visits with host nations in conjunction with other assigned duties. SCOs should perform EUM of defense articles and services exported via the Foreign Military Sales (FMS) and other building partner capacity (BPC) programs (such as 1206, 1208 and 1033 authorities) during visits to the host nation's installations, through interaction with other assigned embassy personnel and USG individuals working with the host nation's military and security forces, embassy and interagency reports and news media information. These EUM visits should be documented in a memorandum for record (MFR) to support DSCA compliance assessment visits (CAV). An MFR template is included in attachment 18-1. DSCA has developed a Routine EUM Summary Report in the EUM-Security Cooperation Information Portal (SCIP) database which provides a "watch list" of specific categories defense articles exported via the FMS system (or other DOD transfer programs). This report appears under the Queries/Reports menu on the EUM-SCIP home page. More information regarding SCIP is available in appendix 1 of this textbook. The routine EUM "watch list" of specific categories of defense items includes:

- Battle tanks

- Armored Combat Vehicles

- Artillery systems

- Fixed wing aircraft & Helicopters

- Unmanned Aerial Systems

- Warships & Military Vessels

- Missiles & Missile Systems

- Military vehicles

- Bombs

- Crew Served and Individual Weapons

- Platform Mounted Night Vision Devices

Enhanced EUM

Enhanced EUM (EEUM) are those actions required by the SAMM and other directives as specified in the appropriate transfer documents for sensitive items which require increased monitoring, physical security and accountability. EEUM articles require actual inventories (by item serial numbers) to be conducted by the purchasing country and SCO, and under certain circumstances, these articles may also require a compliance assessment visit by a DSCA-led team. The following defense articles are EEUM items:

- Communication Security (COMSEC) Equipment

- STINGER Missiles and Gripstocks

- Night Vision Devices

- JAVELIN Missiles and Command Launch Units

- TOW-2B Missiles

- Advanced Medium Range Air-to-Air Missiles AMRAAM (AIM-120)

- AIM-9X Advanced Sidewinder Air-to-Air Missiles

- Standoff Land Attack Missile Expanded Response Missiles (SLAM-ER)

- Harpoon Block II Missiles

- Joint Air-to-Surface Standoff Missiles (JASSM)

- Joint Standoff Weapon (JSOW)

- Standard Missile-3 (SM-3)

- Tomahawk Missile

- Large Aircraft Infrared Countermeasures (LAIRCM)

- Unmanned Aircraft System (UAS)

- Theater High Altitude Area Defense (THAAD)

- Other sensitive items specifically identified by Congress, DOS, or DOD

Standard Operating Procedures (SOPs) and Compliance (Control) Plans

SCOs are required by SAMM chapter 8, C8.T2, to develop EUM SOPs and/or EUM Compliance (Control) Plans to promulgate country-specific EUM policy and implement procedures to conduct routine and enhanced EUM. Copies of the SOPs and/or compliance (control) plans must be provided to DSCA. Written SOPs should contain as a minimum the information below and should be approved by the SCO Chief:

- EUM reference documents including laws, regulations & policy documents

- EUM POCs for all pertinent USG agencies & host nation organizations

- Procedures for conducting routine EUM including the use of FMS Routine EUM Summary Reports provided in the EUM-SCIP database & records of visits

- Procedures for conducting EEUM, including use of EEUM Reconciliation Reports provided in the EUM-SCIP database, use of EEUM checklists, maintaining records of physical security checks & inventories, logging inventories & annotating when items are lost, expended or destroyed in the EUM-SCIP database

- Procedures for assisting the host nation with requests for transfers of defense articles (third party transfers), changes of end use (destruction/disposal), and reporting equipment losses

- Procedures for reporting potential end-use violations, including theft and unauthorized access

- Procedures for recording all expenses for performing EEUM and submitting annual costs and projections under code 210EM through the Security Assistance Automated Resource Management Suite (SAARMS)

- Procedures for supporting attendance to regional EUM forums and coordinating DSCA Compliance Assessment Visits (CAVs) including taking corrective when required

Country Team Assessment (CTA)

If a host nation has a request for Missile Technology Control Regime (MTCR) Category I Intelligence, Surveillance, & Reconnaissance (ISR) Unmanned Aerial Vehicle (UAV)/Unmanned Combat Aerial Vehicle (UCAV), or NVDs, a plan for end-use monitoring for sensitive and advanced war fighting technology and the SCO's plan for compliance verification will need to be addressed in the CTA as referenced in SAMM C5.T1b.

Country Specific EUM

There are some countries that have unique EUM requirements mandated by Congress. The National Defense Authorization Act of 2008 provides the legal basis for the requirement to implement a control program in Iraq. According to law, the President shall implement a policy to control the export and transfer of defense articles delivered to Iraq. This includes all defense article registration and monitoring of all small arms provided to the Iraqi Government, as well as any Iraqi groups or individuals. Additionally, the law requires the USG to maintain detailed records of origin, shipping, and distribution for defense articles transferred under the Iraq Security Forces Fund authorization. This law was implemented by DOD Instruction 4140.66 *Registration and Monitoring of Defense Articles* (dated October 15, 2009).

The National Defense Authorization Act of 2010 provides the legal basis for the requirement to implement control programs in Afghanistan and Pakistan. This law was implemented by the reissuance of DOD Instruction 4140.66 *Registration and End-Use Monitoring of Defense Articles and/or Defense Services* (dated September 7, 2010). This instruction directs the establishment of a registration and monitoring system for DOD government-to-government transfer or export of defense articles and/or defense services transferred to Iraq, Afghanistan, and Pakistan using funds made available to the DOD including, but not limited to, funds made available pursuant to the Iraq Security Forces Fund, Afghanistan Security Forces Fund, Pakistan Counterinsurgency Fund or any other security assistance program.

Specifically, DOD Instruction 4140.66 directs the applicable SCO to develop the necessary compliance plans and procedures to administer and maintain a comprehensive system of registration and monitoring of defense articles and/or defense services provided to Iraq, Afghanistan, and/or Pakistan, including maintaining auditable records sufficient to certify that the system complies with this instruction. These plans and procedures include the necessary steps to ensure the registration of the serial numbers of all small arms to be provided to the governments of Iraq, Afghanistan, and/or Pakistan and/or to other groups, organizations, citizens, or residents of Iraq, Afghanistan, and/or Pakistan. It directs for an EUM program of all lethal defense articles to be provided to the governments of Iraq, Afghanistan, and/or Pakistan and/or to other groups; and it mandates that the SCOs maintain auditable records to certify compliance of maintaining detailed records of the origin, shipping, and distribution of all defense articles provided to the governments of Iraq, Afghanistan, and/or Pakistan, and/or to other groups, organizations, citizens, or residents of Iraq, Afghanistan, and/or Pakistan.

Security Cooperation Office and the Partner Nation End-Use Monitoring Plan

The SCO and the partner nation should develop either a combined EUM compliance (control) plan or individual plans that spell out the procedures that will be followed to ensure the requirements for both routine and enhanced EUM as specified in the appropriate transfer documents are met. The plan should include the following provisions:

- Procedures to be followed for EUM visits

- Partner nation internal accountability procedures

- Procedures for reporting required inventories and inspections

- Procedures for record keeping on the part of the host nation and the SCO. As a minimum, the records maintained by the host country should include:

  ◊ Procedures for reporting possible violations and corrective action required

  ◊ Procedures for use of the SCIP

Visits to assess EUM compliance programs are an important part of the Golden Sentry program. There are three types of visits that the SCO and host nation will be involved with (See SAMM chapter 8, paragraph C8.5). The purpose of the EUM familiarization assessment visit (FAV) is to assist the host nation, the SCO, and the combatant command (CCMD) with the development of EUM compliance plans. The EUM compliance assessment visit (CAV) is to review and evaluate the overall EUM program of the SCO and the host nation and to assess host nation's compliance with the security and accountability provisos contained within the LOAs for EEUM items. FAV and CAV time lines and requirements are detailed in SAMM tables C8.T5 an C8.T6. An EUM investigation visit must be conducted if a possible violation of the AECA, section 3, and/or the FAA, section 505 is suspected. Because of the unique nature and political sensitivity associated with these visits, they are handled on a case-by-case basis in concert with DOS.

The SCIP EUM Community contains detailed information on items that have been transferred to a partner nation. It is to be used to report all inspections and other information concerning EUM and third party transfers. It also provides the capability to generate reports concerning the status of selected items transferred to a partner nation, as well as other information. To enroll or access the SCIP EUM Community, visit the SCIP website: http://www.scportal.us/home/.

Funding for EUM Requirements

Direct costs for EUM are itemized in the budget and include total estimated expenses that will require distribution of funding authority to the SCO. For management purposes, there will be a special exhibit for End-Use Monitoring (EUM) requirements. Enhanced EUM requirements that have just been received in country and were not included within the budget target ceiling level will be submitted as an unfunded requirement (UFR).

The CCMD reviews and modifies the budgets submitted by each SCO. When the CCMDs are satisfied with their budgets, DSCA reviews the overall budget and prepares it for submission to DOD and Congress.

SCOs should start the request for funds as a budget requirement as soon as the country starts the Letter of Request process (LOR) for an EEUM item. This allows time to include the EEUM monitoring requirements in the budget process and thus should have the additional EUM funds when needed. For a more detailed discussion of the overall budgeting process, refer to chapter 17 of this textbook, "Resource Management for the Security Cooperation Organization."

Compliance Assessment Visits

To comply with AECA section 40A, DSCA developed policy guidance in the SAMM to establish the Golden Sentry EUM program. In-country Compliance Assessment Visits (CAV) are required to verify that SCOs and host nations have appropriate EUM control measures in place.

The purpose of a CAV is to review and evaluate the SCO's (or equivalent organization/office) compliance with Golden Sentry EUM policy and the host nation's compliance with the terms and conditions for the transfer of defense articles and services including specific physical security and accountability provisos pertaining to sensitive technologies. Activities during a CAV include facility visits, record reviews, review of routine and enhanced EUM policies and procedures, and inventories of US-origin defense articles and/or services. EUM CAVs are coordinated well in advance with the CCMDs and the SCOs to ensure timely coordination with the host nation.

The EUM Community (i.e. Support/EUM resource tab) in SCIP has defense article checklists to assist the SCO in conducting self-assessments, to help prepare the host nation to receive EEUM defense articles, or to prepare for an upcoming CAV.

Security Cooperation Office CAV Criteria

Compliance with the policies and procedures of the Golden Sentry program and the SCO's responsibilities stated in the SAMM, C8.T2, to include:

- Implementation of written Standard Operating Procedures (EUM Compliance Plan) to perform routine and EEUM;

- Implementation of physical security and accountability plan(s) (NVD Compliance Plan) for the protection, storage, use and accountability of NVDs or other sensitive and advanced war fighting technology;

- Maintenance of records verifying routine and EEUM;

- Accuracy of the EEUM-designated items baseline as per the EEUM Reconciliation Report provided in the SCIP-EUM database;

- Timely performance of physical security and accountability checks of all EEUM-designated defense articles and services in accordance with Golden Sentry checklists;

- Use of the SCIP-EUM database to track inventories and to maintain an accurate disposition of EEUM-designated items;

- Verification and proper coordination with the DOS's Bureau of Political-Military Affairs / Office of Regional Security and Arms Transfers (DOS PM/RSAT) for the demilitarization, disposal, or destruction of EEUM-designated items and sensitive defense articles;

- Accuracy and timeliness of reporting losses, expenditures and destruction of EEUM-designated equipment;

- Proper coordination with DOS PM/RSAT regarding third-party transfer requests and approvals.

Host Nation CAV Criteria

Compliance with the conditions of the transfer agreements for US-provided defense articles and services to include:

- Cooperation and coordination with US officials to implement and maintain a viable EUM program which provides for routine and EEUM, including the CAVs conducted by DSCA;

- Potential end-use violations found during the assessment or previously reported by the SCO;

- Implementation of NVD physical security and accountability plan(s) (NVD Compliance Plan) as required;

- Implementation of physical security and accountability measures at storage sites/facilities maintaining EEUM-designated items in accordance with the special provisions stated in the LOA or other transfer agreement EEUM-designated equipment losses, action taken to prevent future losses (as appropriate) and reporting history;

- Accurate and timely notifications of demilitarization, disposal, destruction, loss, expenditure, or other change of end-use of EEUM-designated equipment and sensitive defense articles.

DSCA sends an annual message to all CCMDs and SCOs listing the countries that are subject to a CAV in the next two years. The two-year CAV plan is validated annually as necessary through coordination between DSCA and SCOs.

DEPARTMENT OF STATE'S BLUE LANTERN PROGRAM

The DOS program to conduct pre-license, pre-shipment/post-license, and a post-shipment check of defense articles and services transferred through direct commercial sales (DCS) is called the Blue Lantern Program. Blue Lantern end-use checks are conducted by US mission personnel abroad or personnel from the DOS.

The purpose of the Directorate of Defense Trade Controls (DDTC) is to verify the destination and specific end-use and end-users of US commercial defense exports and transfers. Blue Lantern cases are targeted based on potential risk, and are not randomly selected. These end-use checks encourage compliance with legal and regulatory requirements and have proven effective in addressing the growing problem of gray arms trade—the use of fraudulent export documentation or other techniques to acquire defense articles through legitimate channels for unauthorized end-users. The US Chief of Mission can request assistance from the SCO to conduct Blue Lantern checks in country. If there are expected temporary duty (TDY) costs, the SCO should request funding from the Embassy.

DEPARTMENT OF COMMERCE'S EXTRANCHECK PROGRAM

Extrancheck is the Department of Commerce (DOC) program that focuses on monitoring dual-use items transferred by US industry to a foreign nation via the *Export Administration Regulation* (EAR). DOC approves the export license and primarily focuses on "pre-delivery" controls (licensing checks) and post-delivery inspections. Post-delivery inspections are performed by Bureau of Industry and Security (BIS) Attachés, "Sentinel Teams" from DOC BIS, and US Foreign and Commercial Service Officers.

THIRD-PARTY TRANSFER AND CHANGES IN END-USE

A third-party transfer is any retransfer of title, physical possession or control of defense articles, training or technical data acquired under authorized USG transfer programs from the authorized recipient to any person or organization which is not an employee, officer or agent of that recipient country. A change in end-use is considered a third party transfer.

Examples of possible third-party transfers include retransfer of possession or title of defense articles or related data to:

- Any other foreign government
- Any private companies
- Bona fide museums within the receiving country
- Private education organizations within the original receiving country

Change of end-use is defined as any change in the usage of defense articles and services that deviates from the original purposes for which the items were sold. Disposal also constitutes a change in end-use for which prior consent from DOS is required for non-consumable items. Cannibalization is viewed as disposal only if the parts being removed will no longer be under the control of the ministry or agency that owns them, or will be used for purposes other than for national defense. Examples of possible changes of end-use could be:

- Withdrawal of military end items from the operational inventory for display at a government run museum
- Use of unserviceable/non-repairable vehicles as targets on a firing range
- Transfer of demilitarized military end items or machinery from the armed forces to civil government or educational institutions
- Transfer of a US-origin military vehicle from an operational military unit to be used as a police vehicle assigned to a police department or other law enforcement agency
- Demilitarization and redistribution of defense articles re-cycled among host government agencies
- Demilitarization and complete disposal of defense articles such that the materiel is no longer considered a defense article

Requirement for Prior Approval

The DOS, on behalf of the President, must consent to the retransfer of defense articles or services originally provided under the provisions of the FAA or the AECA to anyone not an officer, employee, or agent of that recipient country.

In considering a request for approval to retransfer any implement of war to another country, DOS will not agree to the transfer unless the USG itself would transfer the defense article under consideration to that country. In addition, DOS will not consent to the retransfer of any significant defense article on the *United States Munitions List* (USML) unless the item is demilitarized prior to transfer, or the proposed recipient foreign country commits in writing to provide appropriate security and third party transfer assurances.

The transferring government must send a written request either directly or through the SCO by letter, fax, or e-mail to the DOS, Directorate of Regional Security and Arms Transfer if the items were originally provided through a government-to-government program (See attachment 18-2 of this chapter for more details). For previously exported DCS USML articles and technical data, per section 123.9(c) of the *International Traffic in Arms Regulations* (ITAR), the original exporter or recipient may apply directly to the DOS, Directorate of Defense Trade Controls. Some Commerce Department *Commerce Control List* (CCL)-licensed items require a license for initial export, but they may be retransferred within the receiving country, and in selected cases, re-exported without further USG coordination.

The request for retransfer must be supported by end-use and retransfer assurances from the proposed recipient. If the initial recipient is not the final end-user, the final end-user must be identified and appropriate end-use and retransfer assurances must be provided by both the intermediate and final recipients. If proposed recipients are unable or unwilling to identify the final end-user and end-use of the articles, the transfer will not be approved. In addition, if brokers are involved as intermediaries in the transfer, they must be clearly identified in the transfer request, and they must be registered with the DOS PM/DDTC as brokers.

If the receiving country has a blanket end-use and retransfer assurance agreement with the USG, end-use and retransfer assurances specific to individual transfers may not be required. Blanket assurance members under the Defense Trade Security Initiative (DTSI) program have the added benefit of limited advanced consent (see SAMM C8.7.3.2).

The DOS must notify Congress of proposed transfers that meet AECA section 32, "Congressional reporting" thresholds, as described in chapter 2 of this textbook, "Security Cooperation Legislation and Policy."

Disposal

When the recipient government no longer requires an item and there is no other agency that wants it, disposal may be in order. Thus, disposal is the final change of end-use. Normally, title to equipment acquired through a grant program such as Military Assistance Program (MAP) or excess defense articles (EDA) passes to the recipient country. However, the US retains reversionary rights to the equipment so the recipient must agree to return the equipment to the USG when it is no longer required for its intended purpose.

If the Defense Logistics Agency (DLA) Disposition Services determines that the materiel can neither be redistributed nor employed any longer, the recipient is obligated to take responsibility for its proper disposal and seek consent of DOS prior to doing so.

Net proceeds of any such disposal or sale of MAP and grant EDA equipment will be paid to the USG unless another cost sharing arrangement has been previously approved. For guidance on MAP equipment disposal see SAMM, chapter 11 section C11. HR.1.9.3.

For items acquired through FMS with a country's own funds, or through Foreign Military Financing or grant programs other than MAP or EDA, the USG has no reversionary right. All proceeds of approved sales/transfers go to the host nation.

Title to DCS acquired US-origin defense articles passes to the recipient country upon shipment. USG approval is required for third-party transfer and change of end-use only for those DCS purchased defense articles that are subject to export license control, i.e., those items on either the USML or the CCL. Regardless of whether or not the export application was accompanied by a duly executed form DSP-83, all DCS USML exports must have retransfer authorization from the DOS PM/DDTC. All proceeds of approved sales/transfers go to the host nation.

If the partner nation has been granted the right to dispose of materiel, its disposal procedures should follow in form and content those used by DLA Disposition Services in disposing of US excess defense articles, though local forms and channels may be used as appropriate. The following functional areas are those deemed most important in complying with security trade control requirements:

- Determination of demilitarization requirements

- Conduct of sale

- Bidder screening, end-use and retransfer assurance

- Import certificate/delivery verification as required

In some instances, materiel can only be disposed of as scrap, but this does not negate the requirement to follow appropriate security procedures. Details, which must be followed in the conduct of local sales, are found in DOD 4160.21-M. *Defense Materiel Disposition Manual*, and DOD 4160.28-M vol 1-3, *Defense Demilitarization Manual*.

Summary

To preserve American technological advantage, countries receiving weapons and weapons technology must agree to provide the same level of protection for the articles and information as would the US itself. This requirement applies whether a country receives material through commercial channels or through a government-to-government mechanism.

The DOD's EUM program is the Golden Sentry program, which applies to all defense articles, services, and training transferred by DOD. The DOS's EUM program is the Blue Lantern program, which applies to all defense articles, services, and training transferred through commercial channels (e.g. Direct Commercial Sales). The Department of Commerce has an EUM program, Extrancheck, which focuses on the monitoring of dual-use items transferred by commercial channels.

Under Golden Sentry, two levels of EUM are possible (routine and enhanced), depending on the sensitivity of the technology involved. The SCO and the partner nation must jointly develop an EUM control (compliance) plan that will ensure the procedures are taken to protect defense articles, services, and training transferred by the DOD.

Transfers of defense articles, services, and training to a third-party and changes of end-use always require prior approval from USG. These transfers and changes in end-use terms are covered in the standard terms and conditions of the LOA, which are discussed in chapter 8 of this textbook. Disposal of the equipment is the final stage of EUM and must conform to USG demilitarization requirements to safeguard the technology from possible misuse.

REFERENCES

Arms Export Control Act of 1976 (AECA), as amended.

Foreign Assistance Act of 1961 (FAA), as amended.

Export Administration Act of 2001.

DOD Instruction 4140.66, *Registration and Monitoring of Defense Articles and/or Defense Services*, September 7, 2010.

DOD Instruction 4160.28, *DOD Demilitarization (DEMIL) Program*, April 7, 2011

DOD Instruction 4140.01, *DOD Supply Chain Materiel Management Policy*, December 22, 2011

DOD 4160.21-M, *Defense Materiel Disposition Manual*, August 18, 1997.

DOD 4160.28-M, vol 1-3, *Defense Demilitarization*, June 7, 2011.

DOD Directive 4165.06, *Real Property*, November 18, 2008.

DSCA Manual 5105.38-M, *Security Assistance Management Manual* (SAMM). http://www.dsca.mil/samm/.

DSP-83, *Non-transfer and Use Certificate* (Office of Defense Trade Control).

Export Administration Regulations (EAR) (title 15 CFR parts 730–774).

International Traffic in Arms Regulations (ITAR) (title 22, parts 120–130).

GAO/NSIAD-00-208, *Changes Needed to Correct Weaknesses in End-Use-Monitoring Program*, August 2000.

ATTACHMENT 18-1
ROUTINE END-USE-MONITORING (EUM) REPORT TEMPLATE

Routine EUM is conducted to provide reasonable assurance that recipients of defense articles and services provided via government-to-government programs are complying with requirements imposed by the USG with respect to use, transfer and security. All Routine EUM observations will be recorded (at least quarterly) and records will be maintained for five years. This template or a Memorandum for Record (MFR) containing similar information will be filed electronically or physically within the EUM record folders whenever Routine EUM is performed. Potential violations will be reported immediately to the CCMD, DSCA and DOS PM/RSAT through appropriate channels.

1. Reporting Official:

2. Office:

3. Duty Position:

4. Date: CY/QTR:

5. Routine EUM performed through the following (Check all that apply):

    ☐ Inspection/Observation by Reporting Officer

    ☐ Inventory by Reporting Officer

    ☐ Report by US Government Employee/Military Member

    ☐ Report by US Contractor

    ☐ Review of the Host Nation's Records

    ☐ Open Source Media (TV, Newspaper, Magazine, etc.)

    ☐ Other

6. Describe as indicated below the Routine EUM performed.

    a. Defense articles/service(s) monitored:

    b. Circumstances of monitoring (site visit in conjunction with official business, etc.):

    c. Location:

    d. Monitoring performed with respect to proper use, transfer and security. If applicable, annotate the quantity or serials #s observed:

    e. Any issues or problems requiring corrective action:

    f. If there were any potential end-use violations observed and whether the potential violation(s) were reported immediately to the CCMD, DSCA and DOS PM/RSAT through appropriate channels:

    g. Any other pertinent remarks as appropriate:

ATTACHMENT 18-2
DEPARTMENT OF STATE THIRD-PARTY TRANSFER REQUEST FORM

What does the foreign government include in the request?

The following questions should be addressed in a written request by governments proposing to transfer of US-origin defense articles/data to another country or private entity on a permanent or temporary basis prior to US State Department taking action.

Standard questions for requests to US for authority to retransfer government-origin defense articles:

1. Who is the divesting government?

2. What commodity/equipment/service/technical data is to be transferred? (Please provide NSNs.) What are the serial numbers? (These must be provided for significant military equipment.)

3. How did the divesting country originally acquire the defense article(s)?
   - Foreign military sale? (Please provide case identifier or explanation as to why it is unavailable)
   - Military assistance program?
   - Excess defense article grant or sale?
   - Drawdown?
   - Cooperative development program?
   - Memorandum of understanding?
   - Direct commercial sale? If DCS, contact Office of Defense Trade Controls
   - Was this equipment acquired with national funds or with grant funding such as foreign military financing?
   - Other?

4. When was/were the article(s) acquired by the divesting country?

5. What was the original acquisition value (necessary for Congressional approval/reporting)?

6. What is the current value, if applicable?

7. Why does that government wish to divest itself of the equipment?

8. Who is the proposed recipient?

9. Is this a temporary or permanent transfer to the proposed recipient?

10. What is the proposed recipient's planned end-use for the articles (Please provide as much detail as possible)?

11. Does the proposed recipient currently possess this model of equipment?

12. Are there any intermediaries? If so, who? What is their role? Where are they located and what are the points of contact?

13. Will any net proceeds be realized from this sale, transfer, or disposal? If so, what are the estimated net proceeds?

14. Is there a certain date requested for approval? If so, please indicate the date and provide the relevant details.

15. Please provide point of contact details for the divesting government, the proposed recipient, and any intermediaries.

Chapter

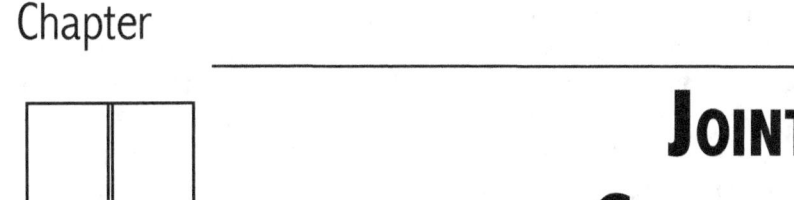

JOINT PLANNING FOR SECURITY COOPERATION

INTRODUCTION

Planning is an essential step in all military operations or activities, security cooperation included. At its simplest, planning is the process by which one understands where they are, where they want to be, and how best to get there. The plan is the product; how one intends to get from "A" to "B."

At the operational level, planning focuses on ends, ways, and means. Planning allows the military professional to clearly identify where the command wants to go—the ends. Through operational art and design, the planner pinpoints how best to get there—the ways. Finally, the means, i.e., resources, are identified and applied. While the plan directs action to achieve the ends, it also serves as the justification for resourcing; planning is how DOD rationalizes security cooperation (SC).

What is different between operational planning and SC planning? In security cooperation, the political and military realms are one, and the planner must be an expert in all aspects of the Partner Nation (PN) and on the USG policy towards it. Also, SC is not war fighting, and SCOs do not wield weapons. The metaphorical weapons in SC are the SC programs—each with highly specific engagement criteria (i.e., the law); hence, it is important to know the rest of this textbook.

This chapter does not represent doctrine. Readers should review JP 5.0, *Joint Operation Planning*, 11 August 2011, prior to reading further, if unfamiliar with the Joint Operational Planning Process (JOPP) or with operational art and design. This chapter will not reiterate joint doctrine but seeks only to present SC aspects and suggest a methodology.

THEATER-LEVEL SC PLANNING

Introduction

Theater-level planning, like all joint planning, is conducted using the Joint Operation Planning Process (JOPP) (see figure 19-1) within the Adaptive Planning and Execution (APEX) system, as described in JP 5.0. While grand in scope and duration, the process is recognizable, and the finished plan has the familiar five-paragraph format. Our intent in this section is to illustrate how national-level guidance from the President flows logically down the chain-of-command, though the various documents and plans, to direct security cooperation.

Figure 19-1
Joint Operation Planning Process

Step 1	Planning Initiation
Step 2	Mission Analysis
Step 3	Course of Action (COA) Development
Step 4	COA Analysis and Wargaming
Step 5	COA Comparison
Step 6	COA Approval
Step 7	Plan or Order Development

Within joint planning there are four planning functions: (1) Strategic Guidance, (2) Concept Development, (3) Plan Development, and (4) Plan Assessment. Strategic guidance is an expression of the "ends," i.e., what should the theater look like after plan is implemented. How does the Combatant Command (CCMD) know it has succeeded? For the CCMD, strategic guidance is stipulated in national-level strategy and defense planning documents. Concept development is the heart of planning, where planners determine how the CCMD is going to achieve its ends. This is codified in the Theater Strategy and the Theater Campaign Plan (TCP). These documents express the "ways." Finally, the "means" are individual activities, events, operations, and investments programmed by various planners and managers and laid out in the Country Plan.

Strategic Guidance

Analysis of Higher Guidance

Security cooperation planning begins at the national level with the National Security Strategy (NSS), produced annually by the President. DOD explains how it will achieve its part of the NSS, in the broadest terms, in the National Defense Strategy (NDS). The National Military Strategy (NMS) is the Chairman of the Joint Chiefs of Staff's (CJCS) military advice on achieving the goals in the NDS (see Glossary for expanded descriptions of these strategies). On the Department of State (DOS) side, strategic planning similarly takes place with the Joint Strategic Goals and the Quadrennial Diplomacy and Development Review (QDDR) (see pp. 19-18 and 19-19 for a full discussion of DOS planning). Figure 19-2 illustrates the national planning flow.

Figure 19-2
Flow Of National Planning

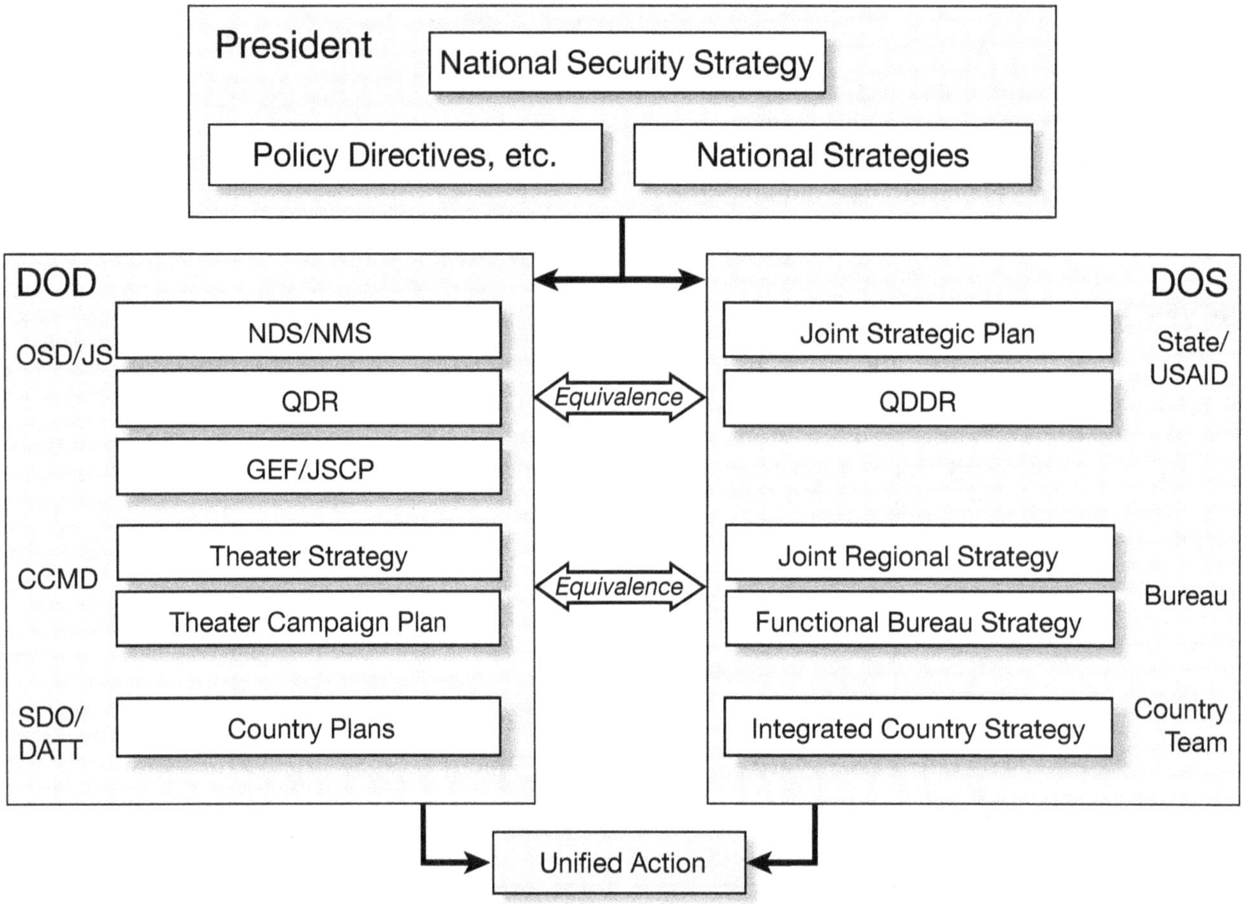

For DOD, these strategies are turned into specific guidance in the Guidance for Employment of the Force (GEF) and the Joint Strategic Capabilities Plan (JSCP). The GEF directs Geographic CCMD to conduct near-term (two year) planning for operational activities and articulates strategic end states that CCMDs are expected to attain (focusing 5-10 years in the future); all with input from the Department of State. While the GEF directs the CCMD to conduct operational planning and articulates strategic end states, the JSCP actually tasks the Combatant Commanders (CCMD) and Service Chiefs to prepare operation, contingency, and theater campaign plans CCMDWhile tasks are specified, the CCMD must also integrate Phase 0 of any contingency plans (CONPLANS) into the TCP. Said differently, theater steady-state activities, e.g. mil-to-mil events run by the SCO, incorporate the Phase 0 actions of CONPLANs to be executed later.

The GEF and JSCP are classified companion documents developed concurrently on a two year cycle, by OSD and the Joint Staff respectively that provide strategic guidance to theater level planners. . It translates the strategic guidance in the NDS into direction on planning, force management, security cooperation, and posture planning. Most importantly for SC planning, it provides the strategic end states for each CCMD. The well-informed planner also will have reviewed the relevant DOS Joint Regional Strategy and Functional Bureau Strategy (see pp. 19-18 and 19-19) as part of Mission Analysis.

Theater posture planning and five-year budgets are important factors that the CCMD must take into account when conducting theater campaign planning. Posture planning may have a direct effect on how forces can be used and the nature and capabilities of those forces in the future.

Understand the Operational Environment

When seeking to understand the operational environment, the theater-level planner should focus on regional dynamics. What are the roles of regional actors in the strategic balance of power? Detailed looks at these major actors are important and country-level experts from J-2 or J-5 will be central to the planning team during this phase. Fitting these pieces together and figuring out the optimal strategy to influence the situation is the result of operational art and design during concept development.

Concept Development

Concept development is the very heart of joint planning. By use of operational design, theater planners develop, analyze, and compare courses of action (COA). CCMDs select a COA, which is approved during the In-Progress Review (IPR) IPR C (see figure 19-3). The approved COA is then fully developed during the third planning function, plan development.

Theater Strategy

The theater strategy is a broad statement of how the CCMD intends to achieve GEF strategic end states, thus serving as the link between national guidance documents and the TCP. It serves as the starting point for the Joint Operational Planning Process, with the TCP seeking to operationalize the theater strategy.

Ends States and Intermediate Military Objectives

The GEF strategic end states are the most specific description of the strategic objectives presented to the CCMD, or the "ends." As specifically tasked in the GEF, the CCMD develops Intermediate Military Objectives (IMO). IMOs must demonstratively move the CCMD toward the strategic end states. It may only take one IMO to reach a strategic end state, but more commonly there will be multiple IMOs over the three- to five-year time frame of the TCP.

IMOs must be specific and achievable to ensure that the CCMD can measure progress. In preparing IMOs, the acronym "SMART" (Specific, Measurable, Achievable, Relevant and Results-oriented, Time-bound) should be observed:

- Specific—the reader knows what exactly must be done

- Measureable—empirically measureable so the CCMD knows when it has achieved the IMO

- Achievable—practicable within the time and resources provided

- Relevant—focused on an objective that moves the CCMD toward the end states

- Results-oriented—Focused on the results of actions, not on the process of doing them

- Time-bound—a clear deadline within the planning horizon

In addition to identifying Strategic End States and IMOs, the CCMD planner must also identify key planning assumptions and define "success and sufficiency," as applicable to the TCP.

Lines of Effort

Lines of Effort (LOE) link related IMOs by purpose, in order to focus efforts toward a GEF End State(s). This approach allows planners to bundle by purpose various activities, events, operations, and investments, thus logically linking more specific planning detail to strategic end states. Thus within an LOE, IMOs step forward in demonstrative ways toward the "Ends." LOEs are useful to group near-term and long-term IMOs that must be completed simultaneously or sequentially.

Lines of Activity

Lines of Activity (LOA) group activities, events, operations, and/or investments supporting a particular IMO. LOAs thus allow the planner to dive down in increasing detail to answer the question, "What activities, events, operations, and/or investments are needed to achieve the IMO?" Figure 19-3 illustrates the relationship between LOEs and LOAs.

Figure 19-3
Notional Concept

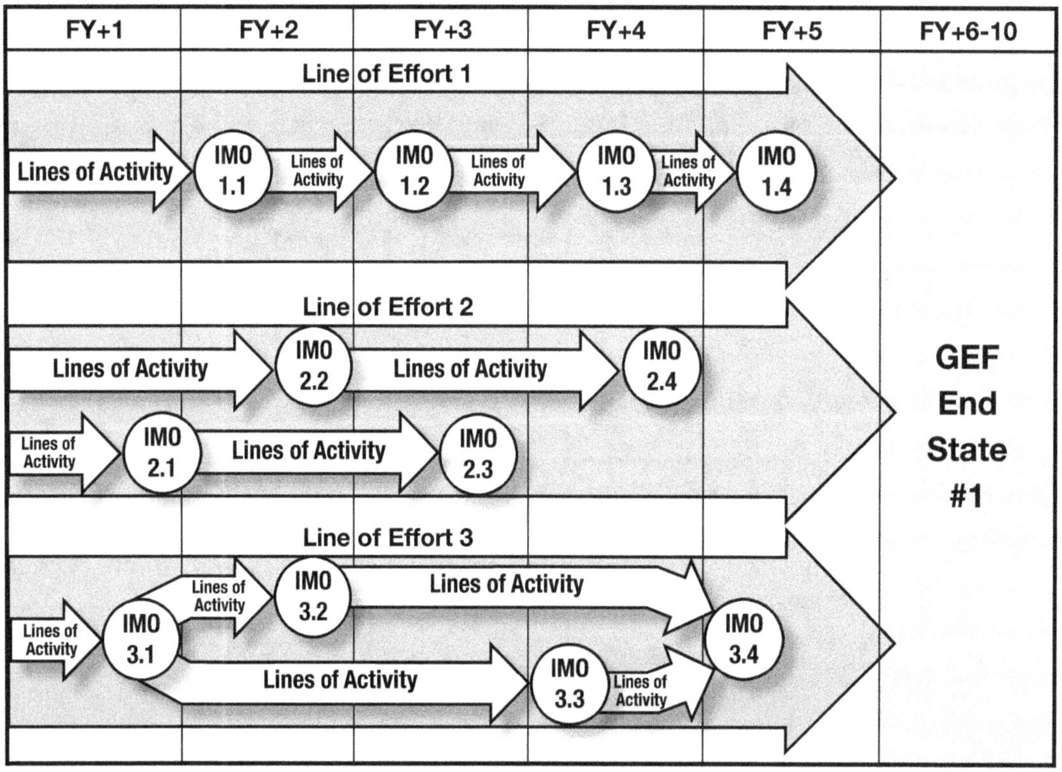

Ends—Ways—Means

Thus, End States are achieved by moving along LOEs, from IMO to IMO. IMOs are achieved by lines of activity, which are made up of specific activities, events, operations, and investments. Just as this process of increasing detail provides the planner a logical way to think through the problem, the plan will provide the program manager with justification as to why specific events must be resourced, i.e., how a particular three-day event fits into the overall plan to achieve the strategic end states. Hence, the TCP provides the "ways" to justify the "means" to achieve the "ends."

Plan Development

The actual plans preparation process will generally follow JOPP, but each CCMD will vary in its internal procedures and products. The TCP itself will generally be similar to the suggested format in JP 5-0, Appendix A, but likewise, this is not doctrinally required. APEX forms the external joint review and approval process through a series of formal In-Progress Reviews (IPR). Reference figure 19-4, each planning function correlates to one or more steps of the JOPP. As each planning function is concluded, an IPR is held to approve progress made so far (see JP 5-0, pg I-4).

Figure 19-4
Joint Operations Planning Functions, Approvals, And Process

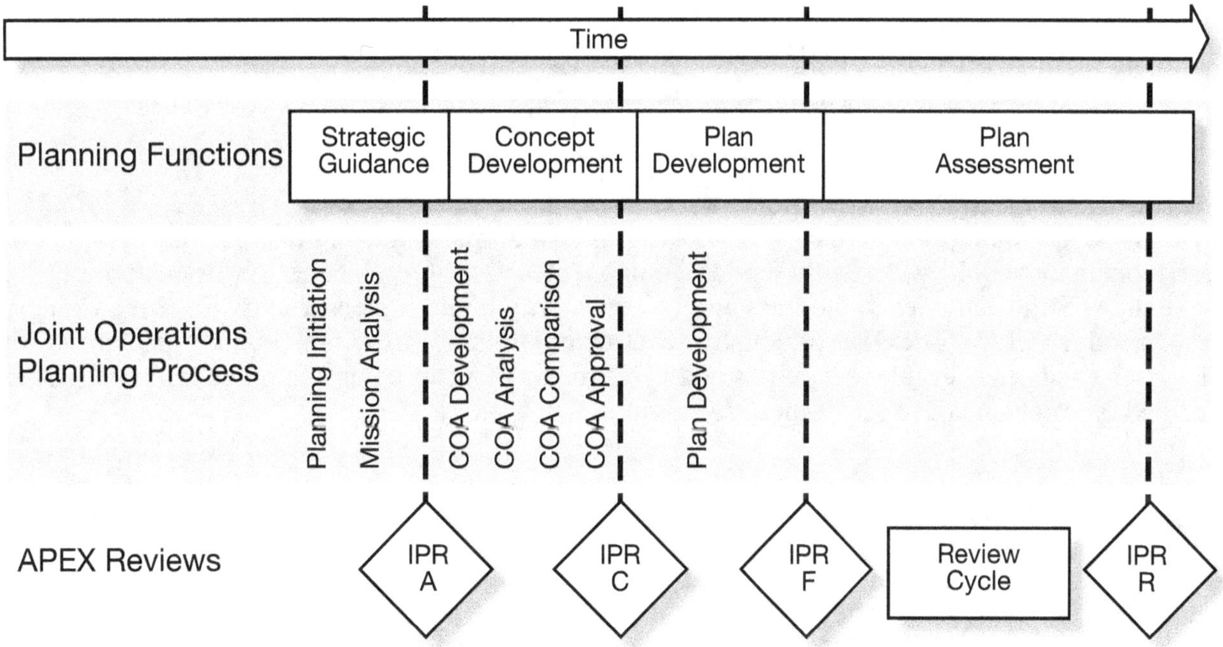

Plan Assessment

The final planning function is plan assessment, which takes place during execution. The purpose of assessments is to tell the CCMD if his plan is working and if the command is succeeding in the mission assigned to it, i.e., reaching the GEF End States. When conducting plan assessments, there are three questions that must be answered:

- Are activities, events, operations, and investments being executed effectively?

- Is the CCMD moving toward its objectives (IMOs and Strategic End States)?

- Are resources being used in the most effective manner?

COUNTRY-LEVEL SC PLANNING

Introduction

What is meant by "country-level" planning? In this chapter, it refers to planning by DOD for SC with a particular nation-state or international organization. Despite the focus on DOD processes, country-level planners must coordinate with interagency counterparts in the Department of State (DOS), US Agency for International Development (USAID), and others agencies. Country-level planning does not necessarily mean "in-country" planning. DOD planning can be done at the CCMD headquarters or in-country by the SCO. Each CCMD differs on this. This section will orient joint country-level planners, typically the J-5 country desk officers, to the overall process and to suggest a methodology that has been successful.

From Theater Campaign Plans to Country Plans

The TCP describes how the theater is going to achieve its Ends, but by definition, the TCP is too general to provide a starting point for scheduling specific SC events. With over fifty countries in some Geographic Combatant Commands (CCMD), the CCMD will typically prepare Regional Campaign Plans (RCP) to provide increasing detail on how it will achieve the Ends in a sub-region.

Figure 19-5
Country-Level Planning Process

1. Mission analysis
2. Capabilities-based analysis
3. Resource
4. Country plan development

Below RCP, Country Plans (CP) will start to leave strategy behind and manifest concrete action. Theater planners should work with service component and SCO personnel on brainstorming and developing specific activities to progress on lines of activity in the subject country toward a Country-level Objective (CLO). The goal of country-level planning is not truly the country appendix to the TCP, but the activities, events, operations and investments that can be programmed into budgets and scheduled on calendars (also see "Lines of Activity," p. 19-4).

Mission Analysis

Analyze Higher Guidance

For the country-level planner, the primary source of higher guidance is the TCP and the RCP. Furthermore, the content of each of the component campaign support plans must be considered. The planner must keep in mind DOS interests in the country, as expressed in the Integrated Country Strategy (ICS), and the national interests of the partner nation (PN). It is where the three interests overlap, those of DOD, DOS, PN, that the "sweet spot" is found (see figure 19-7).

Figure 19-6
Mission Analysis

1. Analyze higher guidance
2. Assess security environment
3. Define the desired security role for the partner nation
4. Identify what resources are available

It is particularly important for the planner at the CCMD to remember that the country plan will serve two roles: (1) it will be a country-specific part of the RCP and the TCP, and (2) it will also be the DOD component of the Integrated Country Strategy (ICS). Neither the planner in the HQ, nor the SCO in the embassy, should lose sight of these dual roles at any time.

Depending on the country and the situation, planners may need to take into account other actors, be they USG agencies (e.g. USAID), international organizations (IO), or other governments. Optimally, each agency would plan in parallel using their respective processes while coordinating. This can seldom happen. What can, and should happen, is that each agency should share information and synchronize plans as they are developed. In fact this is required by Presidential Policy Directive-23 (PPD-23) dated 5 April 2013. Planners at the theater and component headquarters need to ensure open and frequent communications with all stakeholders, particularly the in-country DOD team.

Figure 19-7
Correlation of Interests

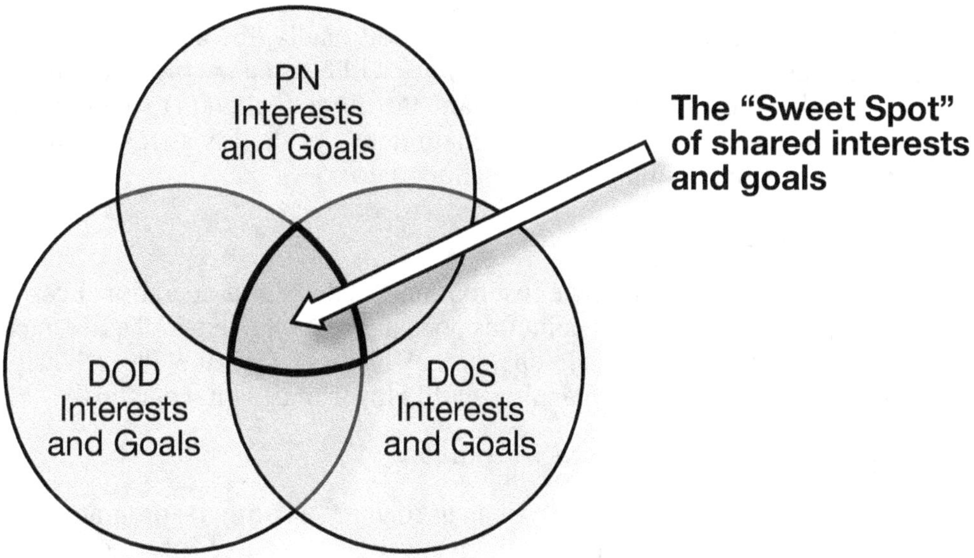

Remember, it is the CCMD who needs the PN (to play a certain role in their TCP). The PN, on the other hand, is a sovereign nation that has its own national interests, which may or may not harmonize well with US desires. It is important for the country planner to understand the true position, policy, and interests of the PN. By doing so, the country planner is more likely to identify how PN efforts can be synchronized with USG policy, i.e., the strategic ends.

Assess Security Environment

There are many ways to study the security environment: Political, Military, Economic, Social, Infrastructure and Information (PMESII), Center of Gravity (COG) analysis, Strengths, Weakneses, Opportunities, and Threats (SWOT) analysis, cultural studies, and terrain analysis. Any way it is done, its importance cannot be understated. Each time the US military has operated in a new corner of the world, it has often had to relearn the lesson that one needs to know culture, environment, or partners of a region. This research will inform the rest of the planning effort. Extra work here will pay off later in preventing false steps and restarts.

As stated earlier, it is critical to have a realistic picture of the PN's security environment; if the PN is to play a constructive role in the TCP, the planner must understand the PN's perspective. It is important the planner identifies: the PN's significant threats (real or perceived); breadth and complexity of operational demands; relevant geopolitical trends; and key security-related opportunities.

Joint Planning for Security Cooperation

Define The Desired Security Role For The Partner Country

This is the central element where the theater strategy, the TCP, and RCP, bear on the country plan. How do these and national planning documents see the PN fitting into the CCMD's operational approach? Within theater and country-level plans, these roles are often labeled Country-level Objectives (CLO).

Not every country can or should play every role. Perhaps one country could play a role in its own internal stability, while another might be looked at as troop contributing country for the United Nations; it all depends on how the CCMD sees these various parts fitting together to achieve the ends. Particularly, in light of current fiscal realities, careful consideration must be given to this question.

Assess Partner Desire to Play That Role

Planners need to assess a PN's overall strategic willingness to play the desired role. Do they have the political and civil society consensus? Critical factors include positions of political leaders, public opinion vis-à-vis the role, national priorities, fiscal realities, security interests, military and political aspirations, and historic role in the region. Additionally, the degree of political accountability of the government and civilian control of the military will bear on the problem. In an often ironic manner, the less accountable the government or military, the more likely it is to act in the desired role. Conversely, if the desired role is counter to the national interest of the PN as it sees them, the plan must take this into account; wishing will not change nation-states.

Determine Ability to Play That Role

Planners must now look at the institutional capacity and operational capability of the PN military to play the desired role. At this point this does not require a detailed assessment, but a general military capabilities study: What is their operational history? Can the PN self-deploy? Can it even leave garrison? Does it have a joint planning staff? How robust is its logistics?

ID What Resources Are Planned or Available

The final step in Mission Analysis is to identify existing or programed resources. While country planning is not "resource constrained," it must be "resource informed" if it is to have any basis in reality. Remember, there is always something currently planned. What are the current program budgets and manpower directed by the USG at the PN forces? What other resources are available? When considering this, look not only at DOD programs but particularly at DOS Title 22-funded programs. Equally, what actions are the PN or third parties already planning? If another country is already planning to address a capability, then the USG need not put resources against it. Perhaps more importantly, does the PN have the resources and will to maintain the capability over the long term.

Capabilities-Based Analysis

Capabilities-Based Analysis (CBA), as presented here, is a modification of the doctrine used within the DOD, but significantly streamlined and re-focused on the Security Cooperation with foreign militaries. This is not by any means the only way planners could analyze the problem and recommend solutions, but this method has been successful. The eight steps are grouped into three phases, shown below. These phases are not so different from any problem-solving process.

Figure 19-8
Capabilities-Based Analysis for Security Cooperation

Problem Analysis
1. Describe the role the CCMD wants the partner nation to play in the TCP
2. Identify military tasks the PN military needs to be able to do to play the desired role
3. Identify capabilities needed to execute the task
Needs Analysis
4. Assess PN current capabilities
5. Identify gaps
6. Assess risks
Solutions Analysis
7. Identify alternate solutions
8. Recommend solutions

Problem Analysis

Problem Analysis seeks to understand the situation in ever greater detail. It starts with clearly defining the "desired role," which was determined during Mission Analysis, and asking what military tasks are needed to achieve that role. Perhaps the CCMD wants the PN to focus on providing peacekeepers to UN missions in the region. One military task for such a role may be "Conduct Stability Operations." Next, capabilities needed to execute this task are listed out in priority order.

Needs Analysis

Needs Analysis takes the generic capabilities determined in Problem Analysis, and determines the actual needs of a particular PN in a specific situation. This process begins with Assessing Current Capabilities. By comparing the generic needs to the current capabilities, gaps can be identified.

Assess the Current Capabilities and Identify Gaps

While SCO and attaché personnel can provide general assessments, the service component commands should play a central role in assessing current capabilities. The Services have technical expertise and manpower to provide a detailed assessment of the PN's capability. During Mission Analysis, a significant effort was made to understand the operational environment, to include PN forces, but this usually takes a more academic look focusing on open sources and intelligence information. During this step, however, service component commands apply detailed standards evolved for their own operations (while recognizing varying tactics, techniques, and procedures) to conduct a detailed on-the-ground evaluation of each capability. The delta between required capabilities and those present in the PN forces are the gaps.

While assessments are often central to wise investment, the country-level planner needs to keep the scale and priority of a particular country and effort in mind. All operations by US forces are expensive, to include assessments, and these assessments will usually consume the same program funds as the eventual assistance. Additionally, if the program is small, the planner must be wary of raising expectations of the PN too high; as if the USG was promising to address all the gaps. Lastly, assessments can wear on the patience of those being assessed; who among us likes inspections? If the scale of the overall effort is modest, it may not be cost effective or wise to conduct detailed, service-specific assessments. Perhaps in these cases, the assessment should be left to the SCO and attachés resident in country.

Joint Planning for Security Cooperation

Assess the Risks

Once these gaps have been identified, a thorough assessment of the risks must be performed. When looking at risk, the military planner must first assess the risk posed to the planned role for the PN if the capability gap persists. If it presents little risk, then there is little point in providing the capability, and limited USG resources should be applied elsewhere. If this capability gap presents a major risk to the proposed role, this would indicate a higher priority for resourcing.

In addition to this operational risk, the planner must also consider political risk. In the case of political risk, a planner must not only be concerned with the fallout from not providing a capability, but also the risk from providing one, e.g., atrocities by US-trained personnel. While the military planner might be reluctant to incorporate political concerns, rest assured the US ambassador to the PN will put these foremost when looking at how the CCMD's country plan (CP) fits into his overall strategy for US relations with the PN.

This provides yet another example of the importance of country-level planning. It is at this level where the military and diplomatic planning efforts come together and must be synchronized. The only other place these planning chains formally come together is in the NSS itself, and then only in the broadest terms.

Solutions Analysis

Identify Alternate Solutions

Solutions Analysis is the longest phase of planning. There are two primary methods for working though a capability to identify alternative solutions to filling the capability gaps. The first is DOTMLPF (Doctrine, Organization, Training, Material, Leadership and Education, Personnel, and Facilities) as outlined in figure 19-9. The second is the War Fighting Functions (mission command, movement and maneuver, intelligence, fires, sustainment, and protection) as outlined in figure 19-10. In either case, each serves as a paradigm by which to logically work one's way though each proposed capability. In each case, the results of this brainstorming effort will be a list of complementary or alternative activities, events, operations, and investments that improve PN capability and move them toward playing the role described during Step 1 of CBA (see p. 19-9).

Figure 19-9
DOTMLPF

Doctrine—the tactics and procedures of military operations and employment of military resources
Organization—the command structure and relationships among military units
Training—the preparation of soldiers, units, commanders and staff to execute their operational missions
Materiel—military equipment, including end items, spares and consumables
Leadership and Education—the preparation of commanders and senior leaders to lead, train, organize, and employ their units and resources
Personnel—the availability of qualified persons for specific missions or tasks
Facilities—the real property and facilities for military production, maintenance and storage

Figure 19-10
War Fighting Functions

Mission Command—develops and integrates those activities enabling a commander to balance the art of command and the science of control
Movement and Maneuver—tasks and systems that move and employ forces to achieve a position of relative advantage over the enemy
Intelligence—tasks and systems that facilitate understanding of the enemy, terrain, and civil considerations
Fires—tasks and systems that provide collective and coordinated use of Army indirect fires, air and missile defense, and joint fires through the targeting process
Sustainment—tasks and systems that provide support and services to ensure freedom of action, extend operational reach, and prolong endurance
Protection—tasks and systems that preserve the force so the commander can apply maximum combat power to accomplish the mission

DOTMLPF is our recommended approach. DISAM feels it provides the planner the most clear and concrete answers to providing a capability. To apply this paradigm, planners work their way through each part of DOTMLPF asking themselves what is needed within each domain. For example, to provide a reconnaissance capability, "What additional doctrine is needed? Do PN forces need to be re-organized? What training is needed? What equipment is needed?" One major benefit of methodically working through DOTMLPF is that lower cost solutions may be identified.

This entire process is informed by the assessments conducted by the service components, and much of this specific step may be done at the service component command level. It is often best for CCMDs to task an Office of Primary Responsibility (OPR) to do the Assessment and Recommended Solutions for particular capabilities. A typical example of this might be assigning the intelligence analysis to the J2.

Recommend Solutions

In analyzing alternatives, the planner must assess each to determine if each is affordable, feasible, and responsive. Thus, often in real-world application, this step becomes very iterative with the next step, resourcing, as possible solutions fail or succeed to secure funding or manpower.

In the end, the planner may find there is not an effective way to address the capability gap. In this case, two policy solutions may be available. First, change or drop the desired role the CCMD wants the PN to play in the TCP (i.e., change the TCP). Second, it might be necessary to change the rules for a program or create a new program to address the gaps over the long term (e.g., propose changes to legislation).

Resourcing

Resourcing is a highly iterative process where the country-level planners seek out resources to fill gaps, often over and over again. This can be due to competition from higher priority efforts, or because the program is a poor fit. There are currently over eighty SC programs which could be used to resource capability gaps. Each program is specifically designed to address a particular need. Each has its strengths and weaknesses, its authorities and prohibitions. It is critical that planners understand these programs if they want to apply them effectively. These programs are the "weapon systems" of SC; if planners do not understand them, they will never employ them effectively.

US Investment Considerations

DOD wants to achieve the greatest overall improvement in the specified capabilities with the lowest possible investment. When looking at where to invest, the country planner must consider the factors listed below. Key among these factors is priority; priority based on risk and based on urgency. Risk represents the likelihood that a capability will not be achieved if resources are not provided, while urgency represents the importance of the resources based on time.

- Deriving—What strategy and environment are the missions and capabilities designed to address?

- Prioritizing—What shortfalls are most important and pressing? (based on risk and urgency)

- Integrating—Have investments been made across all Services to be effective as a joint force?

- Balancing—Are investments and attendant risk balanced across all the capabilities needed during the planning period?

- Sequencing—What is needed now? What can wait until later? Is there a logical order in which investments should be made?

- Resourcing—How much can the USG afford during the planning period?

Requirements Coordination and Integration

In the end, these capabilities will have to be consolidated and prioritized across the all of the PN's military services. The ability of PNs to conduct CBA and requirements integration varies widely across the globe. Many PNs will not present the SCO with a coherent plan and capability requirements. It will often be left to the country-level planer (CCMD or SCO) to integrate PN joint requirements and determine which best fulfills the strategic requirement.

As with competing PN requirements and priorities, there will frequently be competing priorities within the USG. This can be particularly important if the resources are not DOD resources. To avoid this, it is important for the country planner to remember the concept of the sweet spot—where do the interests of DOD, State (or other agencies), and the PN overlap. What investment would have the broadest payoff, and hence, the most support among the interested parties.

If the planning was done correctly and logically, it will also serve as solid justification for program requests as they move up the chain of command. The country planner should remember that this same prioritization takes place across the theater, and at the national level, across the globe. There are over 100 SCOs all competing for scant resources.

Figure 19-11

Resourcing Windows Overlaid on Notational Synchronization Matrix

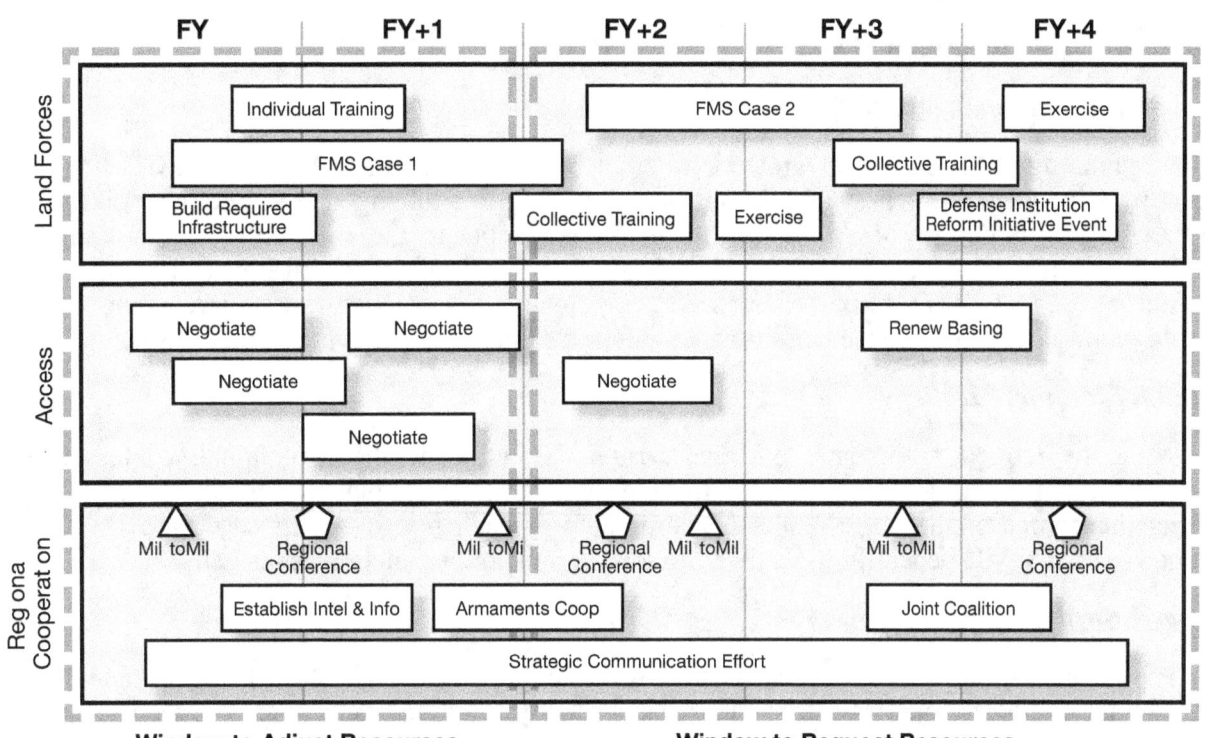

Window to Adjust Resources   **Window to Request Resources**

At this point, proposed activities, events, operations, and investments need to be laid out over time, up to five years into the future. This serves many purposes. As a planner, it will help to determine sequencing and identify critical paths. For the program manager, it will help them request resources in the three- to five-year window, as illustrated in figure 19-11.

Ideally, the planning time lines will take Global Force Management time lines into account, but this is not always so. Often plans have to be made, and events scheduled well after the point that forces need to be requested. Either the event will have to adapt to available forces or, ideally, planning time lines should be moved a year to allow for the Request for Forces (RFF) process.

Country Plan Development

In many ways, country plan (CP) development is the simplest of the four steps in the country-planning process. However, if corners were cut during mission analysis or problem analysis, serious conflicts with stake-holders will develop, mostly from not addressing the actual problem or by doing so in an unacceptable manner. This is particularly true with countries of less military importance or of significant political controversy. These countries may lack rock-solid policy, thus leaving an assessment of the plan open to more interpretation.

Plan development is, at its heart, the simple act of writing the plan. Currently, joint doctrine does not exist for the format of a CP. A notional CP format developed by JFCOM may be found at attachment 1 to this chapter. Typically, CPs are found as an appendix to the TCP. While there is no set doctrine for a CP, the Deputy Under Secretary of Defense for Plans looks for the following issues to be addressed when reviewing CPs:

- Country Assessment

- Country Objectives

- Reference to the TCP and Integrated Country Strategy (ICS) directly

- Concept of Engagement

- Synchronization Matrix

- Coordinating Instructions

SC planning must be fully integrated with other DOD agencies and the DOS. The CP should make direct reference to the embassy's ICS, thus demonstrating this interagency integration. Likewise, the DOD country-planning process can form a significant input to the embassy's ICS and supporting Mission Resource Request (MRR), which feed Title 22 program requirements into the Foreign Operations budget. Plans must be assessed periodically for effectiveness and relevance. Updates should be produced as strategic conditions or funding changes, perhaps every other year.

Annual Planning Meetings

While the frequency of updates to formal, written CPs will generally be biannually, or less, country-level planning is continual. Of particular importance is the series of planning meetings that take place during the course of the year. While the particulars of each meeting will vary by CCMD and by country, each CCMD generally has a meeting to accomplish the function described.

Theater Strategy Conference

The Theater Strategy Conference is hosted by the CCMD to discuss policy direction and initiatives. It is attended by personnel from the embassies, typically the SDO/DATTs and the Deputy Chiefs of Mission, from OSD, and from DOS.

Regional Working Group

Where the Theater Strategy Conference focuses on direction and policy, the Regional Working Group (RWG) focuses on SC activities. Attendees include personnel from the SCO, the service components, OSD, CCMD, and the services. Work will focus on detailed event planning and program by program reviews.

Security Cooperation Education and Training Working Group

The Security Cooperation Education and Training Working Group (SCETWG) is an annual meeting hosted by CCMD, usually between the months of March and June, to project training requirements one and two years out. Members of the SCO, DOS, and the services attend in order to coordinate and approve PN training requirements (See chapter 14, "International Training," for further details).

Annual Planning Conference

The exact nature of these conferences varies widely, but all are intended to coordinate activities directly with PN militaries. They can be hosted in-country or at the CCMD headquarters. They can be joint or single service. These conferences typically focus on coordinating military-to-military events, but could also cover training. During these meetings, the real work gets done on finalizing cooperation plans and getting PN buy-in (See chapter 1 for further discussion).

Putting the Pieces Together in a Country Plan

Please review figure 19-12, Notional Synchronization Matrix with Comments, before reading further. This figure provides a simplified example of how a country-level planner might pull together various SC programs into a synchronized plan to achieve a CLO. In this example, the CLO is seeking to build an airlift capability. The matrix only focuses on load handling, as a component of airlift, which was an identified gap in our scenario.

Initially, the SCO or SDO/DATT needs to build support among the players to support and participate in the effort to build this capability. To do this, the SCO plans a distinguished visitor (DV) visit to promote the idea. We also send observers to a regional exercise to raise awareness and to show how it is done. The airlift familiarization visit builds on this exchange of know-how, and likewise raises the profile of the US program within the PN air force. During the second phase, individual training and equipment acquisition begins in earnest. Trained load handlers are scheduled to complete training before the arrival of load handling equipment in country.

Once trained personnel and equipment are on hand, collective training can begin. A second DV visit is scheduled during this period to highlight the program and the progress, in order to maintain support within the PN and the US militaries. Additionally follow on Traveling Contact Teams, assessment visits or even Subject Matter Expert Exchange visits could take place to make sure the program is still on tract. Finally, a maintenance phased is reached with continued training and spare parts.

Figure 19-12
Notational Synchronization Matrix with Comments

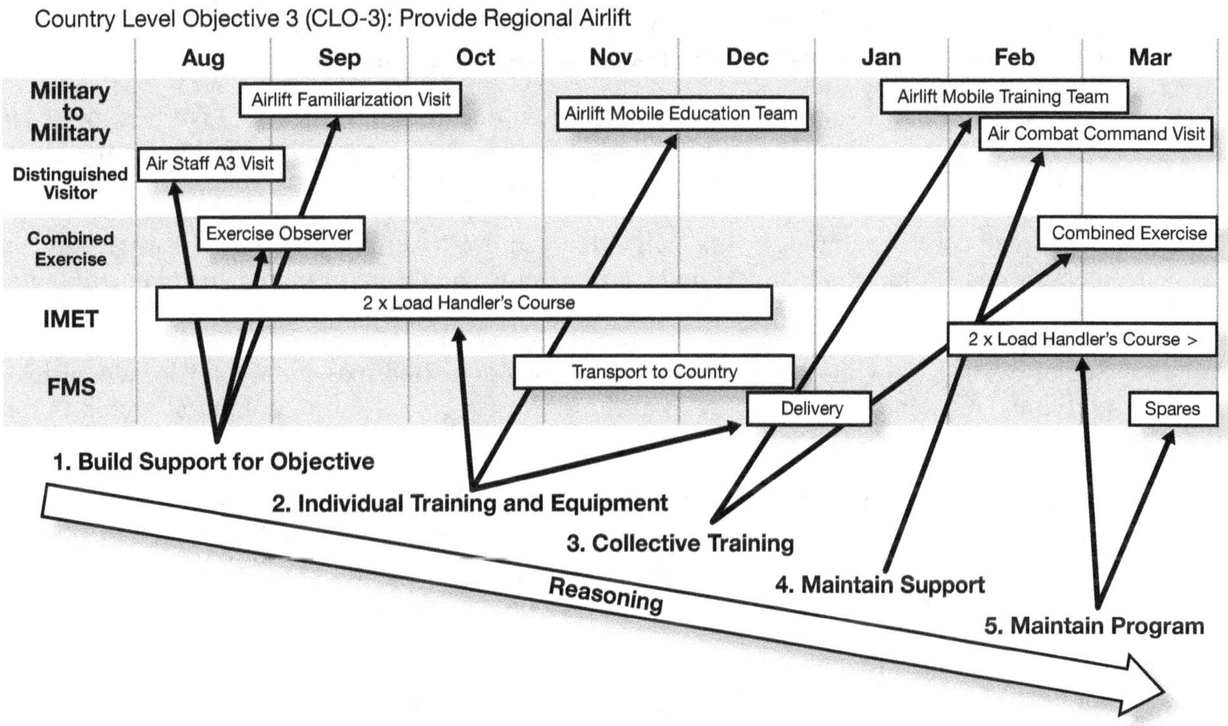

Country Level Objective 3 (CLO-3): Provide Regional Airlift

In-Country Event Planning

A military career is excellent preparation for execution planning of in-country events. The key changes are translating the military infrastructure to that of the embassy and changing operational considerations from those of a soldier to those of a diplomat. Within an embassy and the country team, the organization, responsibilities, and capabilities are different than those of a military organization. For example, if one is trying to have some equipment moved, the General Services Officer (GSO), a sort of logistics officer, would be the person to see; for a funds transfer, the Management Officer (see chapter 4).

As to operational considerations, detailed knowledge of the PN, its military, its bureaucracies, and USG policy considerations, will be critical. The first three points hone in on one of the central roles of the SCO in country—getting things done. To do this, the SCO must have a deep understanding of how the PN military operates in reality. For example, perhaps PN battalions are to rotate through American training, so the SCO knows to work with the junior J-3 planner to ensure the deployment dates and third-country training all mesh seamlessly.

Joint Planning for Security Cooperation

One of the other major duties in country will be ensuring political support continues within the PN and within the country team. The ambassador is the central personality in this issue. It is critical he/she supports the concept and the details of the proposed event, and continues to do so. New ambassadors will need to be briefed, educated, and won over. Additionally, it is important that everyone on the country team understands how military activities they are asked to support are accomplishing not just the military's objective, but that of the embassy as a whole. See chapter 4 for more details on personnel, aircraft, and ship visits.

Common Considerations

- Size: One of the first questions a SCO must ask themselves is "Can I, or should I, support this event internally within the office or do I need DAO or embassy assistance?" What support will be needed from the CCMD, e.g., public affairs or contracting officers?

- Itinerary: This is the very heart of any event planning. Itineraries have multiple lines of operation (LOO) and multiple phases. The itinerary must take into account LOO for separate, simultaneous elements of the event, logistics support, and preparation for future portions of the event. Plans must take into account overlapping phases: preparation, pre-advance party, advance party, main body, trail party, and cleanup.

- Local customs: At every step, keep the local culture in mind; the SCO is the expert. The SCO may need to guide US planning toward more locally acceptable implementation, e.g., avoiding local holidays or greeting the appropriate official.

- Office calls: Even simple events will often require a certain amount of formalities and pleasantries. Talking points and notes on customs should be prepared for planned and ad hoc office calls.

- Social events: As with office calls, social events are often planned even for tactical-level activities, e.g., an ice breaker social at the start of a course, or a cookout at the end of an exercise.

- Press: Have a proactive plan to deal with the press. Not only can unplanned press coverage create a problem, but lost press opportunities will cost the overall USG effort. Get the embassy Public Diplomacy Officer and the CCMD public affairs office involved. Talking points for planned and ad hoc press events should be prepared.

- Clothing/uniform requirements: Be sure to determine uniform policies and requirements for each element of an itinerary. Consider when civilian attire is needed or required.

- Medical: Keep local medical, hygiene, food concerns in mind. Is drinking water safe?

- Interpreter support: Few Americans will speak the local language. The SCO personnel should not attempt to serve as an event interpreter. Not only is interpreting a particular skill that SCOs are not trained to do, but SCO personnel need to be focused on the event. Likewise, if the senior military officer will need to participate in discussions, he/she should bring an extra person along to serve as a note taker.

Logistics

- Customs Clearance: Often equipment brought into country will have to clear customs. The smooth, no-cost clearance should be coordinated in advance. Particular care should be exercised when goods are shipped in advance.

- Contracting support: Many in-country events will require the contracting of PN goods and services. For large military activities, a CCMD contracting officer should be sent into country well in advance of the event. For smaller events or TDYs, the embassy may be willing to provide contracting support.

- Travel services support: If the need for travel services is limited to that of typical TDY personnel, e.g., a rental vehicle or a room, the embassy travel office will usually be willing to support such routine travel. If the scale of the visit or event grows to the point where one is essentially talking about contracted service, the above contracting support applies.

- Funding: If the embassy is going to procure any goods and services for the event, fiscal data will be needed as early as possible. Keeping this business relationship between the embassy and the events' participants cordial will go a long way to ensuring embassy support for the next event. It is also important to confirm exactly which type of money the SCO or SDO/ DATT should use to fund their participation (see chapter 17, "Resource Management").

Security

- Weapons Clearance: If weapons will be required, get the Regional Security Officer (RSO) involved early. Many countries will require permits for USG personnel to carry weapon in the country, particularly concealed weapons.

- Local law enforcement: Discuss any law enforcement liaison requirements with the RSO. In addition to weapons, issues of traffic control, security, border control are often important depending on the PN.

- Classified Information: If classified information will be handled, where is it to be stored? Do the US participants need access to classified computers for communication back to their headquarters?

Contingencies

- Remain flexible

- Remain in communication. Charge your cellphone. Bring a two-way radio.

- Remain mobile. Have your own vehicle standing by.

- Delegate. The senior person needs to be free to escort, politic, respond to contingencies. If he/she is tied down in the mechanics of the visit, they won't be able to direct a contingency response

STATE DEPARTMENT PLANNING

DOS recently updated their planning process. Instead of the Mission Strategic and Resource Plan (MSRP), the DOS has broken their plans at the embassy level into two parts: the Integrated Country Strategy (ICS) and the Mission Resource Request (MRR). This division of the plan into two parts is a logical manifestation of the change to their planning process.

The new planning process starts with the 2010 Quadrennial Diplomacy and Development Review (QDDR). The QDDR defines the strategic priorities that guide global engagement jointly at the DOS/ USAID, and identify the diplomatic and development capabilities needed to advance US interests. As of March 2012, the QDDR also serves as the DOS/USAID Joint Strategic Plan. It sets institutional priorities and provides strategic guidance as a framework for the most efficient allocation of resources, which includes directives for improving how embassies do business, from strengthening interagency collaboration to increasing State and USAID engagement with civil society, the private sector and others. From this guidance, the regional bureaus at DOS and USAID (e.g., the Africa Bureaus) prepare a Joint Regional Strategy laying out their plan to achieve their part of the national strategy.

Separately, USAID also prepares the USAID Policy Framework, to provide its' staff and partners with USAID's core development priorities as well as operational principles. USAID also develops, for some countries, Country Development Cooperation Strategies.

All of thes documents then flow down to the individual embassies and USAID missions, who develop, with SCO input and assistance, their ICS (). At this point in the planning process, plans start to flow back up the "chain-of-command" as resource requests. Individual embassies and missions send consolidated MRRs to bureaus, who prioritize and prepare a Bureau Resource Request (BRR). At the department level, DOS consolidates priorities and submits their budget requests to the Office of Management and Budget.

While DOS plans are coordinated with DOD plans, it is important to remember that the planning process is only hard-wired together at the National Security Strategy and the ICS. It is vital all planners along both planning chains keep their counterparts in the other department aware of institutional direction and planning intentions.

For the SCO or SDO/DATT, this system places a heavy burden of responsibility on their shoulders. It can be said that these two formal planning chains only come together at only two people, the SCO and the President. SCOs must be extremely adept at keeping all parties informed, facilitating cooperation, and deconflicting priorities of the various departments, agencies, and commands involved.

Figure 19-13
Department of State Planning Process

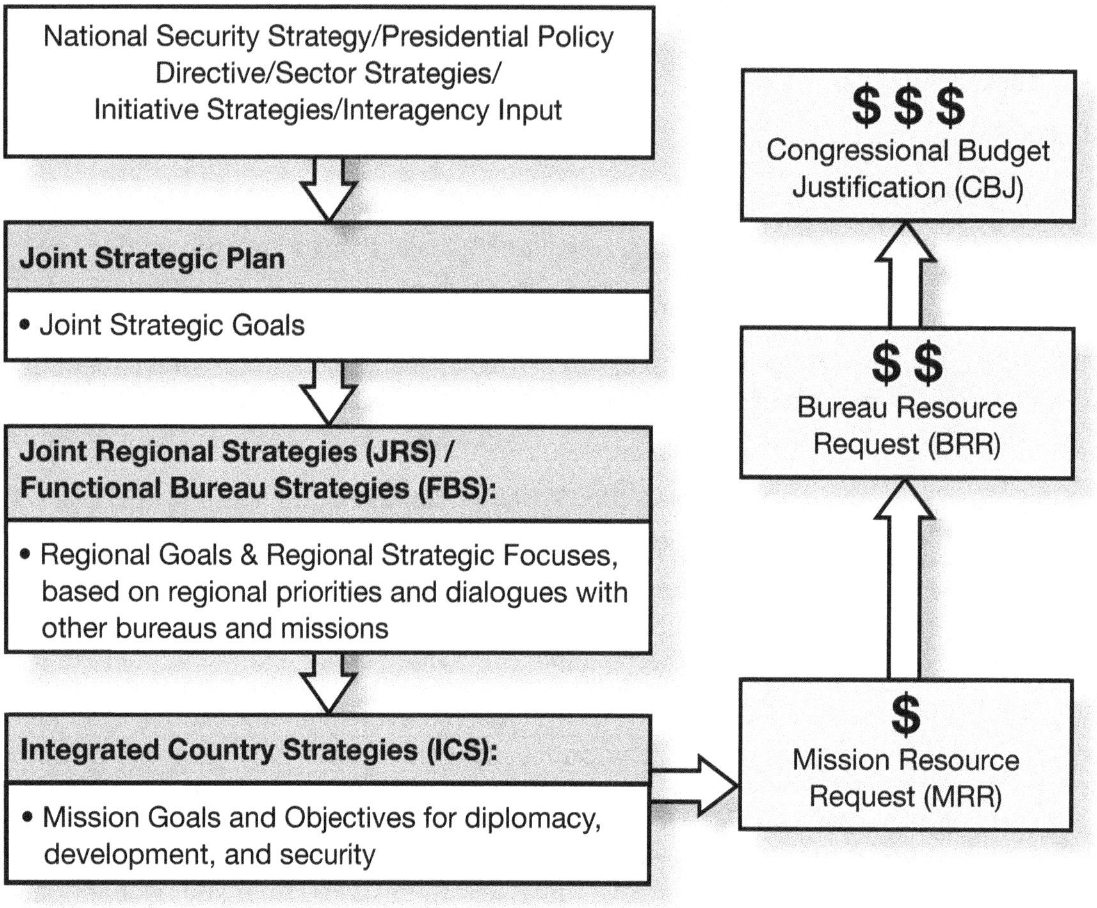

SCO Planning Tools

Partnership Strategy Toolkit

The Partnership Strategy Toolkit (PST) is a web site that provides access to a searchable database of SC programs and partner building tools. An SC planner can use the database to find various SC programs intended to address a particular need. Searches can be limited to certain countries, program objectives, or tasks, e.g. counterterrorism training in country X. The searches will produce a list of applicable programs. Clicking on the program will lead you to program details and POCs. The site is hosted by OSD at https://policyapps.osd.mil/sites/sctools/Pages/default.aspx. To request access, send a digitally signed e-mail to SCToolsAdministrators@osd.mil.

Combined Education and Training Program Plan

The SCO prepares the Combined Education and Training Program Plan (CETPP). This document focuses on the goals and objectives for DOD-sponsored education and training for the PN. Guidance for preparation is contained in the SAMM, paragraph C10.5 and figure C10.F3. The SCO uploads the draft plan electronically onto the Security Assistance Network (SAN) for review and approval by the CCMD. The approved plan is utilized each spring during the CCMD's Security Cooperation Education and Training Working Group (SCETWG). Further training program details are in chapter 14 of this textbook, "International Training." It is critical that the SCO develop a solid working relationship with the training departments of the PN military services early in the tour so their desires can be incorporated into the CETPP.

Security Assistance Budget Web Tool

If the PN receives, or is proposed to receive, appropriated funds through FMF or IMET, the SCO will also make an annual submission and justification for these funds. This request is submitted electronically through the Security Assistance Budget Web Tool, managed by DSCA. This document is forwarded upward through channels for endorsement and comment, i.e., to the CCMDs staff, the Joint Staff, DSCA and Office of Secretary of Defense (OSD) policy offices, where a final DOD position is developed for each country. This position is then used by DOD representatives in round table discussions with DOS in the development of an eventual Congressional budget justification to be submitted by the Secretary of State to Congress. SDO/DATTs must coordinate their submissions (both the amounts of aid requested and the justification) with those in the MRR, because it is the MRR that will form the basis of DOS's proposed budgets.

SCO Annual Forecasting Documents

SCOs are required to submit two forecasting documents annually. It is important to note the distinction between planning documents and forecasting documents. The planning documents listed earlier all reflect a goal which is intended to be achieved. Conversely, a forecasting document simply reflects the SCO's best estimate of what defense articles and services the PN will purchase from the USG. For the below forecasting reports, DSCA sends a call-up message to SCOs (and other organizations) each April with input due in June. Beginning in 2011, DSCA merged the reporting requirements for both the Javits Report and the Sales Forecast Report into one submission for SCOs. It is important for SCOs to be as thorough and as accurate as possible in this submission. SCOs should consider historical FMS activity by the PN, current economic trends, and the availability of unexpended and anticipated FMF grant monies. It may well be appropriate to contact PN counterparts to obtain their estimates of essential and likely FMS sales, but it is important to avoid any "false impression" that the USG will approve (or has already approved) a future request.

Javits Report

Required annually by the AECA, the Javits Report is the President's estimate to Congress of potential or proposed arms transfers during a given calendar year. The Javits Report is designed to identify potential sales by country, whether FMS or DCS. The two thresholds are $7M of major weapons or weapons-related equipment and any proposed sale of $25M or more. The Javits Report is not binding on PNs and is submitted to Congress as an advisory document.

FMS Sales Forecast Report

A companion document to the Javits Report, the FMS Sales Forecast Report helps DSCA determine the resource requirements for FMS implementing agencies. Its reporting requirements are separate from, but largely overlap, those of the Javits Report. This report is a two-year projection by fiscal year (vice one calendar year for Javits) but only addresses potential FMS sales. Unlike Javits, it has no dollar thresholds, so all potential FMS sales should be listed.

Summary

Planning is an essential step in all military operations, including security cooperation. This chapter revealed how country-level SC planning flows from the National Security Strategy (NSS) through DOS and DOD. On the Department of State (DOS) side, strategic planning similarly takes place with the Joint Strategic Goals and the Quadrennial Diplomacy and Development Review (QDDR). Correspondingly, DOD turns the NSS and other strategies into the Guidance for Employment of the Force (GEF) and the Joint Strategic Capabilities Plan (JSCP). The SCO, working with the CCMD and Embassy staffs, collates those over arching goals and objectives and develops the SC portion of the Ambassador's ICS/MRR and the CCMD's country plan.

References

JP 3-0, Joint Operations, 11 August 2011

JP 5-0, Joint Operation Planning, 11 August 2011

Draft Theater Campaign Plan Planner's Handbook, USD(P) Strategy, Plans, and Forces, February 2012

Draft Planner's Handbook for Country-Level Steady State Planning, JFCOM, 4 April 2011

ATTACHMENT 19-1
NOTIONAL COUNTRY PLAN FORMAT

INTRODUCTION SECTION

1. Purpose

2. Overall USG Goals and Objectives

3. Summary of Higher-level DOD Guidance

4. Commander's Vision

    4.1. Commander's Intent

    4.2. End State 1

    4.3. End State 2

    4.4. End State 3

SITUATION SECTION

1. Strategic Context

    1.1. Geopolitical Relevance of Country X

    1.2. Relevant PMESII-C Attributes

    1.3. Historical Relationship between US and Country X

    1.4. Partner Nation Interests, Political Commitment, Priorities

2. Operational Limitations

    2.1. Authorities

    2.2. Restraints

    2.3. Constraints

3. Contextual Assumptions

    3.1. Theater End State Assumptions

    3.2. Trend/Status Assumptions

    3.3. Impact Assumptions

4. Risk Assessment

    4.1. Risks to country and / or regional stability

        4.1.1. Risk 1

        4.1.2. Risk X

    4.2. Risks to country and / or regional partnerships

        4.2.1. Risk 1

        4.2.2. Risk X

    4.3. Risks to DOD plans

        4.3.1. Risk 1

        4.3.2. Risk X

    4.4. Should US posture toward the state be risk acceptant or risk averse and to what degree?

5. Risk Matrix

CAMPAIGN SECTION

1. Overview

    1.1. Concept of Operations

    1.2. DOD Command and Control and Engagement Plan

    1.3. Resource Allocation

Joint Planning for Security Cooperation

2. End State 1

    2.1. Campaign Objective 1

        2.1.1. Background 1

        2.1.2. Theory of Change 1

        2.1.3. Line of Effort 1

            2.1.3.1. Line of Activity 1

                2.1.3.1.1. Implementation / Tasks

                    2.1.3.1.1.1. Assessment Indicators / MOEs / MOPs

                    2.1.3.1.1.2. Assessment Indicators / MOEs / MOPs

                2.1.3.1.2. Implementation / Tasks

                    2.1.3.1.2.1. Assessment Indicators / MOEs / MOPs

                    2.1.3.1.2.2. Assessment Indicators / MOEs / MOPs

            2.1.3.2. Line of Activity 2

                2.1.3.2.1. (similar sub-bullets as Line of Activity 1)

        2.1.4. Line of Effort 2

            2.1.4.1. (similar sub-bullets as Line of Effort 1)

        2.1.5. Related Strategies and Plans 1

    2.2. Campaign Objective 2

        2.2.1. (similar sub-bullets as Campaign Objective 1)

3. End State 2

    3.1. (similar sub-bullets as End State 1)

ANNEX A: TASKS-TO-END STATES

1. End State 1

    1.1. Campaign Objective 1

        1.1.1. Line of Effort 1

            1.1.1.1. Line of Activity 1

                1.1.1.1.1. Implementation / Task 1

                    1.1.1.1.1.1. Task Mission / Description

                    1.1.1.1.1.2. Contact Information for Task Lead

                    1.1.1.1.1.3. Subordinate and Supporting DOD Elements

                    1.1.1.1.1.4. Supporting and Supported non-DOD Elements

                    1.1.1.1.1.5. Coordinating Instructions

                    1.1.1.1.1.6. Potential Adversaries and Obstacles

                    1.1.1.1.1.7. Risk Assessment and Risk Mitigation Strategies

                    1.1.1.1.1.8. Progress Assessment Plan

                1.1.1.1.2. Implementation / Task 2

                    1.1.1.1.2.1. (similar sub-bullets as Implementation / Task 1)

            1.1.1.2. Line of Activity 2 (similar sub-bullets as Line of Activity 1)

        1.1.2. Line of Effort 2 (similar sub-bullets as Line of Effort 1)

    1.2. Campaign Objective 2 (similar sub-bullets as Campaign Objective 1)

2. End State 2 (similar sub-bullets as End State 1)

ANNEX B: DETAILED STRATEGIC CONTEXT

1. Geopolitical Overview of Country X

    1.1. Country X's strategic importance

    1.2. Country X's geographic location

    1.3. Country X's demographics

    1.4. Country X's interests, political commitment, priorities

    1.5. Actors of interest in Country X

2. Relevant PMESII-C Attributes

    2.1. Formal Institutions

    2.2. People

    2.3. Other influential entities

    2.4. Culture

    2.5. Interdependencies and key relationships

3. Relationship between Country X and the US

    3.1. Historical recitation of the overall relationship between US and Country X, including long-term trends and major shifts

    3.2. DOD activities in Country X over the past year

    3.3. Non-DOD activities in Country X over the past year

ANNEX C: RELEVANT NON-DOD ACTORS AND ACTIVITIES

1. US Department of State (DOS)

    1.1. End State(s)

    1.2. Objective(s)

    1.3. Intent

2. US Agency for International Development (USAID)

    2.1. End State(s)

    2.2. Objective(s)

    2.3. Intent

3. Other USG Agencies

    3.1. End State(s)

    3.2. Objective(s)

    3.3. Intent

4. Multinational Partners, Alliances, and Coalitions (NATO, etc.)

    4.1. End State(s)

    4.2. Objective(s)

    4.3. Intent

5. Non-Partner States, Adversaries

    5.1. End State(s)

    5.2. Objective(s)

    5.3. Intent

6. Intergovernmental Organizations (WTO, UN, OSCE, etc.)

    6.1. End State(s)

    6.2. Objective(s)

    6.3. Intent

7. Non-Governmental Organizations

     7.1. End State(s)

     7.2. Objective(s)

     7.3. Intent

8. Interest Groups and Private Sector Actors

     8.1. End State(s)

     8.2. Objective(s)

     8.3. Intent

ANNEX D: COMBATANT COMMAND RESPONSIBILITIES

1. Combatant Command responsibilities

2. Other Geographic Combatant Command

3. Functional Combatant Command

4. Defense Agency Responsibilities

5. Other USG Responsibilities

SECURITY COOPERATION AUTOMATION

INTRODUCTION

This appendix provides an overview of some of the more common automation systems used by the security cooperation (SC) community. The overview includes the system description and functionality, as well as the procedures for requesting a user identification and password, if applicable.

SECURITY ASSISTANCE NETWORK

Background

In the 1990s, there was heightened interest in developing a more efficient way for overseas Security Cooperation Organizations (SCOs) and combatant commands (CCMDs) to exchange information with the Department of Defense (DOD) and military department (MILDEP) security assistance management information systems and with individuals at all echelons within the security assistance community. Early in 1990, Defense Security Cooperation Agency (DSCA) formed a special task group to examine security assistance automation among prospective users. One of the objectives was to enhance the opportunity for access by CCMDs and SCOs, as well as continental United States (CONUS) based security assistance activities, to existing security assistance management information systems and to provide users labor-saving automated data processing (ADP) administrative tools. With this in mind, the director of DSCA established the following goals:

- Tie existing automated systems and users together

- Provide simplified access procedures to a range of automated systems

- Interface automated systems through existing or expanded telecommunications networks, providing automated communication and data exchange support

With the above objectives and goals outlined, the Security Assistance Network (SAN) was initiated, and is currently formalized in DSCA Manual 5105.38-M, *Security Assistance Management Manual* (SAMM), chapter 13. The original telecommunications gateway for the SAN project was the Interoperability Decision Support System (IDSS), operated by the Institute for Defense Analysis (IDA). In the summer of 1996, development began on a web-based SAN. The concept of operations for the SANWeb is quite simple; a web browser is used to connect to the SANWeb home page via a local Internet service provider.

System Description

The SAN is a network used to exchange SC training and budget information between overseas SCOs, CCMDs, MILDEPs, DSCA, DFAS, DOD schoolhouses, Regional Centers, and international host nation organizations. The SANWeb contains many useful internal functions. Figure A1-1 shows many of the internal functions available to SANWeb users. The SANWeb can be accessed at https://www.idss.ida.org/san/login.prg.

Figure A1-1
Security Assistance Network

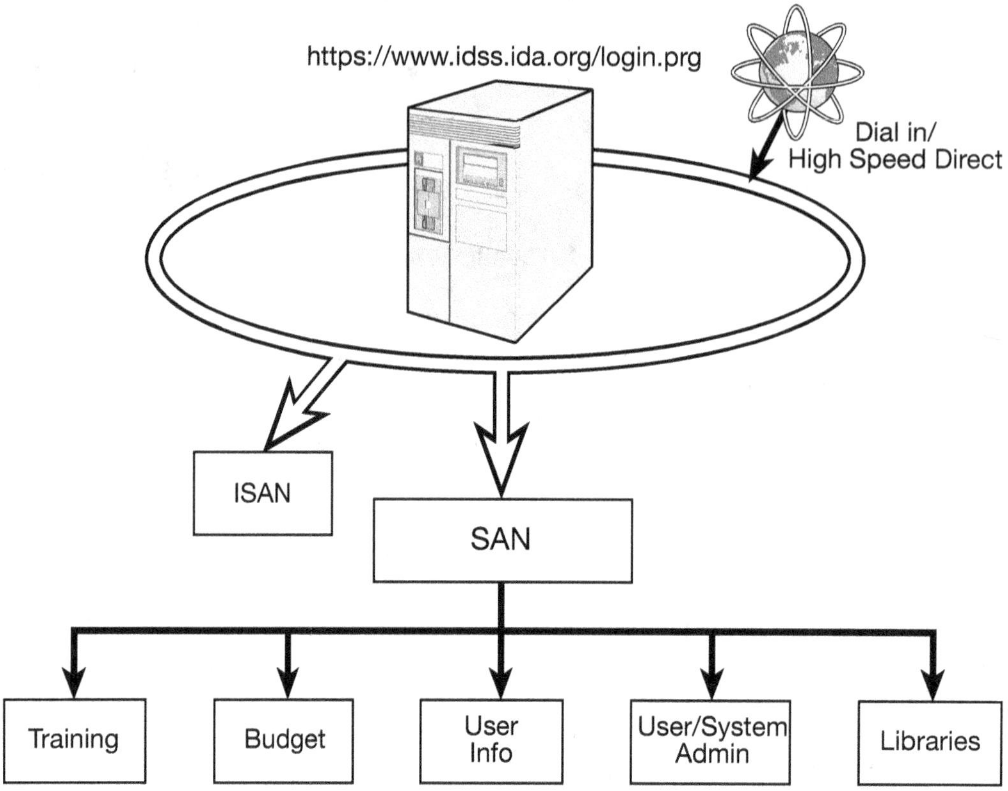

https://www.idss.ida.org/login.prg

Dial in/
High Speed Direct

ISAN

SAN

Training | Budget | User Info | User/System Admin | Libraries

User Database

Students attending the Defense Institute of Security Assistance Management (DISAM) Overseas Course (SCM-O) will automatically be registered as SAN users. Other requests for new SAN accounts can be accomplished by having an existing SAN user, acting as a sponsor, send a request electronically through the system. For detailed information on how to request a SAN account, please see the following web page: https://www.idss.ida.org/sanweb/How%20to%20Request%20a%20SAN%20Acct.doc. Users can locate information about other SAN users by searching the user database. They can search by name, security assistance country code, organization, etc.

Library

Users can share files with other SAN users by uploading them into one of the libraries. Libraries can also be used to overcome smaller file size limitations of e-mail systems. Information in these libraries must be unclassified.

Budget

The budget section provides access to the Security Assistance Automated Resource Management Suite (SAARMS) and the Integrated Security Assistance Automated Resource Management Suite (ISAARMS). SAARMS will be discussed later in this appendix. ISAARMS is an electronic interface among the SCOs, the CCMD, and the Defense Finance and Accounting Service (DFAS). It is only applicable for Security Assistance Administrative (T-20) funds. Twice a week, T-20 financial information is uploaded from SAARMS to ISAARMS for use by the CCMDs and DFAS. DFAS uses this data to update their official accounting records. CCMDs and SCOs can find current and archived data on this site by country or command. In return, DFAS produces a file of active financial documents, which is used to reconcile each country's financial records in SAARMS.

Training

The training section on the SAN provides the user with access to the various international military training databases such as the Training Military Articles and Services List (T-MASL) and the Standardized Training List (STL). SCO users can access this data for their individual countries. MILDEP and CCMD users can access multiple countries. Data updates are on a daily basis for all of the military services.

TRAINING WEBS

The Security Assistance Network (SAN) and the Security Cooperation-Training Management System (SC-TMS) are two essential automation systems utilized by the international training community.

Depending on the user's role, International Military Student Office (IMSO) or SCO, different functions will be available to the user as he or she logs into SC-TMS via the SAN.

SC-TMS for the International Military Student Office

Based on the IMSO role type, various functions are available within SC-TMS for use by IMSOs to manage international military students (IMS) assigned to their schoolhouse. SC-TMS for IMSOs is maintained on and receives its data from the SAN.

SC-TMS for IMSOs provides a means for the IMSO to identify international student quotas assigned to their training activity, receive arrival information on those students and report the student's progress as they advance through the training program. SC-TMS also enables the IMSO to document detailed information about their location and schoolhouse which is available online for the training community.

SC-TMS for the Security Cooperation Office

SC-TMS for SCOs is maintained on the SAN and receives STL and MASL updates from the Defense Security Assistance Management System (DSAMS). In addition to allowing the SCO to view STL and T-MASL information online, the SC-TMS for SCOs has several other very important features. It is where the SCO enters IMS information and creates Invitational Travel Orders (ITO) for the students. The SCO is also able to look up schoolhouse and IMSO information. The SCO can also maintain SCO POC information within the SC-TMS so that it is available to the training community. SC-TMS is required to be used for submission of student nomination packages for the Combating Terrorism Fellowship Program (CTFP). The SC-TMS is also used by the SCO to submit the Combined Education and Training Program Plan (CETPP).

International Security Assistance Network Web

The International Security Assistance Network web (I–SANweb) is an Internet tool that provides essentially the same data accessibility to an international user from a host nation that is provided to US SCO users via the SAN. Thus, international users can access the T-MASL data to identify desired courses of instruction. They can see course location information, and can have complete visibility of all country training programs that have been established for their country by viewing the STL. The I–SAN is a read only tool for the international customer. They cannot enter or change any information via the I–SAN. International customers who would like access to the I–SAN should contact their SCO in-country for further guidance. The SCO can then initiate a request for I–SANweb access for the international customer using the main menu of the SAN. The I–SANweb can be accessed at: https://www.idss.ida.org/isan/login.prg.

FINANCIAL AND LOGISTICS DATABASES

Prior to discussing the financial and logistics databases maintained by DFAS, Army, Navy, and Air Force security assistance agencies, several key points should be noted. First, all access to these databases is read-only, unless special permissions are granted. Although it is recognized that personnel in the SCO and other communities need access to the data, only those personnel responsible for actions have write or change capability. Second, use of the SAN does not require access to or a full understanding of the total database. Thus, SCOs do not see the same screens as the CONUS action offices. Those elements and screens that were deemed necessary were modified and simplified to give the SCO a clear, concise picture of foreign military sales (FMS) case/line/requisition data. Finally, the data viewed is just a snapshot of what is occurring. After viewing, it is considered a historical record because within days, or perhaps hours, the data can change.

Defense Integrated Financial System

System Description

The Defense Integrated Financial System (DIFS), managed by Defense Finance and Accounting Service–Security Cooperation Accounting (DFAS–SCA) in Indianapolis, Indiana, is the integrated system for all security assistance financial data. Financial data from the FMS letter of offer and acceptance (LOA) through case closure is maintained by the DIFS system.

Functionality

Simplified screens have been developed for the SCOs providing required data in an easily readable form. For in-country SCOs, data is available for that country only. For CCMD desk officers, data can be made available for all countries of responsibility. For standard DIFS system users the following data is available:

- Country implementing agency (IA) summary totals

- Financial status-country, and financial status-IA for country level data

- LOA detail summary and financial data

- Billing status data

- Payment schedules for LOA

- LOA line level data

- FMS case inventories

- Case controls

- Budget

- Case closure certificate inventory

- Performance/FMS Detail Delivery History Search Reports (FK)

- Cash

- Financial summary totals

- DIFS tables

Registration

To register for DIFS access the user must submit a completed DD Form 2875, System Authorization Access Request (SAAR), to DFAS. The basic form is available online: http://www.dtic.mil/whs/directives/infomgt/forms/forminfo/forminfopage3211.html.

DFAS has developed a special continuation sheet that explains what is required in block 27 of the form. To request the continuation sheet and submit the completed form, email DFAS–IN-DIFS-ACCESS-REQUEST@DFAS.MIL or contact the administrator at:

DFAS-JAXDC/IN

8899 E. 56th St.

Indianapolis, IN 46249

Fax: (317) 212-1917 (No DSN)

Tel: (317) 212-0977/7396, DSN 699-0977

Management Information System for International Logistics

System Description

The Management Information System for International Logistics (MISIL) is the US Navy's logistics and financial tracking system for security assistance. MISIL has standardized screens for SCO use.

Functionality

Some of the most useful screens and uses are as follows:

- The case management screen depicts material provided, summary case information, and the name and phone number of the case manager.

- The case/amendment/modification screen provides implementation dates of the latest amendments/modifications and the number of any pending case actions.

- The case line summary screen provides a description and dollar value for every line on an LOA and identifies lines supplying major defense equipment (MDE).

- The case line detail screen provides data such as material supplied, source of supply, disbursements, obligations, for a specific case and line.

- The case financial screen provides financial data for each line of a case as well as case totals.

- The case management history screen shows chronologically the impacts on a case by amendments and modifications.

- The requisition screen provides detailed information on the current supply, shipment, and delivery status of any requisition for a given case.

- The supply discrepancy report (SDR) or report of discrepancy screen gives general and specific information on all SDRs submitted against a case.

- The FMS case listing report area enables the user to generate a complete listing of all cases for a specific country.

In addition to these simplified screens, the SCO also has access to selected MISIL screens, which are used by CONUS FMS case managers.

Registration

To obtain access to MISIL, the user must submit a completed DD Form 2875, System Authorization Access Request (SAAR) and forward it to:

NAVSUP WSS-OF

ATTN: P7612 700 Robbins Avenue

Philadelphia PA 19111 Fax: (215) 697-0333

DSN 442-0333 Tel: (215) 697-2774, DSN 442-2774

Centralized Integrated System for International Logistics

System Description

The Centralized Integrated System for International Logistics (CISIL) is the Army's automated system used to support the management of security assistance programs. CISIL is the central repository for all Army security assistance and provides a series of databases, which offer users of the system information needed to manage their specific program. The system is comprised of modules of data which interact within the system and also interface with other external sites/activities for exchange of information. The SCO menu within CISIL provides access to various levels of information to assist the SCOs in managing the programs under their area of responsibility.

Functionality

The CISIL SCO menu provides the user access to logistical and financial information at case, line and requisition levels specific to their programs. It also provides useful case management reports, case history, requisition and supply discrepancy report (SDR) data. One of the areas currently provided under CISIL SCO data is the case requisition review report sometimes referred to as the mini-audit report or case audit report. Although designed for US Army Security Assistance (USASAC) personnel, SCOs may find the open inhibitors option and the case requisition review option very helpful. Much of the same data in CISIL can be viewed in the user-friendly web-based Security Cooperation Information Portal (SCIP).

Registration

To obtain access to CISIL, the user must submit a completed DD Form 2875, System Authorization Access Request (SAAR) and a signed CISIL IT Users Agreement and forward them to:

USASAC-S ATTN: Security Manager

54 M Avenue, Suite 1

New Cumberland, PA 17070-5096

(717) 770-4735 DSN: 771-4735 (Fax)

(717) 770-7052/7845; (DSN) 771-7052/7845

Security Assistance Management Information System

System Description

The Air Force Security Assistance and Cooperation Directorate (AFSAC) is responsible for administration of the security assistance program within the Air Force Materiel Command (AFMC). Security assistance program activities start with the initial negotiation of agreements for AFMC-managed initial and follow-on support cases, continue with the delivery of logistics support and end with the completion of all financial aspects of the programs for which AFMC is responsible. The Security Assistance Management Information System (SAMIS) is the Air Force's primary logistics information system for security assistance.

Functionality

The SAMIS maintains and reports comprehensive data on AFMC-managed security assistance programs. This information comes from many different sources; however, most data originates from various Air Force data systems. SAMIS serves as a repository for FMS case information, requisitions, supply status, shipments, and billing information required by AFSAC to effectively manage security assistance programs. SAMIS provides the security assistance community with accurate and timely information. To accomplish this, SAMIS provides online, real-time data updating as well as batch processing functions.

Registration

The SAMIS is a password protected system. A DD Form 2875, System Authorization Access Request (SAAR) is required for both US government (USG) (including SCOs) and international customers. Access to SAMIS can be requested via the AFSAC web site at https://afsac.wpafb.af.mil, "Apply for AFSAC Online and/or SAMIS Account." Access to SAMIS and AFSAC online is granted based on a person's "need to know." Users are assigned specific permissions and privileges according to their FMS task requirements. Once the SAAR is approved, a user identification and password will be issued. There are four application formats based upon the category of the user:

- USG civilian and military—This category consists of AF, DOD, and other USG employees including those working in overseas locations such as SCOs.

- USG contractor—This category includes contractors employed by USG that need to access FMS data as approved by the command country manager and/or the system administrator.

- CONUS foreign national representatives and support contractors—This group includes foreign representatives and contractors employed directly by the country that work within the continental US (CONUS) such as freight forwarder employees, Foreign Liaison Office (FLO) employees, embassy personnel, and any US citizen employed by a foreign country.

- OCONUS foreign national representatives and support contractors—This category includes individuals listed above that are located outside of CONUS (OCONUS). It is important to note that this category of user is required to forward their request for access through their embassy in Washington, DC.

DEFENSE SECURITY ASSISTANCE MANAGEMENT SYSTEM

System Description

The Defense Security Assistance Management System (DSAMS) is a DOD standard system operating under a modern information technology infrastructure encompassing the migration and reuse of selected features of existing security assistance systems. Incorporating an extensive analysis of the security assistance business area and its processes, DSAMS provides a set of standardized, improved, streamlined, and optimized services. The major benefits of DSAMS are consolidated data, improved data quality, standard reports to the customer, faster building of cases, and a current implemented view when a case is opened in DSAMS.

Functionality

Case Development Module

The case development module (CDM) provides functionality from the entry of an initial request through the development of a FMS LOA and changes resulting in a modification or an amendment. The CDM also initializes centralized reference tables and workflow applications that are used in other modules. Enhancements over the past few years include additional functionality to enable electronic countersignature, and support for other security assistance programs such as leases.

Security Cooperation ⬚uto⬚ation

Case Implementation Module

The case implementation module (CIM) covers the process from receipt of customer acceptance through issuance of implementing directions to the case manager and performing activity.

Training Module

The training module (TM) replaced the three MILDEP legacy training management systems, and includes automated interfaces with the SAN and TMS systems. This allows the automated upload of international student data into DSAMS, and automated the invitational travel order (ITO) funding process. DSAMS TM also allows the automated processing of cross-service training requirements across MILDEP channels.

Registration

DSAMS is a password protected system for use by USG personnel only. A DD Form 2875, System Authorization Access Request (SAAR) is required for access to DSAMS. Access to DSAMS applications is through the Citrix application only. Applicants for Citrix user accounts must email or fax a completed SAAR to the DSAMS help desk. The e-mail address is saar@dsadc.dsca.mil and the fax is DSN 430-9082. However, the user must have a valid DSAMS account, provided by a MILDEP, before a Citrix account is provided.

Once access is approved, a user identification and password for Citrix will be issued. The issuance of the DSAMS accounts is done through the appropriate MILDEP points of contact. Any additional questions should be directed to:

DSAMS Help Desk

dsca.dsadc.servicedesk@mail.mil

717-605-9200; (DSN) 430-9200

DSAMS does not permit system access by international customers. There is a daily interface from DSAMS to the SCIP which provides FMS customers access to selected DSAMS data.

SECURITY COOPERATION INFORMATION PORTAL (SCIP)

System Description

SCIP (https://www.scportal.us/home/) is a secure, controlled, unclassified DOD web-based computer information system that provides authorized users with access to Foreign Military Sales (FMS) and Building Partner Capacity (BPC) programs case-related data and reports to support management responsibilities for those cases. All USG personnel (including Locally Employed Staff—LES, and support contractors), and foreign purchasers (including their authorized freight forwarders) that have job responsibilities requiring access (i.e., need to know) to the SCIP system information are eligible to obtain SCIP accounts. DSCA's policy is that "USG personnel and SCOs are encouraged to become familiar with SCIP's full capabilities."

The SCIP data extracts are obtained (automatically for most of the data) from multiple authoritative DOD and US military department (MILDEP) financial and logistics systems (figure A1-2). The majority of data is updated daily via a batch process at approximately 0700 US Eastern Standard Time. Refresh status indicators and information are provided to users in the "Case Info Community" to document the date/time of the last data refresh from those systems. Depending on the data being sought and the user's permissions, having a single SCIP account can save time from having to obtain separate system accounts to access that data from each individual source system. SCIP became operational in 2003 and has been significantly expanded and improved upon over time. SCIP system access is available world-wide from any computer (i.e. does not have to be from a USG or DOD domain) as long as there is adequate internet access, and an active authorized SCIP user account.

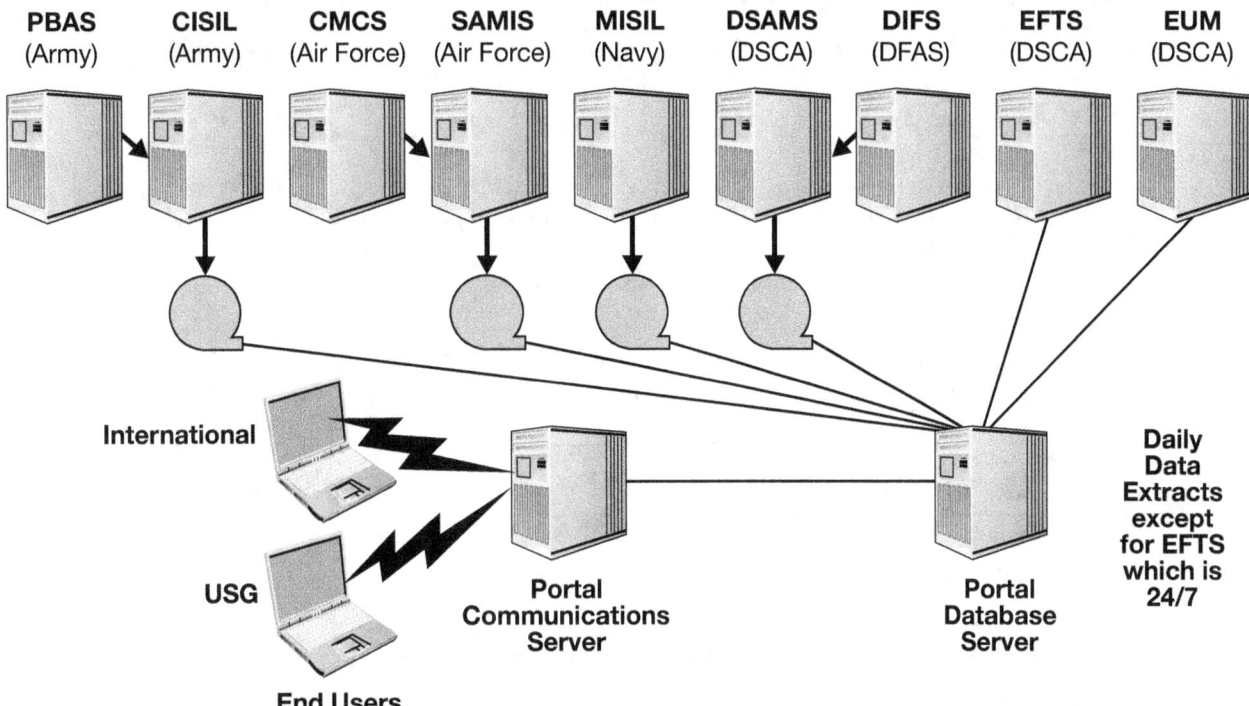

Figure A1-2
SCIP Authoritative Data Sources

Functionality

SCIP capabilities, applications, and reports are separated by tabs into different "communities" (see figure A1-3). Some of the SCIP communities are only authorized for USG users. A brief description of each community and the related capabilities and applications follows.

Home Community

This is the first page users see when they successfully logon to SCIP. Like all the SCIP communities, there are announcements to inform the user of all the recently completed and planned changes to that community. Users can use the community navigation bar (figure A1-3) at the top of the web page to navigate to any of their authorized communities.

Figure A1-3
SCIP Community Menu Bar

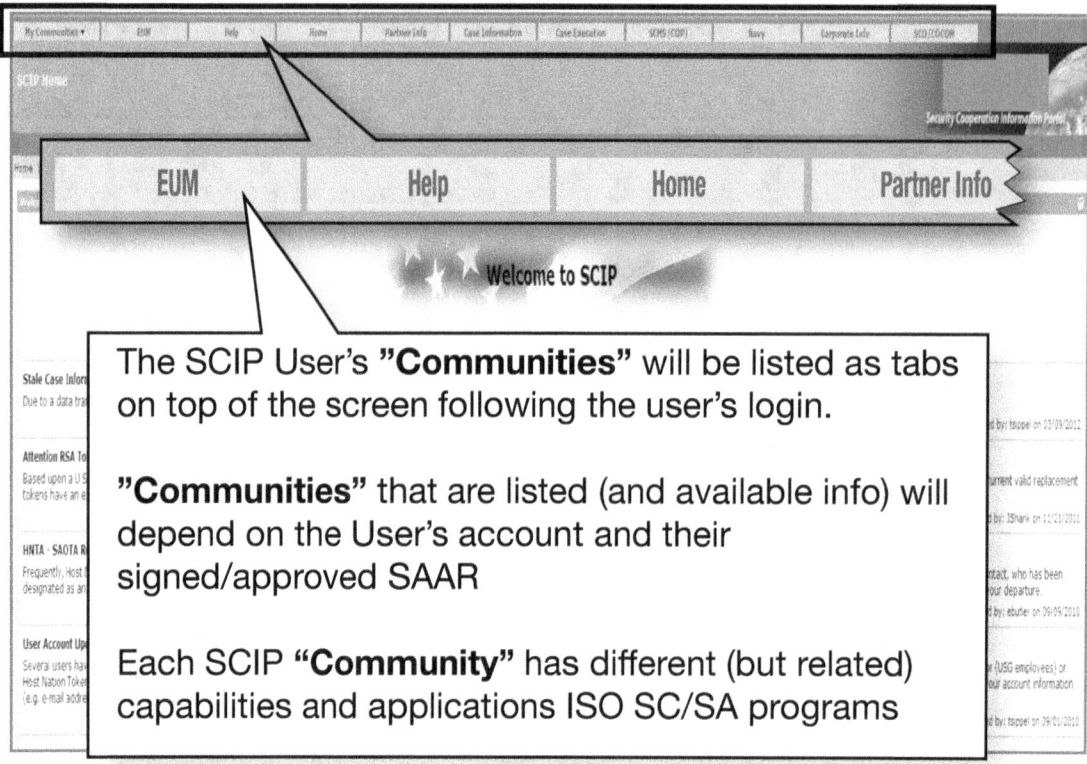

The SCIP User's **"Communities"** will be listed as tabs on top of the screen following the user's login.

"Communities" that are listed (and available info) will depend on the User's account and their signed/approved SAAR

Each SCIP **"Community"** has different (but related) capabilities and applications ISO SC/SA programs

Case Information Community

This community provides a query capability to view all FMS and BPC case information for which the user has been authorized access. SCIP displays region, country, or case data of interest depending upon the user access, application, and filter options that the user chooses. The application is chosen by the user via the "Case Information" menu bar. Each community has a unique menu bar. This unique menu bar is located directly below the "Community" navigation menu bar and available once the desired community is selected. It provides the user with the capability to select their desired community application or report. In the "Case Information" community, some of the applications include real-time metrics (that can be quickly exported to a PowerPoint slide if desired), data inputs (requisitions, supply discrepancy reports [SDRs], freight transactions), Financial Management Reviews (FMRs), Ad Hoc reports, and a Case Status filter to enable the user to quickly find cases of interest. For all cases that the user is authorized to see, the user is presented with a "Pyramid of Choices" (figure A1-4) for all the case's Letter of Offer and Acceptance (LOA) documents (Basic, Amendments, Modifications). Selecting any one of these pyramid levels will provide the user with specific case details (e.g., what is the LOA Anticipated Offer Date, when is the requisition material expected to be shipped, are there any unprogrammed case funds remaining, etc.) pertaining to that level. A summary report of all or a portion of that case data can be exported to a Microsoft Excel file.

Figure A1-4
Case Status Menu Options—A "Pyramid of Choices"

Case Execution Community

This community provides links to several tri-service applications, including the Enhanced Freight Tracking System (EFTS), EMALL, Asset Visibility (AV), and the recently added WebRoR (formerly a Navy-only application that automates the Repair of Repairables process). EFTS is a secure, web-based application that serves as a consolidated source for SC material in-transit information. EFTS does not replace existing shipment systems, but rather, it provides a clearinghouse of all available shipment information in a single supplemental tracking system to provide additional visibility of equipment and material shipments. EFTS receives data from Defense Logistics Agency (DLA), contractors, depots, Defense Transportation System, carriers, freight forwarders, consolidation points, and ports of embarkation and debarkation. This allows EFTS to provide visibility of the SC material distribution pipeline for all classes of supply and modes of transportation either outbound from the US to the purchaser's country or materiel returning to the US or US facilities overseas.

EUM (End-Use Monitoring) Community

This community provides authorized users with specific information, reports, and capabilities applicable to the DOD EUM program. The EUM applications within SCIP provide inventory reports that will help inspectors plan for upcoming inventories and isolate items that are considered "delinquent."

Partner Info Community

This community is an information-sharing type of community instead of a business process or business application community. It includes (among other items) documents, presentations, and files related to the Foreign Procurement Group (FPG) and International Customer User Group (ICUG).

National Geospatial-Intellegience Agency (NGA) Community

This community allows authorized SCIP users to access, review, and download navigation charts (e.g., aeronautical en route and approach charts, terminal procedures, etc. for international navigation and flight safety).

Security Cooperation ⬚uto⬚ation

SCMS (Security Cooperation Management Suite) Community

Access to this community is authorized only for USG personnel to support case management responsibilities for Building Partner Capacity (BPC) and Foreign Military Sales (FMS) cases. SCMS resides within SCIP and is a joint-service, web-based capability that provides a common operating picture of the SC process. SCMS has joint worldwide US military and civilian users, which increases joint communication, resulting in enhanced decision-making. SCMS provides USG personnel with key information used to track high-priority FMS and BPC programs and is especially useful during the oversight process for expiring funds on cases that are funded via US appropriated sources. SCMS allows data input and customization through its multiple reports, showing information by appropriation and program, which allows for vital information-sharing among multiple program participants. Although initially conceived to support the war effort in Iraq, the utility of SCMS was recognized by additional communities throughout DOD. SCMS has been expanded for use with all the BPC programs. It benefits US decision-makers when planning how to best build partner nation capacity.

Corporate Info Community

This community provides information to USG personnel regarding the Security Cooperation Business Forum (SCBF) and Performance Measurement Senior Working Group (PMSWG) meeting, Lean Six Sigma/Continuous Process Improvement, organizational charts, Lessons Learned—Best Practices, etc.

SCO/COCOM Community

Access to this community is authorized only for USG personnel and provides information sharing (e.g., General Information, Lessons Learned & Best Practices, DISAM SCM-O (Overseas) lesson material, etc.) for the USG SCO and CCMD personnel. This community also contains DISAM SCM-O class presentations for the four-week class (and not just SCIP presentations).

Navy Community

This community provides numerous capabilities (e.g., Case Execution Performance Tool [CEPT], Case Reviews, Information Warehouse, Supply Discrepancy Reports, etc.) pertaining to US Navy-managed cases. Case and line financial commitments, obligations, and expenditure details are also provided for those cases.

Help Community

The help desk was developed to provide all SCIP users a common location and interface for submitting and reading SCIP help desk requests. Having the help desk embedded within SCIP provides users with more security and privacy and prevents unauthorized viewing of requests. There are also numerous online help guides (Help Desk User Guide, Case Information User Guide, SCIP Help Descriptions, Corporate Info User Guide, International Customer Token Access Guide, Logon Guide, SCIP Acronyms, SCIP Background, Token Administrators Guide, US Government (USG)/SCO Token Access Guide, and the Partner Info User Guide) posted to assist SCIP users with understanding how to fully use the numerous SCIP capabilities. In addition to the guides and reference documents listed above, there are also other Community specific guides that are posted on SCIP that can be accessed via the Help links on the applicable community navigation menu.

Obtaining a SCIP Account

The online SCIP registration form for both US and international users can be found by accessing the SCIP web site (https://www.scportal.us/home/) and clicking the "REGISTRATION INFO" link on that page. All USG SCO and CCMD students who attend the DISAM Security Cooperation Management Overseas (SCM-O) course are registered for their individual SCIP accounts while in class per DSCA Policy Memo 11-58 (*Policy Update Regarding Security Cooperation Information Portal (SCIP) Account Access for Security Cooperation Officers (SCOs)*). For all other SCIP account applicants, follow the instructions in the SCIP "REGISTRATION INFO" introduction to submit the registration for processing by the SCIP Program Office/Defense Security Assistance Development Center (DSADC). International (i.e., non USG) SCIP applicants must be issued a secure SCIP token by their country's Host Nation Token Administrator (HNTA) prior to completing the registration form. DSCA Policy Memoranda 03-11 (*Enrollment Process for SCIP*), and 05-17 (*SCIP Electronic Token Issuance and Replacement Processes*) are the policy references for details regarding issuance and management of SCIP tokens. The SCIP International Customer Token Access Guide (posted on the SCIP "REGISTRATION INFO" web page), provides further details on SCIP token operations and processes. Additional SCIP DSCA policy memoranda are posted on the DSCA web site. For additional SCIP assistance, users (and prospective users) can contact the SCIP Help Desk at SCIPHelp@dsadc. dsca.mil or via phone at (717) 605-9200.

Accessing the Security Cooperation Information Portal (SCIP) Web Site

To access the SCIP system once a user has obtained a SCIP account, type https://www.scportal.us/home/ in the Internet browser address line and click the "SCIP Logon" link on top of that page. Both Internet Explorer (IE) and Mozilla Firefox can be used to access SCIP, though SCIP functionality appears to work best on IE. The browser advanced security settings and DOD root certificates need to be correct to gain access. Contact the SCIP Help Desk regarding SCIP log-on issues.

If logging into SCIP with a USG Common Access Card (CAC) certificate, (which is the usual means for USG DOD users to log-on to SCIP if the account has been CAC enabled), select the non-e-mail certificate. Logging into the SCIP system with a token will be via the subsequent SCIP login screens requiring entry of the SCIP user ID and passcode.

To keep the SCIP account active, users need to periodically log-on. Failure to log into SCIP for forty-five days will result in an automatic e-mail advising the user to log in or risk the loss of SCIP account privileges. Failure to log in for sixty days results in account suspension, requiring a USG supervisor or country HNTA to contact the SCIP Help desk to reactivate the account. If a user fails to log in for 180 days, the account will be permanently deleted, requiring submission of a new registration form to obtain another account.

SCIP Training

DISAM provides SCIP basic through advanced topic training in the majority of the DISAM-offered classes. The DISAM SCIP classroom training, which includes in-residence and Mobile Education Teams—METs, has expanded by 125 percent in the last year due to the increasing importance of SCIP to the SC users. Electronic copies of all the current DISAM SCIP presentations are posted on the SCIP Corporate Info Community and are accessible via the "Training>DISAM Presentations>SCIP" links to authorized USG users. The DISAM SCIP training maximizes the online demonstration of the system capabilities by the instructors and the 'hands-on' practical exercises by the students.

Additional SCIP information and training may be accessed on the DISAM home page (http://www.disam.dsca.mil/) via the "SC Tools" link on that page. These DISAM SCIP training resources (figure A1-5) include an overview presentation, a SCIP exercise handbook, DSCA SCIP policy letters, SCIP frequently asked questions (FAQs), and a link to access the SCIP system. The SCIP handbook is a familiarization tool and training guide for SCIP users to better understand the capabilities of the SCIP system. It is intended for both initial system instruction and also to provide users with a future reference handbook when using the SCIP system. All the exercise questions (Process, Logistics, Financial, and Miscellaneous Advanced) in the handbook are based on information provided in the DISAM class lessons and can be completed even without a SCIP account using the case examples in the handbook. A basic understanding of the FMS process, logistics, and finance subjects is needed to understand and interpret the materials and complete the exercises in the SCIP exercise handbook. Future DISAM SCIP training will include online training module 'vignettes' (e.g., how do I log in...develop a real time metrics...develop an Ad Hoc report...track a requisition shipment, etc.), which students can access and complete via the DISAM web page.

Figure A1-5
SCIP on DISAM Web Page

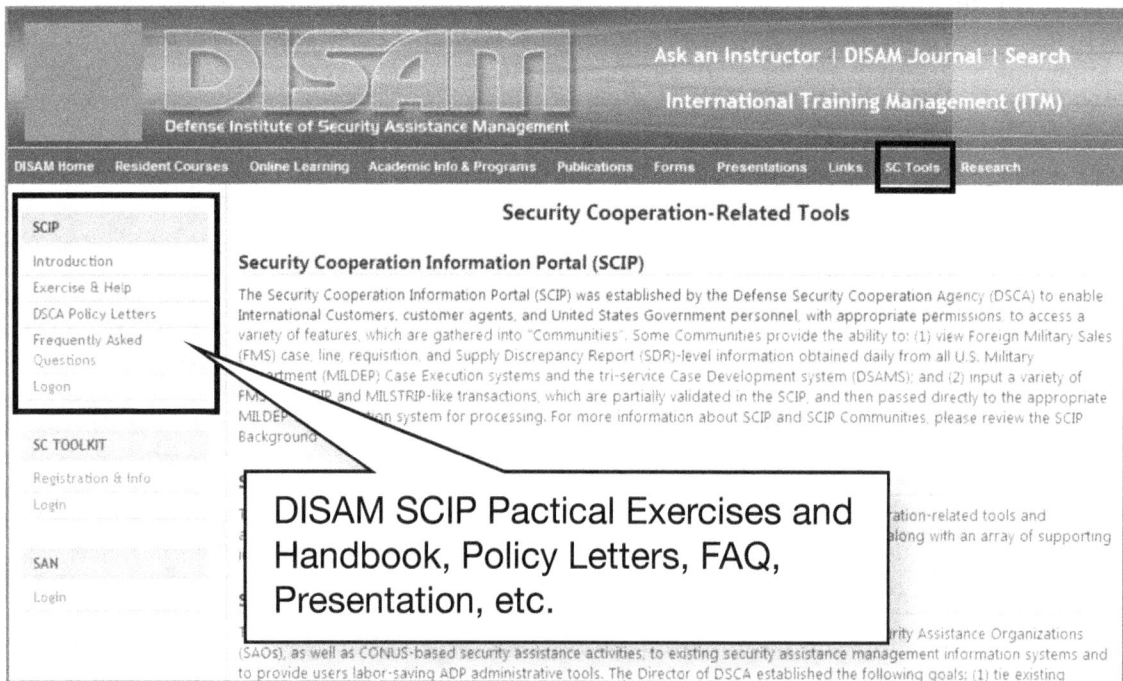

ADDITIONAL SOFTWARE PACKAGES

Security Assistance Automated Resource Management Suite

System Description

The Security Assistance Automated Resource Management Suite (SAARMS) is a group of one stand-alone and two web-based software applications used by SCOs and CCMDs to manage their security assistance funded resources. The SAARMS applications are Budget Preparation, Budget Execution, and Property.

Functionality

Budget Preparation—This program standardizes the budget preparation process in a web-based format. It uses relevant historical data from previous budget submissions and periods of financial execution and generates the required budget submission reports that SCOs and CCMDs are required to submit to DSCA during the budget submission cycle.

Budget Execution—This program is a web-based funds management feeder system that automates the record keeping of the SCO budget management functions. SAARMS feeds into the official DFAS BQ accounting system by conducting twice-weekly electronic transfers of data via the SAN.

Property—This program is a stand-alone application that is used for property book management, to include accounting for property and tracking property acquisition, use, and disposition.

International Training Management Web Site

The International Training Management (ITM) web site is an informational web site intended for all US and foreign international training managers. It provides a full range of international training management information, including references, policy and procedural messages, articles, lessons, exercises, FAQ sheets, links, and specific functional information.

The ITM web site is available to anyone at http://www.disam.dsca.mil/itm/ and does not require the use of a password.

DOD Acquisition Portal

System Description

The DOD Acquisition Portal (http://dap.dau.mil) is designed to be a single point of access to DOD acquisition related resources and information. This web-based system easily links users to the myriad of acquisition source documents, references, and other related information. The acquisition portal replaces its two predecessors, the Acquisition Knowledge Sharing System (AKSS) and the previous Defense Acquisition Deskbook (DAD) system.

Functionality

Acquisition Process—Covers the three primary acquisition processes of the Joint Capabilities Integration and Development System (JCIDS), the Defense Acquisition System (DAS), and the Planning, Programming, Budgeting and Execution (PPBE) system. This includes links to DOD and MILDEP policies, guidance, tools and other resources.

Workforce—Provides information on acquisition career management, the DOD human capital initiative, career planning, leadership training, and relevant professional organizations.

Policy—Serves as an encyclopedic source of acquisition policy that follows a hierarchy of policy issuance that can also be filtered by organization, career field and special topics.

Communities of Practice—Offers links to the various acquisition communities of practice and special interest areas.

Training and Continuous Learning—Outlines various training resources and continuous learning opportunities applicable to DOD acquisition professionals.

Industry—Functions as a one-stop source for information and links about industry partner support and participation in defense acquisition.

Workforce Support—The acquisition portal also provides a link to the DAU's "Ask a Professor" (AAP) program (http://dap.dau.mil/aap/). AAP serves as a vehicle for practitioners within the DOD workforce to submit acquisition related questions that are routed to the appropriate subject matter expert for a response. AAP contains a user accessible Frequently Asked Question (FAQ) database that can be searched by key word or by category. FMS related questions are contained within the "International Foreign Military Sales" sub-category within the overall "Contracting" category.

Registration

The acquisition portal is hosted by the Defense Acquisition University (DAU) on behalf of the DOD acquisition community. You can access the acquisition portal at http://dap.dau.mil. The portal structure consists of a home page with general acquisition information and links.

SUMMARY

Security cooperation personnel have access to numerous automated systems, some that have been in existence since as early as 1976. Access has transformed from direct links for a few specific users to worldwide access via the Internet. Newer systems such as the SAN and SCIP have been specifically designed with the needs of the end-user in mind. SC users in the far-flung corners of the globe are freed from the constraints of time zone differences and slow mail delivery by virtue of Internet connectivity and interaction. Use of these systems has greatly enhanced communication between the SCO, CCMDs, and CONUS-based logistics and training activities such as the MILDEPs and IMSOs and the international customers. The impact the increased access to the systems discussed in this annex has been profoundly beneficial, not only to security cooperation activities, but ultimately to the international customer as well.

REFERENCES

DSCA Manual 5105.38-M. *Security Assistance Management Manual* (SAMM). Chap. 13, sections C13.6.3.2.2, C13.6.3.2.3. http://www.samm.dsca.mil/.

DSCA Policy 03-11. *Enrollment for the Security Cooperation Information Portal.* June 25, 2003. http://www.dsca.mil/samm/PolicyMemos/2003/DSCA%2003-11.htm

DSCA Policy 5-17. *Security Cooperation Information Portal (SCIP) Electronic Token Issuance and Replacement Processes.* June 24, 2005. http://www.dsca.mil/samm/PolicyMemos/2005/DSCA%2005-17.htm

DSCA Policy 11-08. *Security Cooperation Information Portal (SCIP) Background Document.* February 10, 2011. http://www.dsca.mil/samm/PolicyMemos/2011/DSCA%2011-08.htm.

DSCA Policy 11-58. *Policy Update Regarding Security Cooperation Information Portal (SCIP) Account Access for Security Cooperation Officers (SCOs).* November 15, 2011. http://www.dsca.mil/samm/PolicyMemos/2011/DSCA%2011-58.htmhttp://www.dsca.mil/samm/PolicyMemos/2003/DSCA%2003-11.htm

SCIP International Customer Token Access Guide. October 2012. https://www.scportal.us/home/docs/IntlCustAccessGuide.pdf

HISTORY OF SECURITY ASSISTANCE AND SECURITY COOPERATION

SECURITY ASSISTANCE AND FOREIGN POLICY

One of the primary methods used to carry out US foreign and national security policy has been, and still remains, the transfer of defense articles, defense services, military training, and economic assistance; i.e., the provision of security assistance (SA). The various programs that comprise SA are described in some detail in chapter 1, "Introduction to Security Cooperation," of this text. In general, the term encompasses various programs of military and economic assistance for allied and friendly foreign countries.

The use of SA has been a major tool in the formulation and conduct of US foreign policy, especially beginning with World War II. It has helped countries in peril to actively defend themselves, reconstruct or strengthen their militaries against a variety of threats, promote the establishment of democracies with a strong emphasis on internationally acceptable human rights, promote interoperability within strategic alliances, and strengthen coalition efforts against unacceptable use of force. US SA is authorized only when determined by the President to be in the US national interest. This powerful determination has been made many times since World War II by American Presidents responding to crises throughout the world ranging from the Soviet threat of the Cold War to the Global War on Terrorism (GWOT) following 11 September 2001.

HISTORICAL PRECEDENTS OF SECURITY ASSISTANCE

SA (or, in a narrower sense, the transfer of arms and articles of warfare) has been part of international relations as long as societies have been preparing for and engaging in war. Whenever it was assumed to be in the best interests of one nation to give or sell arms or other military support to another, arms transfers of some type have taken place. The supply and demand for arms has been, and remains, a natural consequence of the desire to achieve national goals and maintain national security.

Early History

The practice of military assistance/arms transfers can be traced to the earliest recorded military histories. A classic example of problems associated with such transfers can be found in Thucydides' *History of the Peloponnesian War*, written some twenty-five hundred years ago. The transfer of arms was as controversial then as now, as illustrated by the declaration of Aristophanes, the classical playwright, when he held that the armaments industry was hindering peace in ancient Greece. Throughout history one can find the roles that military assistance and opposition to it have played in international relationships. US history is a case in point.

The American War of Independence

The very emergence of the US as a nation-state was supported to a large extent by the transfer of arms and other military assistance from France. Such assistance was not entirely altruistic on the part of the French, however, for they saw in the American Revolution an opportunity to limit British expansion in North America. It was in France's national interest to have the British engaged in a protracted American war while the French sought to expand and reinforce their military and commercial positions in North America and elsewhere.

The newly independent nation under President Washington had many postwar problems, not the least of which was to convince the nations of the world that the US was, in fact, an established sovereign state. Washington spent two terms in office consolidating and expanding the country, and trying to establish a foreign policy. When urged to stay on for a third term, he declined and stated that after eight years the country needed a change of administration. As one of his last official acts, he wrote his often quoted "Farewell Address" to Congress in which he warned of the danger of foreign entanglements, a view that has influenced the foreign and domestic policy of the US ever since.

The Nineteenth Century

The period after the War of Independence saw the efforts of the US turn toward the internal development of its political and economic structures, and the expansion of its borders from coast to coast. American foreign policy focused on the development of markets for the growing US industrial capacity and the acquisition of non-indigenous materials for US industry. Little effort was made to expand US foreign relations much beyond commercial interests.

There were, however, a few instances when circumstances arose that required a policy of greater magnitude. One of these was the Monroe Doctrine. The doctrine, initially conceived by John Quincy Adams, was first announced by President James Monroe in his annual message to Congress in 1823. The doctrine, in essence, declared that the Americas, i.e., North, Central, and South, were off limits to incursions from European powers. In the event such incursions were to occur, the doctrine implied that the US would vigorously oppose such actions by whatever means seemed appropriate to meet the real or implied threats to the safety of the US or its neighbors in the Western Hemisphere.

The principles of the Monroe Doctrine have been invoked or used as part of the decision making processes by a number of Presidents since 1823. Examples include:

- President William A. McKinley's involvement in the Spanish-American War

- President Theodore Roosevelt's actions to acquire the Panama Canal

- The stationing of US Marines in Nicaragua by President Calvin Coolidge to stabilize that country

- President John F. Kennedy's invocation of the Doctrine during the Cuban Missile Crisis

- President Johnson's movement of troops into the Dominican Republic

- US assistance in restoring democratic governments in Grenada and Panama

- President Clinton's continuing concerns over events in Haiti and Cuba

The Early Twentieth Century

The acquisition of Guam, the Philippines, and Puerto Rico as a result of the Spanish-American War of 1898 thrust the US into the role of an international power, a role that the US, as a nation, may not have been psychologically prepared to accept. Thus, events at the turn of the century generated many debates as to the direction that US foreign policy should take. While many saw US policies as dictated by our interests, others considered them the US entrance into a morally questionable world. The ambivalence of US foreign policy, combined with certain deep-seated sentiments, led to the resurgence of a strong sense of isolationism in this country.

Feeling secure behind its ocean barriers, the US again turned its attention to internal development. Few international threats were posed against America's security; its armed forces were allowed to decline, reflecting a continuing US aversion to large standing armies and entangling foreign alliances. Thus, as America moved into the twentieth century, it retained strong convictions against foreign adventures. Those convictions were soon to be challenged.

World War I

With the onset of World War I, the US, despite its declared neutrality, rapidly emerged as the leading participant in the international munitions trade. During the period of its neutrality, August 1914 to March 1917, the US exported approximately $2.2 billion in war supplies to Europe. In 1916, the US shipped more than $1 billion of arms in a single year. By 1920, the US accounted for more than 52 percent of global arms exports.

The fact that the US, despite its proclaimed neutrality, was engaged in arms trade during the war served as an indirect cause of US entry into the war. The British, seeking to stop the movement of arms to the Central Powers, established a naval blockade to deny aid to the German forces. Germany, in retaliation, resorted to increased submarine warfare, and on 17 May 1915 sank, among other ships, the British ocean liner Lusitania with a loss of 1,000 lives, many of them American. The Germans claimed that the ship was being used to carry war materiel to Britain and was thus a legitimate target of war. Nonetheless, the attack was seen by the Americans as wanton perdition on an unarmed merchant vessel, and this event accelerated the movement to entanglement in the broils of Europe. Coincidentally, German submarine warfare began to erode American confidence in its "sea barriers."

As an item of further note, a prominent international lawyer of that period, Charles Hyde, petitioned Secretary of State Lansing to reduce the US arms trade. Hyde noted that during World War I, the US was becoming "a base of supplies of such magnitude that unless retarded, the success of armies, possibly the fate of empires, may ultimately rest upon the output of American factories."

However, President Wilson saw this American output of munitions as "an arsenal of freedom." Nevertheless, despite that sentiment, the fact that the US ranked high among the world's leading arms exporters caused a great controversy that was reflected in much public debate and discussion throughout the 1920s and 1930s. Books of that period mirrored the American public's concern about this unwanted, yet thriving arms industry. Examples of the literature of that period which nagged the American conscience included such titles as:

- *Merchants of Death: A Study of the International Armaments Industry*

- *Iron, Blood and Profits*

- *War for Profit*

- *Death and Profit*

Between the World Wars

Continuing debate about America's role as an arms merchant saw the establishment in the 1930s of a special Senate Munitions Investigating Committee, known as the Nye Committee, after its Chairman, Senator Gerald P. Nye (R-ND). The committee's charter called for an investigation of the international arms trade to determine if a commercial profit motive was the primary cause of the continued sustenance of war. The investigation, conducted from 1934 to 1936, also sought to determine whether the arms trade could be regulated under existing laws and treaties, and whether a government monopoly in arms production was a practical alternative. As Senator Nye, an avowed isolationist, interpreted the committee's mandate, he concluded that the way to stop war was to take away the opportunity for private gain. His personal convictions influenced the committee to recommend the nationalization of the US arms industry; a minority opinion held out for close government control rather than nationalization.

Although the concept of nationalization was subsequently rejected, greater government control and oversight over the US arms industry was an outcome of the Nye Committee's efforts. This included the establishment of a munitions control board. A further recommendation of the committee was to seek the international adoption of arms controls, but after some ineffectual multinational efforts, the international arms trade remained unchecked.

One accompanying feature of the Nye Committee findings was an increased US public sentiment for withdrawing from world affairs and returning to America's characteristic isolationism. Despite a resurgence of isolationism and the limited results of the Nye Committee, however, little impact was made on American involvement in the international arms trade. In fact, in 1936, the US ranked third in world arms sales, immediately behind France and Great Britain, a position it was to hold until the outbreak of World War II.

World War II

The arms trade that played such a significant role in US foreign policy during the initial phases of World War I had a similar influence in the period immediately prior to US entry into World War II. Thus, in 1939, Congress revised the Neutrality Act, thereby permitting the sale of arms during peacetime to the British on a cash-and-carry basis. Eventually, US policies were broadened to include arms support for other allies.

The commitment to the British cause by a neutral US took still another direction. In September 1940, President Roosevelt negotiated the destroyers-for-bases agreement in which fifty over-aged US destroyers were exchanged for ninety-nine-year leases on several British bases in the Western Hemisphere under the rationale that the bases might become critical to American defense. The isolationist-minded critics considered Roosevelt's action a gross violation of American neutral status, and regarded his efforts as a device to embroil the US in the war.

The next major US decision to aid the British was the Lend-Lease Program initiated by an act of Congress on March 11, 1941. Lend-Lease eventually supplied about $50 billion of arms, food, and other aid to allies, including, as they became engaged in the war, the Russians and the Chinese. Under Lend-Lease, the US loaned materials to the allies under the premise that it would be paid back when they were able to do so. The program also allowed the lease of other materials and services for which payment could be made by "reverse lend-lease" whereby the allies would provide certain materials and services to the US in payment. As a matter of historical interest, less than $10 billion were repaid to the US for America's lend-lease contributions.

THE TRUMAN DOCTRINE

The stage upon which the post-war scene was to be acted out was dominated by two players – the US and the USSR, the superpowers. The diametrically opposed philosophies of these nations influenced the formulation of major international doctrines by all of the postwar American Presidents, beginning in March 1947 with President Harry S. Truman's landmark proclamation, the Truman Doctrine.

Truman found himself beset by new and serious problems when the war ended in 1945. In Europe, the former US ally, the Soviet Union, had become hostile to US interests. Additionally, the Soviets heightened international anxiety when they seized control of several small Eastern European countries and threatened the independence of Turkey and Greece. Soviet-supported communist guerrilla actions in Greece, and Soviet diplomatic pressures in Turkey, were causes for great concern to President Truman. He believed the unrest in Greece and the overt Soviet political actions in Turkey were blatant attempts to establish a strong communist presence in the region. Truman also felt that the spread of Soviet hegemony was contrary to the national interests of the US, especially in the non-Communist parts of the Balkans, Asia Minor, and the Persian Gulf region.

In support of his views, Truman initiated an emergency request in March 1947 for $400 million to aid Greece and Turkey, a request which came to be known as the Truman Doctrine. In justifying his request, Truman declared:

I believe that it must be the policy of the United States to support free peoples who are resisting attempted subjugation by armed minorities or by outside pressure.

I believe that we must assist free peoples to work out their own destinies in their own way.

I believe that our help should be primarily through economic and financial aid which is essential to economic stability and orderly political processes.

In addition to funds, I ask the Congress to authorize the detail of American civilian and military personnel to Greece and Turkey, at the request of those countries, to assist in the tasks of reconstruction and for the purpose of supervising the use of such financial and material assistance as may be furnished, I recommend that authority also be provided for the instruction and training of selected Greek and Turkish personnel.

Congress was reluctant to act on the request because the US had never before entered into a formal assistance program with a foreign state during general peacetime conditions. Truman persisted, however, and the Greece-Turkey Aid Act of 1947 was enacted, thus introducing the instrument of assistance as a significant factor in US post-war foreign policy.

In the ensuing three years, Greece and Turkey received well over $600 million in both US military and economic aid. The legislation authorizing that aid stipulated that US military advisers would administer the programs within the respective countries. By mid-1949, there were over 527 US armed forces personnel in the Joint United States Military Advisory and Planning Group in Greece and over four hundred in a similar organization in Turkey. With the establishment of these units, the administration of military assistance acquired another dimension, that of creating advisory groups which would eventually operate in many areas of the world and involve US military personnel by the thousands. Thus, the Truman Doctrine was to provide a precedent for the principle of collective security. It was cited as the foundation of subsequent similar programs under the premise that to promote the security and well-being of friendly foreign nations was in the best national interest of the US.

US military assistance in the early post-war period focused primarily on the transfer of US arms from stockpiles of surplus war materiel. These arms transfers were made to participants in an emerging network of US alliances, and were provided as grant aid, i.e., gratis, under what became known as the Military Assistance Program (MAP). The giveaway nature of this grant assistance program would later become a point of extended discussion as the assistance programs matured and as the economies of US war-ravaged allies experienced regeneration and substantial growth. Further, with the establishment of MAP, US arms transfers, economic aid, and collective security began to merge as programs sharing a common purpose, a concept that later, in the Nixon Administration, would come to be known as SA. As part of the continuing evolution of SA, Congress terminated MAP funding in fiscal year (FY) 1990 and integrated all former MAP grant funding into the Foreign Military Financing Program (FMFP) which is discussed in detail in Chapter 1, "Introduction to Security Cooperation," of this text.

The Cold War and Containment

Europe's post-World War II economy was in a shambles. Although the US provided some economic assistance immediately after the war, the slow rate of economic recovery was such that the basic fabric of Western European civilization was being pulled apart. The US feared that the failure of the democratic governments to cope with their fundamental economic and related social problems would open the door to communist opportunism-external or internal. To counter that threat, Secretary of State George C. Marshall, in 1947, proposed a massive program of American aid to help rebuild the shattered economies of Europe. The proposal was not initially presented as an anti-communist measure and the offer of aid was open to any European state.

In 1948, Congress endorsed the proposal and established the European Recovery Plan (ERP) under which sixteen nations of Western Europe (later including West Germany) received $15 billion in loans and grants between 1948 and 1952. The ERP, better known as the "Marshall Plan," was also offered to Russia and other communist states, but it was declined by the Soviets, who denounced the program as an anti-communist effort. As it turned out, the ERP did become anticommunist by application, and it emerged as an essential element of the containment policy.

Containment, as a policy launched by the Truman Administration, was designed to frustrate Soviet attempts to expand their military, political, and economic base in Europe. The Greece-Turkey Aid Act of 1947 reflects the policy's initial application. In theory, the policy held that if the USSR could not expand its influence or borders, communism would eventually collapse of its own inherent weaknesses. The containment policy and its role in Cold War strategy took another turn when the US joined with other nations in creating the North Atlantic Treaty Organization (NATO) in 1949.

The Beginnings of the North Atlantic Treaty Organization

The term "alliance" has been defined as a multilateral agreement by states to improve their power position by joining together in defense of their common interests. Hence, an alliance is a way of informing friend and foe that an attack against any individual nation may precipitate a general war. The NATO alliance explicitly follows that formula, stating in article 5 that, "The Parties agree that an armed attack against one or more of them in Europe or North America shall be considered an attack against them all."

This concept was implemented for the first time, after the 11 September 2001 terrorist attacks on the US, by both the NATO alliance and Rio Pact alliance which includes the countries within North and South America. For the first time since the War of 1812, foreign armed forces were deployed to the US to assist in anti-terrorism protection.

Historically, NATO is considered a most advanced defensive alliance system. It was founded by the Brussels Treaty of 1948 between France, the United Kingdom, Belgium, Netherlands, and Luxembourg. American negotiations with the Brussels powers began with the "Vandenberg Resolution," which was passed by the Senate on 11 June 1948. The resolution, named for Senator Arthur H. Vandenberg of Michigan, expressed the desirability of the US associating itself with others in a system of collective self defense. This goal was fulfilled with the signing of the North Atlantic Treaty in Washington, DC, April 1949.

The close relationships established between the US and its NATO allies have had a corresponding effect on subsequent SA management, to include:

- The provision of arms on a preferential basis to NATO member countries

- Certain exclusions for NATO members for arms control legislative provisions

- International cooperative armaments projects with NATO countries with the F-16 being a case in point

All of these special legislative provisions have placed the NATO alliance in a uniquely favorable position. NATO, in fact, through its political-military infrastructure, provided the prime barrier against communist expansion in Europe. Major elements of US foreign policy, such as the establishment of US bases in Western Europe, the storage and deployment of American nuclear weapons, and the initial post-World War II rearmament of West Germany, were put into effect through the military and political framework of this infrastructure.

Until 1965, NATO countries, as the major beneficiaries of SA, received approximately 56 percent of all American arms transferred under the military assistance and Foreign Military Sales (FMS) programs. However, during the mid-1950s, certain new developments began to have an impact. As the stockpile of surplus World War II materiel declined, the US embarked on a program to furnish technical assistance and industrial equipment to help expand local European defense production. In 1954, those NATO countries receiving this assistance agreed to provide other NATO allies with arms at reasonable prices. Such agreements gradually evolved into joint or coproduction arrangements, including electronics, command and control systems, aircraft, and missiles. However, this arrangement was not long lived, because as each country grew in productive capability, its government demanded arms of local design, development, and production wherever these could meet internal military needs. The end result was widespread competition and limited compatibility between the separate NATO armed forces' military equipment. Thus, the separate systems and their unique support requirements created a logistics nightmare. This lack of standardization would do little to help sustain a war in Europe.

The penalties of such an operational and logistics hodgepodge of equipment, and the waste of valuable technical resources devoted to its development, were obvious. A more rational approach to NATO weapons development and production would be required if the standardization of equipment was to be achieved. Treaty members could either manufacture or sell weapons with unique features, share with others in development and production projects, or share in the manufacture and assembly of components of major systems (as was done by the European consortium members in the original sales agreement for F-16 aircraft).

The NATO alliance, as mentioned, was developed as the primary bulwark for European defenses against communist intervention and was the first alliance to serve the broader US foreign policy goal of containment of the Soviet Union and its allies. This policy was destined to become even more rigid during the Eisenhower Administration when the positions of the East and West hardened in the difficult climate of the Cold War.

THE EISENHOWER DOCTRINE

Military assistance, as a building block of the US containment policy, continued to grow in scope and influence. In 1949, a special foreign aid bill consolidated and expanded military aid programs to include NATO and reflected the importance that the defense of Western Europe occupied in Truman's containment policy. Several incidents in the 1950s inspired further expansion of that policy.

Political and military crises around the globe, such as the Korean War in 1950, Egyptian initiatives to acquire Soviet arms in 1955, and the increasing involvement of the US in Indochina in the late 1950s, caused a reassessment of the containment policy and the foreign aid bill designed for its support. In essence, US foreign aid policy was broadened from the exclusive support of US allies to also include the support of friendly, but non-allied nations. As the US defense of Northeast and Southeast Asia took on prominence, the program of 'arms to allies' was enlarged to include 'arms to friends.' To the concepts of containment and forward defense were added new precepts of internal security, counterinsurgency, civic action, and nation building. The policy of containment was expanded politically to the protection not only of nations on the periphery of the Soviet Union, but to the world at large, including many nations regarded by their leaders as nonaligned.

As a corollary to the expanded containment policy, the Eisenhower Doctrine was initiated on 9 March 1957. This second major post-war doctrine asserted the right of the US to employ force, if necessary, to assist any nation or group of nations in the general region of the Middle East requesting assistance against armed aggression from any country controlled by international communism. The Eisenhower Doctrine resulted from the apparent increase in Soviet influence in Syria and Egypt and the threat of Soviet assistance to Egypt during the Suez Crisis in 1956. As formulated, US assistance was to be based upon a request from any endangered country; however, the doctrine was to be evoked only in the event of external, communist armed aggression, and was not to be applied in response to an internal insurrection or civil war.

Eisenhower saw the maintenance of regional stability in the Middle East as an extended American commitment with a long term impact on our foreign policy. He saw the issue as supporting not only American interests, but also the interests of allies. Basically, US economic interests, as well as those of the allies, were linked to the vast oil reserves in that region just as they are today. There was a prevailing belief that, should the Middle East fall under Soviet domination, the western economies would suffer so severely that the governments of Western Europe would succumb to communism.

Eisenhower further speculated that if the Soviets were to gain control of the Middle East, it would allow them to strategically outflank Pakistan and India. Their position thus established, the Soviets then could slip down into India and Africa at will, thus securing their long-sought permanent warm water port and impinging on American and Western national interests every step of the way.

Strategically, as well as economically, the Eisenhower Administration perceived that the loss of the Middle East to international communism would constitute a severe blow to American national interests. It should be noted that it was primarily US interests, and only secondarily the well being of the nations of the Middle East, that the US was attempting to promote with the Eisenhower Doctrine. The conventional global assistance pattern established by that doctrine, as well as the nuclear policy of strategic reliance on "massive retaliation" developed during the Eisenhower Administration, continue to influence US foreign policy.

THE KENNEDY AND JOHNSON ADMINISTRATIONS

President Kennedy became heir to the policy of massive retaliation as the set piece of our strategic deterrence against Soviet aggression. Events in Eastern Europe, however, including the short-lived 1956 Hungarian Revolution and the 1961 crisis in Berlin, demanded a reassessment of US conventional force capabilities. In Central Europe (and elsewhere), the US and NATO forces seemed unacceptably inferior in conventional military power to Soviet Bloc forces. The new President was alarmed to discover how few options he had (and how little time he had to exercise them) in any conflict in Germany before he would either have to accept defeat or initiate the use of nuclear weapons. While it was clear that in the immediate future NATO could not hope to match the Warsaw Pact man-for-man along the Central European front, the gross disparity of forces struck Kennedy as both unnecessary and dangerous, and he pushed for improvements in NATO conventional force structure

Kennedy initiated other aid and diplomatic actions. First, the Alliance for Progress was created to provide increased economic assistance to Latin America. This alliance program was designed to speed economic growth in the region in order to create a stable social structure capable of fending off revolutionary threats, both internal and external. Although never stated, an implied objective of the Alliance was to erect a restraining fence around Cuba, which had begun to export its brand of communism.

Latin America initially viewed the Alliance with enthusiasm and saw it as an opportunity to overcome the long neglect of the region by the US. Increased economic assistance funds were made available, and military assistance expanded after 1961. After a rather uneven performance in which US political interest and subsequent support of the aid programs ran hot and cold, the Alliance for Progress died out by the end of the 1960s, and US foreign policy south of the border again lapsed into benign neglect.

Another area of the world that had a major impact on the administrations of both Kennedy and Johnson was Southeast Asia. The US had been involved in some part of the Southern and Eastern Asia regions for generations. The intensity of involvement, however, heightened during and after World

War II. The US found that no region in the world was more dynamic, more diverse, or more complex than Asia, particularly as communist inspired insurgencies began to threaten the stability of the entire region.

During the Truman and Eisenhower years, military aid and other SA grants were given to the French to shore up their efforts to regain control over Indochina after World War II. These funds were but a prelude to a much deeper commitment that led the US into the protracted Vietnam War. Over $29 billion was funneled to East Asia and the Pacific areas. Although approximately half of this amount was granted to South Vietnam, the balance is indicative of the importance attached to this region.

The Middle East continued to be an area of high interest during the Kennedy-Johnson era. Arab-Israeli conflicts, difficulties between Iraq and Iran, the Egyptian-Russian disaffection, and the growing realization that the US and much of Western Europe remained heavily dependent on an undisturbed flow of Middle East oil provided the motivation to maintain regional stability virtually at any cost. Military assistance was the primary element used to assure a stable environment. The enormous initial MAP grants were soon overtaken by rapidly escalating arms sales under the FMS program. Thus, the gradual reduction of grant aid accompanied by an increase in military sales radically altered the face of military assistance. This process was to gain momentum under the Nixon Administration.

THE NIXON DOCTRINE

By the late 1960s, America had its fill of the seemingly interminable war in Southeast Asia. The enormous cost in lives and dollars, coupled with domestic turmoil and general public discontent, led to negotiations for an early end of the war. The experiences of the Southeast Asia entanglement led to changed directives and initiatives in US foreign policy; changes that had a major impact on the American approach to military assistance. One of the primary aspects of the changed policy was the transfer of immediate self defense responsibilities to indigenous forces, with the US continuing to provide material assistance and economic support. Further, the concept of self-sufficiency increased the emphasis on military sales, as opposed to grants. Additionally, the linkage of a variety of security-related military and economic assistance programs led to the use of an umbrella term for these programs, security assistance. Thus, it was during the Nixon Administration that many of the major features of the present US SA program were formalized.

The Nixon Doctrine enunciated new guidelines for American foreign policy. Initially termed the Guam Doctrine (in recognition of the site of its original proclamation in 1969), and limited to Asian nations, the doctrine was later broadened to encompass the entire globe, and was renamed for President Nixon. Critical to the doctrine was the view that although the US would continue to bear responsibility for the deterrence of nuclear and conventional war, the responsibility for the deterrence of localized wars would rest with the countries threatened by such wars. The US would continue to furnish limited grant assistance to such countries, but they would be expected to assume primary responsibility for their own defense, including the marshaling of the necessary manpower and resources. The major effort would have to be made by the governments and peoples of these states. The doctrine was mainly a product of public reaction against the largely unsuccessful military intervention by the US in Vietnam during the 1960s.

Earlier in his administration, Nixon had reviewed prior US foreign policies in other parts of the world, especially in the traditional sphere of US influence, Latin America. In a major speech, he criticized the Latin American policies of his predecessors by implying that the Alliance for Progress had been based on the illusion that the US knew what was best for everyone else. He instead pledged a new approach that would deal realistically with governments in the inter-American system. The former dictatorial role of the US would be shifted to one of partnership.

In the Middle East, Nixon was again confronted with continuing strife between Israel and its neighbors. Wars in 1967 and again in 1973 demonstrated that the deep-seated enmity between these nations and their conflicting territorial claims would not soon or easily go away. Continued regional instability and the real possibility that it could spill over to the Persian Gulf area were constant reminders to the governments of the US, Western Europe, and Japan of the fragility of their dependence on that region's energy resources. If the US were to play the role of a peacemaker, any attempt to achieve a peace agreement and regional stability had to consider first and foremost the impact that such an agreement would have on the flow of oil. With that thought in mind and the desire to establish and maintain a regional balance, the US transfer of arms to the Middle East increased dramatically, with Iran, Israel, and Saudi Arabia being the principal recipients. Additionally, arms shipments by France, Great Britain, and other nations also contributed to the Middle East's growing stockpile of weapons.

As a direct outgrowth of the US experiences in Vietnam and what appeared to be a seemingly uncontrolled race to arm the world and the Middle East-Persian Gulf states in particular, US public awareness of SA was heightened. Congress legislated more efficient SA management procedures and greater control over the future transfer of arms. The new legislation, later incorporated in the Arms Export Control Act (AECA) was to have a significant influence on all subsequent SA management.

THE FORD ADMINISTRATION

The interplay of many political and economic factors launched the Ford Administration. Political trauma on the domestic front, continuing disagreements with the Soviets and among the allies, rapidly escalating oil prices, and an incipient recession were included in the inheritance welcoming Gerald Ford to the presidency. Added to this disturbing legacy was a growing apprehension by the Congress over the increase in US arms transfers abroad. Congressional concern over US involvement in the international arms trade stimulated legislative requirements for closer scrutiny by the Department of State (DOS) and Department of Defense (DOD) of potential arms transfers. These concerns also led to the strengthening of legislation giving Congress the right to block certain types of sales. A more definitive explanation of these controls and other legislative processes are covered in chapter 2 of this text, titled "Security Assistance Legislation and Policy."

Yet another element in the legacy inherited by the Ford Administration was the accelerated movement toward détente with the Soviets and the opening of discussions with the Peoples Republic of China (PRC), in both instances, following policies previously put in place by President Nixon. With détente as a major foreign policy goal of his administration, it became increasingly more difficult for Ford to use the containment of communism as a justification for his SA requests, especially those pertaining to military grant aid. In the view of much of the public and Congress, the Cold War was almost a thing of the past.

Further complicating Ford's relationship with Congress was the continued high foreign demand for American armaments, despite growing Congressional pressure to restrain arms sales. The President was now faced with the dilemma of meeting the requests for arms as part of our foreign policy while still remaining within the bounds of existing or pending legislation. Illustrative of that dilemma were the SA requests from Latin America. US motivations for sales to Latin America were primarily political, aimed at restoring good will and preserving access. However, this opening, perceived by the Latin Americans as the most supportive US response to their demands since 1945, proved very short-lived. Congressional, media, and public concerns began to focus on human rights violations in the region and the apparent lack of effective controls on US arms sales. Demands were made for new controls, and these concerns found expression in the International Security Assistance and Arms Export Control Act (AECA) of 1976.

The AECA prohibited arms transfers to any nation found to be in systematic violation of human rights; it terminated (with few exceptions) grant aid and military assistance advisory groups (MAAGs) by September 1977, unless the MAP recipients and MAAGs were subsequently authorized by the Congress in applicable legislation; and it established closer oversight by Congress of arms transfers. The 1976 AECA, as amended by 1977 legislation, was considered by both Presidents Ford and Carter as extremely restrictive and as impinging on the executive branch's prerogative to implement foreign policy.

THE CARTER ADMINISTRATION

Early in his term of office, President Carter issued a statement decrying the unrestrained global spread of conventional weaponry. He critically cited reports stating that total worldwide arms sales had risen to over $20 billion annually, and that the US was responsible for over half of that amount. Based on that assessment, he directed a comprehensive review of existing arms transfer control policies and all of the associated military, political, and economic factors.

In order to reverse the trend of increasing conventional arms sales, President Carter announced on 19 May 1977 that arms transfers would henceforth be viewed as an exceptional foreign policy implement and the burden of persuasion for a sale would fall on those who favored a particular arms sale, rather than those who opposed it. He further established a set of controls to apply to all transfers except to those countries with which the US had major defense treaties, i.e., NATO, Japan, Australia, and New Zealand.

Carter further stated that the conduct of his administration's SA efforts would be governed by the promotion and advancement of internationally recognized human rights in the recipient countries. This statement, in effect, provided added emphasis to the human rights provisions already contained in the Foreign Assistance Act (FAA) of 1961 and the AECA. As a result of the Congressional and Presidential focus in this area, all SA programs were subjected to closer review under the human rights provisions of these statutes. Thus, the human rights issue became a major feature of the Carter foreign policy.

Middle East Policy

Carter's initial foreign policy effort focused on the Middle East, much like that of his predecessors. Of significance, however, was his personal intervention in seeking a resolution to the long-standing enmity between Israel and Egypt. Carter hoped to achieve a resolution of Israeli-Egyptian border disputes and find some answer to the Palestinian question. Through his initiatives, a series of meetings were held with top-level Israeli and Egyptian officials, first in Cairo and Jerusalem, and then at Camp David, the Presidential retreat in Maryland. These efforts led to the so-called Camp David Accord, which, in essence, adjusted the Israeli-Egyptian border, resolved territorial claims in the Sinai, and produced the 1979 Egyptian-Israeli Peace Treaty.

As a part of the Camp David Accord, the US agreed to assist both governments in upgrading their military capabilities. In the case of Egypt, replacement of the obsolete Russian equipment with which Egyptian forces were outfitted became a major long term SA objective whereby the US was to become Egypt's, as well as Israel's, prime supplier. This assistance has continued under all the subsequent administrations, with other Western European nations also providing assistance.

Carter's interest in the Middle East took on additional and complicating dimensions:

- The overthrow of the Shah of Iran in 1979

- The subsequent seizure of the American embassy in Tehran and the taking of diplomatic hostages by militant Iranians

- The burning of the American embassy in Pakistan

- The Russian invasion of Afghanistan in December 1979

As a result of these events, the President concluded that the turmoil in the Persian Gulf area was a most serious threat to regional stability and contrary to the national interests of the US.

The Carter Doctrine

Reflecting his concern over the Persian Gulf area, Carter, in his 1980 State of the Union address warned, "Let our position be absolutely clear: an attempt by any outside force to gain control of the Persian Gulf region will be regarded as an assault on the vital interests of the United States of America. And such an assault will be repelled by any means necessary, including military force."

His words were broadly compared by many in the press to be a restatement of the containment policy of the Truman Doctrine of 1947. In fact, the press speculatively labeled the message the Carter Doctrine. By whatever label, it was the first Presidential public pronouncement since Vietnam of the possible commitment of US troops to protect essential US national interests. In so doing, the US extended its military shield to the Persian Gulf region and, in effect, modified the Nixon Doctrine which primarily relied on the allies in a region not only to defend themselves with US materiel aid, but to also protect American regional interests. Carter's policy was designed to forestall further Soviet aggression and to deter actions which might eventually expand ongoing conflicts in the region.

People's Republic of China Status

Carter's foreign policy assumed another change of direction when he asked for, and Congress granted, most-favored-nation status to the People's Republic of China (PRC), with which formal diplomatic relations were established on 31 December 1978. This, in essence, meant that Beijing's exports to the US would be permitted at tariff (or tax) levels reduced to the lowest levels enjoyed by other American trading partners, a status which was long sought by the Soviets but was continually denied by Congress. Also reflecting the increased US and China rapport, which began with visits by Nixon and Ford, was Carter's decision to sell China dual use (i.e., civilian/military) materiel limited to trucks, communications equipment, and early warning radar. No weapons were included in this arrangement. The first FMS agreement was not notified to Congress until 1985 to allow the modernization of China's large caliber artillery ammunition production facilities. Additional agreements were notified to Congress in 1986 for the sale of Mark 46 MOD 2 torpedoes and for an avionics upgrade of Chinese F-8 air defense interceptors.

Raw Materials and Foreign Policy

A key element in the rapid changes in US foreign policy was the perceived dwindling supply of available foreign source oil. However, oil availability was not the only matter of concern for the world's economies. The scramble for scarce resources was becoming more hectic as the world's demand and consumption of metals and other materials reached new heights. Emerging third world countries, some of which were the only source of certain critical minerals, were learning how to bargain more intensively and collectively in the same manner as the Organization of Petroleum Exporting Countries (OPEC). The finite supply and imminent shortages of certain critical minerals and other raw materials threatened to place the economies of the US, Western Europe, and Japan, in a precarious position.

While the US had maintained, since World War II, some strategic stockpiles of critical minerals and materiel for use in the event of a national emergency, the threat to the overall US economy became apparent. Even with the reserve stocks on hand, the US was not nearly as self-sufficient in everything required to maintain an effective base of production. Critical choices faced Carter and his planners. One choice was to increase, wherever practical, exploration for and development of domestic resources. Such action had its attendant difficulties and often conflicted with quality of life standards, environmental goals, and national economic targets.

A second choice was to maintain friendly relationships with the countries exporting critical materials. Such relationships could be enhanced through the judicious application of SA by grants, government-to-government sales, or by direct commercial sales (DCS). Further, direct barter by the USG of SA for critical materials is authorized by the FAA, section 663, if the President determines it to be in the national interest to exchange strategic raw for weapons.

Although this is an apparently desirable option for countries with ample mineral holdings but limited financial resources, complex economic considerations (e.g., varying requirements for different materials and the need to convert resources to dollars to reimburse US contractors) have precluded any use of this statutory provision.

THE REAGAN ADMINISTRATION

At the onset of President Ronald Reagan's presidency, the international fabric of world arms transfers and national interests remained basically unchanged from that which existed during previous administrations. On 8 July 1981, however, President Reagan announced a new conventional arms transfer policy which viewed arms transfers as an essential element of our global defense policy and an indispensable component of US foreign policy. Reagan's approach, which differed considerably from the Carter Administration's view of arms transfers as an "exceptional foreign policy implement," reflected a more pragmatic view of SA. The US, as a matter of policy, will only transfer arms in order to:

- Reinforce military capabilities to assist in the deterrence of aggression, especially from the USSR and its surrogates, and reduce the requirement for direct US involvement in regional conflict.

- Reinforce the perception of friends and allies that the US is a partner and a reliable supplier with a measurable stake in the security of the recipient country.

- Point out to potential enemies that the US will not abandon its allies or friend.

- Improve the American economy by assuring a more stable defense production base, and by enhancing the balance of payments. However, this objective should not mean that the approval of the transfer of arms will be based solely on economic considerations and gain.

- Enhance the effectiveness of the US military through improved possibilities of access to regional bases, ports, or facilities needed by deployed forces during contingencies. Further, SA should improve the ability of the recipient nations to complement US forces during deployments.

- Strengthen the stability of a region by fostering a sense of a recipient nation's security and its willingness to settle disputes amicably. A government that feels secure is more likely to cope with such challenges in a more progressive and enlightened manner.

A pivotal point of the Reagan policy was that the US could not alone defend western security interests. Thus, the US would heed the security requirements of friends and allies, not as an alternative to a US commitment or capability, but as a complement thereto. The US would assess the transfer of arms in light of the net contribution such transfers would make to US global or regional security, thereby complementing and reinforcing the earlier Nixon Doctrine.

The Reagan policy identified arms transfers to America's major alliance partners as its first priority. Thus, the principal focus was on transfers to those nations with which we enjoy a long association of cooperative and mutually beneficial relationships, and which permit access to support or basing facilities in the interest of mutual defense. Because of the diversity of US interests and the security needs of our allies and friends, the assessment of needs would be pragmatically but strategically derived, and tailored to the specific circumstance of each instance. However, the Reagan arms transfer policy would maintain an inherent flexibility to respond quickly to changing conditions and shifting Soviet strategies. The Reagan policy statement concluded with the following comments:

> The realities of today's world demand that we pursue a sober, responsible, and balanced arms transfer policy, a policy that will advance our national security interests and those of the free world. Both in addressing decisions as to specific transfers and opportunities for restraint among producers, we will be guided by principle as well as practical necessity. We will deal with the world as it is.

THE GEORGE H. W. BUSH ADMINISTRATION

Arms transfer and overall SA policies of the George H. W. Bush Administration essentially represented a continuation of the approach which evolved during the Reagan presidency. Various events occurred in the world, however, each of which had a significant impact on US foreign policy and SA:

- The December 1989 collapse of the Iron Curtain and the subsequent emergence of democracy in the former Warsaw Pact countries

- The August 1990 Iraqi invasion of Kuwait and the subsequent January/February 1991 Operation Desert Storm which liberated Kuwait;

- Middle East peace talks; the December 1991 economic and political dissolution of the USSR

- The far reaching worldwide economic recession of 1991 and 1992, which largely grew out of a convergence of the consequences of the monumental events of the previous year

The political collapse of the Iron Curtain countries, with the almost immediate introduction of democratically elected governments and market-driven capitalism, prompted the flow of US foreign assistance in FY 1991 to Czechoslovakia, Hungry, and Poland. This aid also included grant military assistance in the form of International Military Education and Training (IMET). FY 1992 foreign assistance for Eastern Europe included the addition of Albania, Bulgaria, Estonia, Latvia, Lithuania, Russia, and Ukraine. Foreign assistance was further extended in the region during FY 1993 to Belarus, Kazakhstan, and Romania. The growing political revolution in Eastern Europe extended dramatically to Russia itself, producing force reductions in the region during FY 1993 and withdrawals from Eastern Europe. This action also impacted the West, especially the US, where a defense reduction of 25 percent both in forces and budget was begun. Initially, the vision of large supplies of cheap excess defense articles being made available for transfer became prominent, and legal provisions were made for broader eligibility and simpler implementation. However, the Iraqi invasion of Kuwait put the transfers on temporary hold. Also related to the downsizing were the cutbacks and cancellations in DOD weapons acquisitions. The resulting reduction in system development and production caused industry to seek more overseas markets and to request the assistance of various USG officials and their agencies for entry into the foreign marketplace.

The Iraqi invasion of Kuwait on 2 August 1990 clearly demonstrated the value of past SA programs during the conduct of war and also the responsiveness of the SA community during the war. It also boosted the overall level of FMS agreements which totaled $14.2 billion in FY 1990 and a record $23.5 billion in FY 1991. The deployment, reception, and support of coalition forces in the Persian Gulf (specifically, in Saudi Arabia) was accomplished with comparative ease and was greatly benefited by the over $15 billion in FMS construction projects completed prior to FY 1990. These included runways and ramps for both strategic lift and tactical aircraft, improved piers and equipment marshaling areas for the offload of strategic sealift materiel, and protected facilities with limited command and control capability to build upon for in-theater command elements and associated support. SA also provided for equipment and procedural compatibilities among many of the coalition forces through past sales of US equipment and technical and professional training in US military classrooms. The requirement for international military students to know English during their US training contributed significantly to improved communications during the war. The war generated over 350 new FMS cases valued at about $12 billion, the majority of which were immediately filled and delivered. Section 506, FAA, drawdown procedures were used during FY 1990 and 1991 to meet emergency military and war refugee requirements. These were valued at $225 million for the immediate delivery of Patriot missiles to Israel, aircraft missiles and artillery munitions to Turkey, and humanitarian aid to the Kurds in northern Iraq. Third country transfer authorization procedures were streamlined so transfers of equipment from past FMS could take place with minimal loss of time. The Gulf War proved that US military systems, though expensive, work most effectively. The demonstration of American equipment in the Gulf War probably served as the best marketing effort for years afterwards to promote the value of US arms to foreign purchasers.

As the Bush administration completed its final year in office in January 1993, the resolution of serious domestic economic problems tended to overshadow SA and related foreign policy matters. As tens of thousands of workers throughout America were either released or laid off, as numerous major American corporations shut down factories or went into bankruptcy, and as drugs and crime increasingly plagued US cities, such issues as aiding the emergent democracies of Eastern Europe, pressing the Israelis and Arabs into a peaceful resolution of their long conflict, and supporting allied and friendly nations throughout the world tended to lose their urgency for many Americans. Funding for improvements in American medical care, education, and infrastructure modernization eclipsed national interest in foreign assistance.

THE CLINTON ADMINISTRATION

Bill Clinton assumed the presidency in 1993 with a full foreign policy plate. The humanitarian military mission in Somalia, the downward spiraling situation in Bosnia, sustained defiance by Saddam Hussein against the United Nations (UN) sanctions on Iraq, political and economic chaos in the former Soviet Union that would soon lead to an unsuccessful coup attempt in October 1993, a soft US economy and a worldwide economy recovering from a short but severe recession, the continued down-sizing of the US military to approach forty percent less than at end of the Reagan era, and the continuing saga of the Middle East peace talks, were some of the major challenges facing his administration.

Despite these significant world problems, the Clinton Administration's initial emphasis was on strengthening the US economy and on establishing a predominantly domestic agenda. In terms of the administration's foreign policy and national security interests, initially there was little departure from the previously stated goals of building democracy, promoting and maintaining peace, promoting economic growth and sustainable development, addressing global problems, and meeting urgent humanitarian needs. However, in order to accomplish these foreign policy goals, the Clinton Administration laid as its bedrock a proactive domestic agenda. The overall concern and top priority was to improve and restore the domestic strength of the US through a number of internal and external measures which both directly and indirectly affected SA.

President Clinton's Secretary of State, Warren Christopher, reiterated a previous policy encouraging US embassies to actively assist US marketing efforts overseas. This was interpreted to include aiding US defense contractors in the pursuit of both DCS and FMS of defense articles, services, and training overseas. Additionally, as an example of this new emphasis on domestic economic growth, when the Kingdom of Saudi Arabia was considering upgrading its commercial passenger jet fleet, President Clinton successfully interceded with King Fahd on behalf of the Boeing Corporation to secure the sale of their commercial aircraft.

FY 1993 ended on a bright note in terms of the positive impact of FMS on the US economy. Primarily due to major defense equipment sales to countries in the Arabian Gulf area and Taiwan, FMS topped $33 billion, a record high. Those sales kept US production lines open and defense industry employment up, especially for the great number of companies involved in the production of the F-15s for Saudi Arabia, F-16s for Taiwan, and the M1A2 main battle tank for Kuwait.

The long awaited post-Cold War era US conventional arms transfer policy was announced on 17 February 1995 by the White House as Presidential Decision Directive (PDD-34), "US on Conventional Arms Transfer Policy." This new policy did not represent a dramatic change from previous policy; rather, it was introduced "as a summation and codification" of the Clinton Administration's "decision-making in the arms transfer arena . . . and efforts at restraint over the past two years" (i.e., 1993-1994). The policy, however, does place an increased weight in the post-Cold War era on the dynamics of regional power balances and the potential for destabilizing changes in those regions. The transfer of conventional weapons is reinforced as a legitimate instrument of US foreign policy, deserving USG support as it enables the US to help allies and friends deter aggression, promotes regional security, and increases US and allied force interoperability. Emphasis is on restraint by both the US and other arms suppliers when the transfer of weapons systems or technologies would be destabilizing or dangerous to international peace or balance of power in a region.

In addition to restraint, other key elements of the new US arms transfer policy include the promotion of control and transparency. Improvement of arms transfer controls would be accomplished:

Through continued political efforts by the US in establishing an international control regime successor (the Wassenaar Arrangement) to the Cold-War era Coordinating Committee for Multilateral Export Controls (COCOM).

Through vigorous support of established regimes including regional and weapons specific ones (e.g., Missile Technology Control Regime (MTCR) or the US, proposed moratorium on the transfer of anti-personnel landmines.

Going a step further, the US would assist other arms supplier nations in developing effective export controls in support of responsible export policies. Finally, international arms transfer control is to be sought by the US pushing for increased international participation in the U.N. Register of Conventional Arms, and the expansion of this Register to include military inventories and procurement.

While restraint is most important in arms transfers, the policy also supports legitimate defense requirements of US allies and friends. The policy serves the following five US goals:

- To ensure that US military forces continue to enjoy technological advantages over adversaries

- To help allies and friends deter or defend themselves against aggression, while promoting interoperability with US forces when combined operations are required

- To promote regional stability in areas critical to US interests while preventing the proliferation of weapons of mass destruction and their missile delivery systems

- To promote peaceful conflict resolution and arms control, human rights, democratization, and other US foreign policy objectives

- To support the ability of the US defense industrial base to meet US defense requirements and maintain long-term military technological superiority at lower costs

Another feature of the Clinton Administration US foreign policy was the expansion of NATO. In March 1999, three of the former Warsaw Pact countries, the Czech Republic, Hungary, and Poland, became members of NATO. Both the Administration and Congress concurred with the further political, economic, and military development of other Central European countries for the goal of future membership in NATO.

As the Clinton Administration ended, the Administration had $3.576 billion for FMFP, $57.875 million for IMET, and $2.295 billion for Economic Support Fund (ESF) programs during FY 2001. The prediction for FMS was for a robust $15.9 billion. However, this prediction was made without an anticipated economic slowdown which began at the start of the new FY. The final figure for FY 2001 FMS was $13.3 billion.

THE GEORGE W. BUSH ADMINISTRATION

Continuing the Clinton administration's conventional arms transfer policy of aggressively supporting SA transfers on a case-by-case basis, the Bush Administration experienced new FMS at about the same annual level as before with $12.5 billion completed in FY 2002. FMS for FY 2003 and FY 2004 would turn out to be $13 billion and $13.5 billion, respectively. The biggest difference in FMFP was the successfully legislated authority for a direct loan guarantee of $3.8 billion for Poland during FY 2003 primarily for the purchase of F-16s. The IMET program continued its dramatic growth from $50 million in FY 2000 to a FY 2004 level of $90 million.

The Global War on Terrorism following the 11 September 2001 coordinated attacks on the continental US caused a large aggressive deployment of US armed forces throughout the world especially in the Southwest Asia region along with significant troop support from many other nations. Including an emergency supplemental, FMFP funding increased to $4,052 million in FY 2002 and $4,045 million in FY 2003. The ESF program also experienced growth during the same two FYs with $3,289 million for FY 2002 and $2,280 million for FY 2003.

Continuing the Global War on Terrorism, operations and reconstruction in Iraq, and the US "Road Map for Peace" between Israel and the Palestinian Authority, an emergency supplemental budget request for SA was appropriated and authorized by Congress for the President in April 2003. This included an additional $2,059 million in grant FMFP and $2,475 million in grant ESF. The ESF program was further increased with authorized ESF loan guarantees of $9.0 billion for Israel, $2.0 billion for Egypt, and $8.5 billion for Turkey. This significant funding assistance to key countries has been indicative of the Bush Administration with the legislative support of Congress to use SA as an implement of US foreign policy.

Continuing the Clinton administration policy for the enlargement of NATO and at the Bush Administration's request, in May 2003, the Senate ratified the change to the NATO Treaty to admit seven new members:

Bulgaria   Estonia   Latvia   Lithuania
Romania   Slovakia   Slovenia

This brought the total NATO membership to twenty-six countries. The Senate ratification language included the finding that the US will keep its door open for the future enlargement to possibly include Albania, Croatia, and Macedonia. Albania and Croatia were later invited to join NATO in 2008, bringing the membership to twenty-eight countries.

The Bush administration ended with a record FMS level of $29.2 billion during FY 2008. However, the biggest US military assistance difference during the administration was the use of DOD funding to purchase defense articles, services, and training for Iraq, Afghanistan and friendly countries supporting Southwest Asia coalition operations. This military assistance effort by DOD was included along with other DOD international activities under the classification of "Security Cooperation (SC)." The Bush Administration was provided authority for providing this assistance using DOD funding via the annual national defense authorization acts. Until accountability and management became issues, FMS was not used as the acquisition or management process for security cooperation. Pseudo case procedures were developed using DOD funds to provide military assistance into Southwest Asia. Pseudo case sales during FY 2008 totaled $7.2 billion. Prior to Southwest Asia, pseudo FMS was generally relegated to DOD authorized funding of counter-narcotics activities in Latin America during the 1990s.

There were four other foreign assistance initiatives during the Bush Administration to include:

- The 2003 announced Millennium Challenge Account (MCA) to provide accountable non-military economic assistance

- The 2004 Global Peace Operations Initiative (GPOI) for a professional international peacekeeping capability

- The 2007 announced Merida Initiative to counter trafficking in drugs and other international criminal activities in Mexico and Central America

- The two later 2007 announcements for increased FMFP assistance for Israel and additional FMS to the Persian Gulf countries

The goal of the MCA program was to significantly increase US developmental assistance to countries that demonstrate a commitment to ruling justly, investing in their people, and encouraging economic freedom. Special attention was to be given to countries fighting corruption emphasizing financial accountability and development successful. The June 2004 G-8 summit announced the participant's commitment to fund and support the new GPOI to meet the persistent demand for international peacekeepers especially in Africa. The five year goal included training and equipping 75,000 peace-keepers by 2010 (including transportation and logistics support). The US plan included a contribution of about $660 million over five years which required the combination of the PKO Africa Contingency Operations Training and Assistance (ACOTA) and the IMET and FMFP Enhanced International Peacekeeping Capabilities (EPIC) programs into a singular PKO GPOI program.

The Merida Summit of March 2007 resulted in the bilateral Mexico and US cooperation agreement against transnational crime and drug trafficking. FY 2008 was the first year of International Narcotics and Law Enforcement (INCLE) and FMFP funding for a multi-year program of about $1.4 billion primarily for Mexico but with funding also for certain Central America countries. The 2007 announcement of increased military assistance for the Middle East included a ten year agreement starting in FY 2009 to provide $30 billion overall in FMFP assistance to Israel and the nearly simultaneous pledge to allow $20 billion in military assistance sales collectively to the Persian Gulf countries. The Israeli and US agreement also included the understanding that 26.3 percent of the annual FMFP assistance would be authorized for offshore procurement (OSP) by Israel.

THE OBAMA ADMINISTRATION

The Obama administration began with the revival of the former Clinton administration Assistant Secretary of Defense for International Security Affairs [ASD(ISA)] and influential scholar Dr. Joseph S. Nye, Jr.'s early 1990s concept of "soft power." Soft power, which has its roots in the ancient Chinese philosophers such as Lao Tsu, is defined as the ability to achieve goals through co-option and attraction rather than the "hard power" of coercion and payment.

During her January 2009 Senate confirmation hearings, the nominated Secretary of State Hillary Rodham Clinton went further by using the term "smart power." Smart power is using the full range of tools at one's disposal to achieve objectives or solve problems to include the combination of both soft and hard power. The new Obama administration immediately retooled the FY 2009 supplemental appropriations request and the FY 2010 request for foreign assistance with the initial smart power investment for long term ESF and FMFP coupled with DOD appropriations for Iraq, Afghanistan, and Pakistan as hard power lethal and soft power non-lethal assistance. The collaborative DOD and DOS funding program for Pakistan was titled the Pakistan Counterinsurgency Capability Fund (PCCF) and initially included $500 million in DOD funding and a combined $700 million in FMFP and ESF funding assistance. The military assistance portion used the previously developed security cooperation pseudo case process for management. The Obama administration has also continued funding the Bush-announced MCA, Merida, increased Israeli assistance, and G-8 GPOI initiatives.

Using the widely accepted smart power policy, the Pakistan assistance program has been significantly enhanced by the Enhanced Partnership with Pakistan Act of 2009, P.L.111-73, 15 October 2009, which authorizes the annual appropriation of $1.5 billion in FAA-authorized assistance for Pakistan during FYs 2010 through 2014 with an expressed sense of Congress to extend this program through FY 2019. This law, sometimes referred to as the Kerry-Lugar-Berman bill, likewise authorized undetermined amounts of IMET and FMFP for Pakistan during FYs 2010 through 2014. FY 2010 and FY 2011 legislation also continued to provide significant amounts of DOD funding for Afghanistan security cooperation. However, these Southwest Asia assistance authorities also included the requirement for periodic activity and accountability assessments with detailed reporting by the President to Congress.

Providing a term to long ongoing operations in Southwest Asia, the concept of "security force assistance (SFA)" is formally adopted and promulgated in late 2010. SFA is defined as DOD activities that contribute to unified action by the USG to support the development of the capacity and capability of foreign security forces (FSF) and their supporting institutions. SFA is stated to be a subset of DOD security cooperation initiatives with security assistance programs identified as critical tools to fund and enable SFA activities by DOD special operations forces (SOF), general purpose forces (GPF), and the civilian expeditionary workforce (CEW). Going beyond the traditional support of just ministry of defense forces, foreign security forces are to also include the paramilitary, police, and intelligence forces; border police, coast guard, and customs officials; and prison guards and correctional personnel, that provide security for a host nation and its relevant population.

Military assistance legislation for FY 2012 includes continued DOD funding of the Afghanistan Security Force Fund (ASFF) with US support for Iraq transitioning from the prior DOD Iraq Security Force Fund (ISFF) to the traditional Department of State security assistance programs of International Narcotics Control and Law Enforcement (INCLE), Foreign Military Financing Program (FMFP), and cash FMS. FY 2011 marked the fourth year in a row where total annual FMS sales exceed $30 billion worldwide.

SUMMARY

Foreign policy, regardless of country of origin, is formulated and implemented in a country's national interest. This certainly applies to the US. The roots of its national interests are firmly embedded in the Constitution and have guided its foreign and domestic policies for over two centuries.

SA, SC and SFA remain important instruments of US foreign policy. Arms transfers and related services have reached enormous dimensions and involve most of the world's nations, either as a seller/provider or buyer/recipient.

As a case in point, US early history might have been entirely different if the SA provided by France was denied to the American revolutionaries. Subsequent SA milestones throughout the years following are marked either by arms being received or by furnishing arms support to the allies during World Wars I and II and thereafter.

The period from 1945 until 1991 saw the emergence of the two superpowers and their competition over spheres of influence. The Truman Doctrine of aid to Greece and Turkey in 1947, in an effort to stem the flow of communism, set a pattern for SA that developed for four decades. Concurrently, the Marshall Plan became a model upon which much economic aid was later based.

The policy of containment begun under Truman has impacted on US-USSR relations during every administration from 1945 to 1990. Containment also left a heavy imprint on SA policy, for it became a factor in the determination of who would receive aid, what type of assistance and how much would be furnished, and whether it would be provided through grant or sale.

Another ramification of the containment policy was the joining by the US in formal security alliances, such as NATO. Alliance membership had significant influence on SA priorities and special accommodations for the needs of allies. Every administration made those special accommodations keystones of their own foreign policy pronouncements.

The Middle East, never a quiet sector of the world, assumed a preeminent role in US SA. Five Arab-Israeli wars, countless border clashes, the rise and fall of the Shah of Iran, the assassinations of President Sadat of Egypt and Prime Minister Rabin of Israel, the bombing of the US embassy and the Marine barracks in Beirut and of the Khobar Towers in Saudi Arabia, continuing Middle East-based international terrorism, the Iraqi invasion of Kuwait, and the shifting world dependence on the region's petroleum reserves have placed the Middle East at the top of the US's regional foreign policy concerns. No other part of the world, outside of Southeast Asia, has demanded so much Presidential attention in the post-World War II period. From Truman to Obama, Presidential statements have dwelled on peace conferences, agreements, exchanges, SA, human rights, and hostages. Not only has the political climate remained volatile, but the unsettled worldwide oil situation, Russian adventures into Afghanistan, and the Iranian-Iraqi War continued to emphasize how deeply US national interests have been enmeshed in maintaining the stability of the Middle East and the regions of the Persian Gulf. The 2001 invasion of Afghanistan, the subsequent invasion of Iraq to eliminate the threat of weapons of mass destruction, and the support of the "Road Map for Peace" have all influenced an increased use of US SA to attain the goal of world peace through the Kennedy-era FAA and Ford-era AECA and recent DOD security cooperation authorities.

Finally, growing economic difficulties, recession-induced increases in unemployment, and company failures have produced a political environment in the US which lacks support for foreign assistance programs of any kind. In this atmosphere, the Administration will be hard pressed to induce Congressional support for the funding of the US SC programs which are the subjects of this text. Marketing efforts necessary to support the sale of US defense articles overseas continue to intensify. Strong, directed effort by US embassies to promote the products of US companies may be expected to continue as the US defense industrial base adjusts to the post-Cold War downsizing.

REFERENCES

Grimmett, Richard F. *Conventional Arms Transfers to the Developing Nations*, 2001-2008, Washington, DC: Congressional Research Service, September 2008.

Department of State. *Country Reports on Human Rights Practices for (year)*. Report prepared for the Committee on Foreign Affairs, US House of Representatives, and the Committee on Foreign Relations, US Senate. Washington, DC: Government Printing Office.

Department of State: http://www.state.gov. Among many other resources available at this site are the current *State Department Strategic Plan*, *International Affairs Strategic Plan*, *The Country Reports on Human Rights Practices*, *Country Background Notes*, and the annual *Congressional Budget Justification for the Department of State and Foreign Operations*.

ABBREVIATIONS AND ACRONYMS

A

A&T	Administrative and Technical
AAC	Acquisition Advice Code
AAR	After Action Review
AA&E	Arms, Ammunition and Explosives
ACAT	Acquisition Category
ACCP	Accelerated Case Closure Procedures
ACO	Administrative Contracting Officer
ACOTA	Africa Contingency Operations Training and Assistance
ACRL	Accessorial Cost
ACRN	Accounting Classification Record Number
ACSA	Acquisition and Cross-Servicing Agreement
ACSS	Africa Center for Strategic Studies
ADM	Administrative Surcharge
AECA	Arms Export Control Act
AES	Automated Export System
AETC	Air Education and Training Command (USAF)
AFIT	Air Force Institute of Technology
AFLCMC	Air Force Life Cycle Management Center
AFMC	Air Force Materiel Command
AFRICOM	African Command
AFSA	Afghanistan Freedom Support Act
AFSAC	Air Force Security Assistance and Cooperation Directorate
AFSAT	Air Force Security Assistance Training Squadron
AFSC	Air Force Sustainment Center
AGATRS	ACSA Global Automated Tracking and Reporting System
AIA	Aerospace Industries Association
AIK	Assistance-in-Kind / Aid-in-Kind
ALC	Air Logistics Complex (USAF)
ALESA	American League for Exports and Security Assistance
ALP	Aviation Leadership Program
AMARG	309th Aerospace Maintenance and Regeneration Group
AMC	Army Materiel Command / Air Mobility Command (USAF)
AMCOM	Aviation and Missile Command (Army)
AMEMB	American Embassy

ANA	Afghanistan National Army
ANZUS	Security treaty between Australia, New Zealand, and the United States
AOD	Anticipated Offer Date
APACS	Aircraft and Personnel Automated Clearance System
APCSS	Asia-Pacific Center for Security Studies
APEX	Adaptive Planning and Execution System
APO	Air Force or Army Post Office
APOD	Aerial Port of Debarkation (Delivery)
APOE	Aerial Port of Embarkation
ARC	Adjustment Reply Code
ASA(ALT)	Assistant Secretary of the Army for Acquisition, Logistics and Technology
ASD	Assistant Secretary of Defense
ASDA	Automated State Department Approval
ASFF	Afghanistan Security Forces Fund (DOD)
ASIP	Aircraft Structural Integrity Program
ASN(RD&A)	Assistant Secretary of the Navy for Research, Development and Acquisition
AT	Anti-Tamper (Protection)
ATF	Bureau of Alcohol, Tobacco, Firearms, and Explosives
AT/FP	Antiterrorism/Force Protection
ATTRSSG	Arms Transfer and Technology Release Senior Steering Group
AWACS	Airborne Warning and Control System
AWC	Air War College / Army War College

B

BAC	Billing Advice Code
BAH	Basic Allowance for Housing
BAO	Bilateral Affairs Officer
B&F	Embassy Budget and Finance Office (DOS)
BIS	Bureau of Industry and Security (DOC)
B/L	Bill of Lading
BO	Back Order (Supply) / Blanket Order (FMS Case)
BOE	Blanket Open End (FMS Case)
BPC	Building Partner Capacity

C

C-SAN	Commercial Security Assistance Network
C3I	Command, Control, Communications, and Intelligence
C4I	Command, Control, Communications, Computers, and Intelligence
C4ISR	Command, Control, Communications, Computers, Intelligence, Surveillance and Reconnaissance
CA	Contract Authority / Competent Authority
CAA	Competent Authority Approval / Controlled Access Area
CAC	Common Access Card/Cancellation Administrative Charges

CAD/PAD	Cartridge Actuated Device/Propellant Actuated Device
CAE	Component Acquisition Executive
CAS	Contract Administrative Services / Cost Accounting Standard
CASREP	Casualty Report (USN)
CATP	Conventional Arms Transfer Policy
CAV	Compliance Assessment Visit
CBA	Commercial Bank Account/Capabilities Based Analysis
CBJ	Congressional Budget Justification
CBL	Commercial Bill of Lading
CBO	Congressional Budget Office
CBP	US Customs and Border Protection (DHS)
CBS	Commercial Buying Service
CBW	Chemical and Biological Weapons
CC	Country Code / Customer-Within-Country (Transportation Code)
CCBL	Collect Commercial Bill of Lading
CCDR	Combatant Commander
CCIF	Combatant Commander Initiative Fund
CCL	Commerce Control List
CCM	Central Case Manager (Army) / Command Country Manager
CCMD	Combatant Command
CCO	Center for Complex Operations
CCSA	Case Closure Suspense Account
CD	Case Designator / Counter Drug / Country Director (USAF)
CDM	Case Development Module (DSAMS)
CDRL	Contract Data Requirements List
CE	Communications and Electronic / Civil Engineering
CECOM	Communications - Electronics Command (Army)
CEMIS	Case Execution Management Information System (DOD)
CENTCOM	US Central Command
CERP	Commander's Emergency Response Program
CERPS	Consolidated & Expenditure Reporting System (USN)
CETPP	Combined Education and Training Program Plan
CETS	Contractor Engineering Technical Services
CEW	Civilian Expeditionary Workforce
CFIUS	Committee on Foreign Investment in the United States
CFR	US Code of Federal Regulations / Concept Funding Request
CFS	Contract Field Services
CFSP	Contractor Field Services Personnel
CGSC	Command and General Staff College (Army)
CHDS	Center for Hemispheric Defense Studies
CI	Case Identifier / Counterintelligence

CICA	Competition in Contracting Act
CIIC	Controlled Inventory Item Code
CIM	Corporate Information Management/Case Implementation Module (DSAMS)/Case Initiation Meeting (Army)
CIP	Component Improvement Program (Engines)
CISIL	Centralized Integrated System for International Logistics (Army)
CISMOA	Communication Interoperability and Security Memorandum of Agreement
CJ	Commodity Jurisdition
CJCS	Chairman, Joint Chiefs of Staff (Joint Staff)
CLIN	Contract Line Item Number
CLO	Country Liaison Officer (Foreign Country Representative) / Community
CLSSA	Cooperative Logistics Supply Support Arrangement
CM	Configuration Management / Case Manager / Country Manager
CMCS	Case Management Control System (USAF)
CMI	Classified Military Information
CMO	Contract Management Office
CN	Counter Narcotics
CNAD	Conference of National Armaments Directors (NATO)
CNET	Chief of Naval Education and Training
CNO	Chief of Naval Operations
CO	Contracting Officer / Change Order / Commanding Officer
COA	Courses of Action
COD	Cooperative Opportunities Document
COE	US Army Corps of Engineers
COLA	Cost of Living Allowance
COM	Chief of Mission (US Ambassador)
COMSEC	Communications Security
CONPLANS	Contingency Plans
CONUS	Continental United States
COR	Contracting Officer's Representative
COTS	Commercial Off-the-Shelf
CP	Country Plan / Control Plan
CPD	Congressional Presentation Document (obsolete, see CBJ)
CPI	Critical Program Information
CPM	Country Program Manager
CPX	Command Post Exercise
CR	Cost Reimbursement / Continuing Resolution
CRA	Continuing Resolution Authority
CRMIT	Congressional Report on Military International Training
CRS	Congressional Research Service
CRSP	Coalition Readiness Support Program
CSCS	Capital Security Cost Sharing

CSF	Coalition Support Fund
CSO	Cognizant Security Office
CSP	Concurrent (or initial) Spare Parts
CSTO	Country Standard Technical Order
CTA	Country Team Assessment
CTFP	Combating Terrorism Fellowship Program (DOD)
CTR	Cooperative Threat Reduction
CUI	Controlled Unclassified Information
CUSR	Central US Registry (NATO)
CWD	Case Writing Division (DSCA)
CWP	Coalition Warfare Program
CY	Calendar Year / Current Year

D

DAE	Defense Acquisition Executive
DAMES	DLA Automated Message Exchange System
DAO	Defense Attaché Office / Disbursing Accounting Officer
DAS	Defense Attaché System / Defense Acquisition System
DASA-DEC	Deputy Secretary of the Army for Defense Exports and Cooperation
DATT	Defense Attaché (see SDO/DATT)
DAU	Defense Acquisition University
DCA	Defense Cooperation in Armaments
DCAA	Defense Contract Audit Agency
DCC	Direct Commercial Contract (also DCS)
DCCEP	Developing Country Combined Exercise Program
DCM	Deputy Chief of Mission (US Embassy)
DCMA	Defense Contract Management Agency
DCN	Document Control Number / Design Change Notice
DCS	Direct Commercial Sales (also DCC)
DD Form 250	Department of Defense Material Inspection and Receiving Report
DD Form 645	Department of Defense FMS Quarterly Billing Statement
DD Form 1513	Department of Defense Letter of Offer and Acceptance (obsolete)
DD Form 2285	Invitational Travel Order for International Military Student
DD Form 2875	System Authorization Access Request
DDRE	Director Defense Research and Engineering
DDL	Delegation of Disclosure Letter
DDN	Defense Data Network
DDTC	Directorate of Defense Trade Control (DOS)
DDESB	DOD Explosives Safety Board
DEA	Drug Enforcement Agency
DEF	Defense Exportability Features
DELP	Defense English Language Program

DEMIL	Demilitarize
DEPSECDEF	Deputy Secretary of Defense
DFARS	Defense Federal Acquisition Regulation Supplement
DFAS	Defense Finance and Accounting Service
DFAS-IN	Defense Finance and Accounting Service-Indianapolis Center
DGR	Designated Government Representative
DHS	Department of Homeland Security
DIA	Defense Intelligence Agency
DIFS	Defense Integrated Financial System
DIILS	Defense Institute of International Legal Studies
DISA	Defense Information Systems Agency
DISAM	Defense Institute of Security Assistance Management
DISCO	Defense Industrial Security Clearance Office
DLA	Defense Logistics Agency
DLI	Defense Language Institute
DLIELC	Defense Language Institute English Language Center (Lackland AFB, TX)
DLIFLC	Defense Language Institute Foreign Language Center (Presidio of Monterey, CA)
DLIS	Defense Logistics Information Service (DLA)
DLMS	Defense Logistics Management Standards
DLMSO	Defense Logistics Management Standards Office (DLA)
DLP	Defense Language Program
DMSMS	Diminishing Manufacturing Sources and Material Shortages (Navy)
DO	Defined Order (FMS Case)
DOC	Department of Commerce
DOD	Department of Defense
DODAAC	Department of Defense Activity Address Code
DODD	DOD Directive
DODESB	Department of Defense Explosives Safety Board
DODI	DOD Instruction
DODIG	DOD Inspector General
DOJ	Department of Justice
DON	Department of the Navy
DOS	Department of State
DOT	Department of Transportation
DOTMLPF	Doctrine, Organization, Training, Material, Leadership, Personnel, Facilities
DPAP	Defense Procurement and Acquisition Policy
DPEP	Defense Personnel Exchange Program
DRI	Diplomatic Readiness Initiative / Defense Reform Initiative
DRP	Direct Requisitioning Procedure (USN)
DSADC	Defense Security Assistance Development Center
DSAMS	Defense Security Assistance Management System

DSC	Delivery Source Code
DSCA	Defense Security Cooperation Agency
DSS	Defense Security Service
DTC	Delivery Term Code
DTDT	Domicile to Duty Transportation
DTIC	Defense Technical Information Center
DTM	Directive-Type Memorandum (DOD)
DTR	Defense Transportation Regulation, DOD 4500.9-R
DTRA	Defense Threat Reduction Agency
DTS	Defense Transportation System / Defense Travel System
DTSA	Defense Technology Security Administration
DTSI	Defense Trade Security Initiative
DU	Dependable Undertaking / Depleted Uranium Anti-Tank Shells
DV	Distinguished Visitor
DVO	Defense Visit Office
DVOT	Distinguished Visitor Orientation Tour
DWCF	Defense Working Capital Fund (see WCF)
DX	Direct Exchange (Army)

E

E-NDP	Exception to National Disclosure Policy
EA	Expenditure Authority / Each
EAA	Export Administration Act of 1979
EAC	Emergency Action Committee
EAP	Emergency Action Plan
EACC	Enhanced Accelerated Case Closure
EAR	Export Administration Regulations
ECL	English Comprehension Level
ECISAP	Electronic Combat International Security Assistance Program (USAF)
ECP	Engineering Change Proposal
EDA	Excess Defense Articles / European Defense Agency (E.U.)
EEUM	Enhanced End Use Monitoring
EFT	Electronic Funds Transfer
EFTS	Enhanced Freight Tracking System
E-IMET	Expanded International Military Education and Training Program
EIPC	Enhanced International Peacekeeping Capabilities
ELT	English Language Training
EML	Environmental and Morale Leave
EO	Executive Order
EOQ	Economic Order Quantity
EPPA	Enhanced Partnership with Pakistan Act
ERC	Exercise Related Construction

ERGT	Expeditionary Requirement Generation Team
ESD	Estimated Shipment Date
ESEP	Engineer and Scientist Exchange Program
ESF	Economic Support Fund
ETSS	Extended Training Services Specialist
EUCOM	US European Command
EUM	End-Use Monitoring
EW	Electronic Warfare
EX	Explosive Hazard (number)

F

FAA	Foreign Assistance Act of 1961
FAD	Force/Activity Designator
FAM	Familiarization Visit
FAO	Foreign Area Officer (Army)
FAV	Familiarization Assessment Visit
FAR	Federal Acquisition Regulation
FAST	Fleet Antiterrorism Security Team
FCG	Foreign Clearance Guide
FCT	Foreign Comparative Test Program
FDPO	Foreign Disclosure Policy Office
FDR/ER	Foreign Disaster Relief/Emergency Response
FDS	Foreign Disclosure System
FED LOG	Federal Logistics Data
FEDEX	Federal Express Corporation (also FEC)
FEML	Funded Environmental and Morale Leave
FF	Freight Forwarder
FFP	Firm Fixed Price
FGI	Foreign Government Information
FHC	Final Hazard Classification
FICS	FMS Integrated Control System / Financial Integrated Control System
FID	Foreign Internal Defense
FIFO	First In, First Out
FLIS	Federal Logistics Information System
FLO	Foreign Liaison Office (or Officer) (located INCONUS)
FMCS	Foreign Military Construction Sales / Services
FMF	Foreign Military Financing (Program)
FMFP	Foreign Military Financing Program
FMR	Financial Management Review / Financial Management Regulation
FMS	Foreign Military Sales
FMSA	Foreign Military Sales Act of 1968 (now AECA)
FMSCR	Foreign Military Sales Credit (also FMFP)

FMSO I	Foreign Military Sales Order No. I (stock level case)
FMSO II	Foreign Military Sales Order No. II (requisition case)
FOAA	Foreign Operations, Export Financing, & Related Programs Appropriations Act
FOB	Free On Board
FOCI	Foreign Ownership Control or Influence
FOIA	Freedom of Information Act
FOT	Follow-On Training
FOUO	For Official Use Only
FPG	Foreign Placement Group
FPO	Fleet Post Office
FR	Federal Register and Federal Regulation
FRB	Federal Reserve Bank, New York
FREEDOM	Freedom for Russia and Emerging Eurasian Democracies and Open Markets
FSC	Federal Supply Class / Financial Service Center / Facility Security Clearance
FSF	Foreign Security Forces
FSN	Foreign Service National (local hire overseas)
FSO	Foreign Service Officer (DOS)
FSSP	Fair Share Sustainment Program (Army)
FSP	Field Studies Program
FTS	Field Training Service
FTX	Field Training Exercises
FVS	Foreign Visit System
FY	Fiscal Year
FYDP	Future Years Defense Program
FYROM	Former Yugoslav Republic of Macedonia

G

G&A	General and Administrative Expense (e.g., overhead)
GAO	Government Accountability Office
GBL	Government Bill of Lading
GC	Generic Code
GCC	Geographic Combatant Command / Gulf Cooperation Council
GEF	Guidance for Employment of the Force / Global Environmental Fund
GEOINT	Geospatial-Intelligence
GET	General English Training
GFE	Government Furnished Equipment
GFEBS	General Funds Enterprise Business System (Army)
GFM	Government Furnished Materiel
GFSC	Global Financial Service Center
GPO	Government Printing Office
GPOI	Global Peace Operations Initiative
GPS/PPS	Global Positioning System / Precise Positioning System

GSA	General Services Administration / General Security Agreement
GSCF	Global Security Contingency Fund
GSOIA	General Security of Information Agreement
GSOMIA	General Security of Military Information Agreement
GWOT	Global War on Terrorism

H

HA	Humanitarian Assistance
HAC	House Appropriations Committee
HASC	House Armed Services Committee
HAZMAT	Hazardous Materiel
HC	Host Country
HCA	Humanitarian and Civic Action Projects
HDA	Humanitarian Demining Assistance
HDR	Humanitarian Daily Rations
HDTC	Humanitarian Demining Training Center
HFAC	House Foreign Affairs Committee
HMA	Humanitarian Mine Action
HNS	Host Nation Support
HNTA	Host Nation Token Administrator (SCIP)

I

IA	Implementing Agency
IAAFA	Inter-American Air Forces Academy
IAC	International Armaments Cooperation
IACP	International Acquisition Career Path
IAEA	International Atomic Energy Commission
IATA	International Air Transport Association
IBA	Interest Bearing Account
ICASS	International Cooperative Administrative Support Services
ICE	US Immigration and Customs Enforcement (DHS)
ICP	Inventory Control Point / International Cooperative Programs (now IACP)
ICR&D	International Cooperative Research and Development
ICS	Integrated Country Strategy
ICUG	International Customer User Group
IDA	Institute for Defense Analysis
IDIQ	Indefinite Delivery, Indefinite Quantity
IEMG	International Engine Management Group (USAF)
IEP	Information Exchange Program
IFOR	Implementation Force (Kosovo)
IG	Inspector General
ILCO	International Logistics Control Office

ILCS	International Logistics Communication System
ILS	Integrated Logistics Support
IM	Item or Inventory Manager
IMDGC	International Maritime Dangerous Goods Code
IMET	International Military Education and Training
IMF	International Monetary Fund
IMO	Interim Military Objectives
IMS	International Military Student
IMSO	International Military Student Officer (or Office or Organization)
INCA	International Narcotics Control Act
INCLE	International Narcotics Control and Law Enforcement (DOS)
INFOSEC	Information Security
IPC	Indirect Pricing Components (DSAMS)
IPD	Issue Priority Designator / Implementing Project Directive
IPO	International Programs Office
IPR	In Process Review
IPS	International Programs Security
IPSR	International Programs Security Requirements
IRIS	Interrogation Requirements Information system (DRMS)
ISAF	International Security Assistance Force [in Afghanistan]
I-SAN	International Security Assistance Network
ISFF	Iraq Security Forces Fund (DOD)
ISOO	International Security Oversight Office
ISP	Initial Spare Parts
ISS	In-Service Support (Navy)
ITAR	International Traffic in Arms Regulations
ITM	International Training Management Website
ITO	Invitational Travel Order
IVP	International Visits Program

J

JCET	Joint Combined Exchange Training
JCIDS	Joint Capabilities Integration and Development System
JCS	Joint Chiefs of Staff (Joint Staff)
JER	Joint Ethics Regulation
JFTR	Joint Federal Travel Regulations
JHCS	Joint Hazard Classification System
JMC	Joint Munitions Command
JMP	Joint Manpower Program
JOPP	Joint Operational Planning Process
JSCP	Joint Strategic Capabilities Plan
JSF	Joint Strike Fighter

JTR	Joint Travel Regulations
JVI	Joint Visual Inspection (normally for EDA)

L

LCMC	Life Cycle Management Command (Army)
LE Staff	Locally Employed Staff
LES	Leave and Earning Statement
LIFO	Last In, First Out
LOA	Letter of Offer and Acceptance (DOD) / Letter of Assist (UN) / Lines of Activity
LOAD	Letter of Offer and Acceptance Data
LOC	Location Code / Library of Congress
LO/CLO	Low Observable / Counter Low Observable
LOE	Lines of Effort
LOO	Lines of Operation
LOR	Letter of Request
LRA	Lord's Resistance Army
LRIP	Low Rate Initial Production
LSC	Logistics Support Charge (obsolete term)
LTD	Language Training Detachment

M

M2M	Military-to-Military
MAAG	Military Assistance Advisory Group
MAG	Military Assistance Group
MANPADS	Man-Portable Air Defense System
MAP	Military Assistance Program / Membership Action Plan (NATO)
MAPAC	Military Assistance Program Address Code
MAPAD	Military Assistance Program Address Directory
MARAD	US Maritime Administration (DOT)
MARCORSYSCOM	US Marine Corps Systems Command
MASL	Military Articles and Services List(s) (for materiel and training)
MC	George C. Marshall European Center for Security Studies / US Marine Corps
MCSCG	Marine Corps Security Cooperation Group
MCTL	Militarily Critical Technologies List
MDA	Milestone Delegation Authority / Missile Defense Agency
MDE	Major Defense Equipment
MET	Mobile Education Team
MEU	Marine Expeditionary Unit
MFA	Ministry of Foreign Affairs
MFO	Multinational Force and Observers (in the Sinai)
MIA/POW	Missing in Action/Prisoner of War
MILCON	Military Construction (Appropriation)

MILDEP	Military Department
MILGP	Military Group
MILPERS	Military Personnel
MILSBILLS	Military Standard Billing System
MILSPEC	Military Specification
MILSTRIP	Military Standard Requisitioning and Issue Procedures
MILSVC	Military Service
MIL-STD	Military Standard
MIPR	Military Interdepartmental Purchase Request
MIRR	Material Inspection and Receiving Report (DD Form 250)
MISIL	Management Information System for International Logistics (USN)
MISWG	Multinational Industrial Security Working Group
MLA	Manufacturing Licensing Agreement
MNNA	Major Non-NATO Allies
MOA	Memorandum of Agreement
MOD	Ministry of Defense (international equivalent of US DOD)
MOI	Ministry of Interior
MOR	Memorandum of Request (Security Cooperation)
MOU	Memorandum of Understanding
MRAP	Mine Resistant Armor Protected vehicles
MRO	Materiel Release Order
MRR	Mission Resource Request
MRRL	Materiel Repair Requirements List (USAF)
MSC	Military Sealift Command (USN) / Medical Services Corps
MSG	Message / Marine Security Guard
MTBF	Mean Time between Failures
MTCR	Missile Technology Control Regime
MTDS	Manpower Travel Data Sheet
MTT	Mobile Training Team
MTTR	Mean Time to Repair, Return, or Restore
MWR	Morale, Welfare, and Recreation

N

NAD	National Armaments Director(s)
NADR	Nonproliferation, Anti-terrorism, Demining, and Related Programs (DOS)
NAF	Non-Appropriated Fund(s)
NAMSA	NATO Maintenance and Supply Agency
NAMSO	NATO Maintenance and Supply Organization
NATO	North Atlantic Treaty Organization
NAVAIR	Naval Air Systems Command
NAVSEA	Naval Sea Systems Command
NAVSUP	Naval Supply Systems Command

NAVSUP WSS	Naval Supply Systems Command Weapon Systems Support
NAVY IPO	Navy International Programs Office
NBC	Nuclear Biological Chemical
NC	Nonrecurring Cost (also NRC)
NCB	National Codification Bureau
NCBFAA	National Customs Brokers and Forwarders Association of America, Inc.
NCIS	Naval Criminal Investigative Service
NCS	NATO Codification System
NDAA	National Defense Authorization Act
NDI	Non-Developmental Items
NDP	National Disclosure Policy
NDP-1	National Disclosure Policy Publication
NDPC	National Disclosure Policy Committee
NDS	National Defense Strategy
NDU	National Defense University
NECTC	Naval Education and Training Command
NESA	Near East-South Asia Center for Strategic Studies
NETSAFA	Naval Education and Training Security Assistance Field Activity
NGA	National Geospatial-Intelligence Agency
NGO	Non-governmental organization
NICN	Navy Item Control Number
NIIN	National Item Identification Number
NISP	National Industrial Security Program
NISPOM	National Industrial Security Programs Operating Manual, DOD 5220.22-M
NLL	Navy Logistics Library
NMCS	Not Mission Capable Supply
NMS	National Military Strategy
NOA	Notice of Availability
NORTHCOM	US Northern Command
NPA	NATO Participation Act of 1994
NPS	Naval Post Graduate School
NRC	Nonrecurring Cost (also NC) / Non-Repayable Credits
NSA	National Security Agency
NSC	National Security Council
NSDD	National Security Decision Directive
NSDM	National Security Decision Memorandum
NSN	National Stock Number / NATO Stock Number
NSS	National Security Strategy / National Supply System
NVD	Night Vision Device
NWC	National War College / Naval War College

O

O&M	Operations and Maintenance (DOD Funding)
OA/FCA	Obligation Authority / Fund Certification Authorization (SAARMS)
OAC	Operating Agency Code
OBL	Ocean Bill of Lading
OBS	Observer Training
OCONUS	Outside the Continental United States
ODC	Office of Defense Cooperation
OED	Offer Expiration Date (LOA)
OEF	Operation Enduring Freedom (Afghanistan)
OEM	Original Equipment Manufacturer
OGC	Office of General Counsel
OHA	Overseas Housing Allowance
OHDACA	Overseas Humanitarian, Disaster, and Civic Aid Program (DOD)
OIF	Operation Iraqi Freedom
OJT	On-the-Job Training
OMA	Operations and Maintenance (Army)
OMB	Office of Management and Budget
OPI	Oral Proficiency Interview
OSC	Office of Security Cooperation
OSCE	Organization for Security and Cooperation in Europe
OSD	Office of the Secretary of Defense
OSP	Offshore Procurement
OT	Orientation Tour / Observer Training
OT&E	Operational Test and Evaluation

P

P&A	Price and Availability Data
PACOM	US Pacific Command
PAO	Public Affairs Officer
PASS	Post Administrative Support System
PBAS	Program, Budget, & Accounting System (Army)
PBL	Performance Based Logistics
PC&H	Packaging, Crating, and Handling
PCF	Pakistan Counterinsurgency Fund
PCCF	Pakistan Counterinsurgency Capability Fund
PCH&T	Packaging, Crating, Handling, and Transportation
PCO	Procurement Contracting Officer
PCS	Permanent Change of Station
PD	Presidential Determination
PDD	Presidential Decision Directive

PDM	Programmed Depot Maintenance
PEO	Program Executive Officer
PEO-STRI	Program Executive Office for Simulation, Training & Instrumentation (Army)
PEP	Personnel Exchange Program
PfP	Partnership for Peace (NATO)
PICA	Primary Inventory Control Activity
PKO	Peacekeeping Operations
PL	Public Law
PLT	Procurement Lead Time
PM	Bureau of Political-Military Affairs (DOS) / Program Manager
PM/DDTC	Bureau of Political-Military Affairs, Directorate of Defense Trade Controls
PM/RSAT	Bureau of Political-Military Affairs, Office of Regional Security and Arms Transfer
PME	Professional Military Education / Precision Measuring Equipment
PMESII	Political, military, economic, social, infrastructure, information systems
PML	Program Management Line
PMR	Program Management Review
PN	Part Number / Partner Nation
POD	Port of Debarkation
POE	Port of Embarkation / Port of Entry
POL	Petroleum, Oil, and Lubricants
POL/MIL	Political-Military
POM	Program Objective Memorandum
POTUS	President of the United States
PPBES	Planning, Programming, Budgeting, and Execution System
PPP	Program Protection Plan
PQDR	Product Quality Deficiency Report
PR	Purchase Request
PROS	Parts and Repair Ordering System
PSI	Program Security Instruction
PST	Partnership Strategy Toolkit
PSVR	Payment Schedule Variance Report
PVST	Port Visit
PWS	Performance Work Statement

Q

QA	Quality Assurance
QAT	Quality Assurance Team
QDDR	Quadrennial Diplomacy and Development Review
QDR	Quality Deficiency Report
QRR	Quarterly Requisition Report

R

R&D	Research & Development
R&R	Repair and Return / Repair and Replace
RAD	Required Availability Date / Request Authority to Develop
RCM	FMS Case Reconciliation and Closure Manual, DOD 5105.65-M
RCN	Record Control Number
RCP	Regional Campaign Plan
RCSS	Regional Centers for Security Studies
RD&A	Research, Development and Acquisition
RDD	Required Delivery Date
RDO	Redistribution Order
RDT&E	Research, Development, Test, and Evaluation
RFP	Request for Proposal
RFQ	Request for Quotation
RIC	Routing Identifier Code
RIK	Replacement in Kind
RIM	Retainable Instructional Material
RIRO	Repairable Item Replacement Option (USN)
ROM	Rough Order of Magnitude
ROR	Repair of Repairables or Reparables
RSI	Rationalization, Standardization, and Interoperability
RSN	Record Serial Number
RSAT	Office of Regional Security and Arms Transfer (DOS)
RSO	Regional Security Office (or Officer)

S

S/FOAA	State/Foreign Operations Appropriations Acts
S&T	Science and Technology
SA	Security Assistance
SAAF	Security Assistance Administrative Funds
SAAM	Special Assignment Airlift Mission
SAAR	System Authorization Access Request (DD Form 2875)
SAARMS	Security Assistance Automated Resource Management Suite
SAC	Senate Appropriations Committee
SAF/AQ	Assistant Secretary of the Air Force for Acquisition
SAF/IA	Deputy Under Secretary of the Air Force for International Affairs
SAFR	Security Assistance Foreign Representative [located within CONUS (USN)]
SALO	Security Assistance Liaison Officer (Army)
SAMD	Security Assistance Management Directorate (Army)
SAMIS	Security Assistance Management Information System (USAF)
SAMM	Security Assistance Management Manual (DSCA Manual 5105.38-M)

SAMR	Security Assistance Management Review
SAMRS	Security Assistance Manpower Requirements System (USAF)
SAN	Security Assistance Network
SAO	Security Assistance Organization (or Office or Officer)
SAP	Security Assistance Program / Simplified Acquisition Procedures
SAPM	Security Assistance Program Manager (USAF)
SASC	Senate Armed Services Committee
SAT	Security Assistance Team / Survey Assessment Team
SATP	Security Assistance Training Program
SATFA	Security Assistance Training Field Activity (Army)
SATMO	Security Assistance Training Management Organization (Army)
SATODS	Security Assistance Technical Order Program (USAF)
SATP	Security Assistance Training Program
SBLC	Stand By Letter of Credit
SBU	Sensitive But Unclassified
SC	Security Cooperation
SC-TMS	Security Cooperation-Training Management System
SCES	Security Cooperation Enterprise System
SCET	Security Cooperation Education and Training
SCETWG	Security Cooperation Education and Training Working Group (replaced TPMR)
SCIP	Security Cooperation Information Portal
SCML	Small Case Management Line
SCO	Security Cooperation Office / Officer
SDAF	Special Defense Acquisition Fund
SDDC	Surface Deployment and Distribution Command (Army)
SDO/DATT	Senior Defense Official/Defense Attache
SDR	Supply Discrepancy Report, SF 364
SECDEF	Secretary of Defense
SECNAV	Secretary of the Navy
SECSTATE	Secretary of State
SED	Shippers Export Declaration (SED Form 7525-V)
SEED	Support for East European Democracy (SEED) Act of 1989
SET	Specialized English Training
SF 361	Standard Form 361, Transportation Discrepancy Report (TDR)
SF 364	Standard Form 364, Report of Discrepancy [SDR (ROD)]
SFA	Security Force Assistance
SFRC	Senate Foreign Relations Committee
SIPRNET	Secure Internet Protocol Router Network
SLC	Shelf Life Code
SLS	Standard Level of Service
SMC	Space and Missile Systems Center (USAF)

SME	Significant Military Equipment
SNR	Senior National Representative
SNAP	Simplified Nonstandard Acquisition Process (Army)
SOF	Special Operations Forces
SOFA	Status of Forces Agreement
SOLIC	Special Operations/Low-Intensity Conflict
SOO	Statement of Objective
SOP	Standard Operating Procedure
SOUTHCOM	US Southern Command
SOW	Statement of Work
SPAN	Security Policy Automation Network
SPAWAR	Space & Naval Warfare Systems Command (USN)
SPO	System Program Office (USAF)
SPP	State Partnership Program
SRBMD	Short Range Ballistic Missile Defense
SRC	Security Risk Category
SSC	Supply and Services Complete
SSE	System Security Engineering
STARR/PC	Supply Tracking and Repairable Return / Personal Computer
STL	Standardized Training List
SVI	Single Vendor Integrity
SYSCOM	Systems Command (Army/USN)

T

T&E	Test and Evaluation
T-MASL	Training Military Articles and Services List
TA	Type of Assistance (or Finance) / Technology Assessment
TAA	Technical Assistance Agreement / Trade Agreement Act
TAC	Type of Address Code / Type of Assistance (or Finance) Code
TACOM	Tank, Automotive, and Armaments Command (Army)
TA/CP	Technology Assessment/Control Plan
TAFT	Technical Assistance Field Team
TAT	Technical Assistance Team
TBC	Transportation Bill Code
TCA	Traditional CCMD Activities (also TCCA)
TCG	Technical Coordination Group (USAF)
TCN	Transportation Control Number / Third Country National
TCO	Test Control Officer / Termination Contracting Officer
TCP	Technical Coordination Program / Technology Control Plan
TCT	Traveling Contact Team
TCTO	Time Compliance Technical Order
TDP	Technical Data Package

TDR	Transportation Discrepancy Report, SF 361
TDS	Technology Development Strategy
TDY	Temporary Duty (Army and USAF)
TECOM	Training and Education Command (USMC)
TIP	Trafficking in People
TL	Termination Liability
TLA	Temporary Living Allowance / Travel and Living Allowance
TMS	Training Management System
TO	Technical Order (USAF) / Training Officer
TP	Transportation Plan
TPA	Total Package Approach (also TPC)
TRADOC	Training and Doctrine Command (Army)
TRANSCOM	US Transportation Command
TS&FD	Technology Security and Foreign Disclosure
TSCMIS	Theater Security Cooperation Management Information System
TSCS	Theater Security Cooperation Strategy (DOD)
TSFDO	Technology Security and Foreign Disclosure Office
TTP	Tactics, Techniques, and Procedures

U

UAV	Unmanned Aerial Vehicle
UCA	Undefinitized Contractual Action (s)
UCMJ	US Uniform Code of Military Justice
UDHR	Universal Declaration of Human Rights
UFR	Unfunded Requirement
ULO	Unliquidated Obligation
UMMIPS	Uniform Materiel Movement and Issue Priority System
UN	United Nations
UND	Urgency of Need Designator
UNFICYP	United Nations Forces in Cyprus
UPS	United Parcel Service
USA	US Army
USAF	US Air Force
USAID	US Agency for International Development
USASAC	US Army Security Assistance Command
USASATMO	US Army Security Assistance Training Management Organization (also SATMO)
USC	US Code (as in law)
USCENTCOM	US Central Command
USCG	US Coast Guard
USD (AT&L)	Under Secretary of Defense for Acquisition, Technology and Logistics
USD (C)	Under Secretary of Defense (Comptroller)
USD (I)	Under Secretary of Defense for Intelligence

USD (P)	Under Secretary of Defense for Policy
USDOT	US Department of Transportation
USDR	US Defense Representative (see SDO/DATT)
USEUCOM	US European Command
USG	US Government
USJFCOM	US Joint Forces Command
USMC	US Marine Corps
USML	US Munitions List
USMTM	US Military Training Mission (SAO in Saudi Arabia)
USN	US Navy
USNORTHCOM	US Northern Command
USPACOM	US Pacific Command
USPS	US Postal Service
USSOCOM	US Special Operations Command
USSOUTHCOM	US Southern Command
USTR	US Trade Representative

V

VT	Voting Trust

W

WCN	Worksheet Control Number
WebFLIS	Federal Logistics Information System Web Search
WIF	Warsaw Initiative Fund
WIP	Work in Progress
WMD	Weapons of Mass Destruction
WPOD	Water Port of Discharge
WRSA	War Reserve Stockpiles for Allies
WSLO	Weapon System Logistics Office (or Officer)
WWRS	Worldwide Warehouse Redistribution Service (USAF)

GLOSSARY OF SELECTED TERMS

A

Above-the-line-cost (obsolete terminology). Costs and the related material/services that are the responsibility of the cognizant implementing agency during execution and closure of an FMS case. Specifically, line 21 of the DD Form 1513 (estimated costs) or line 8 of the LOA (Net Estimated Cost) sometimes referred to as the "Net Estimated Case Value."

Acceptance. The act of an authorized representative of the government by which the government assumes for itself, or as agent of another, ownership of existing and identified supplies tendered, or approves specific services rendered, as partial or complete performance of the contract on the part of the contractor. See also letter of offer and acceptance.

Acceptance date. The date that appears on the acceptance portion of the LOA and indicates the calendar date on which a foreign buyer agrees to accept the items and conditions contained in the FMS offer portion.

Accessorial cost. The cost of packing, crating, and handling (PC&H), and transportation which are incidental to issues, sales, and transfers of materiel and are not included in the standard price or contract cost of materiel. An exception to this is working capital fund (WCF) items.

Accrued costs. The financial value of delivered articles and services and incurred costs reported to DFAS–IN via Delivery Transactions. Incurred costs represent disbursements for which no physical deliveries have yet occurred. Examples are: progress payments to contractors, GFM/GFE provided to contractors, and nonrecurring costs.

Act. The term for legislation once it has passed both houses of Congress and has been signed (enacted) by the president or passed over his veto, thus becoming law.

Actual cost. A cost sustained in fact, on the basis of costs incurred, as distinguished from forecasted or estimated costs.

Adjustment reply code (ARC). A code that identifies the type of action being taken in reply to the FMS customer supply discrepancy report [SDR (ROD)]. ARCs are transmitted to DFAS–IN by an FMS case Implementing Agency in FMS Delivery/Performance Reports.

Administrative contracting officer (ACO). The US government contracting officer who is assigned the responsibility for the administration of US government contracts.

Administrative cost. The value of costs associated with the administration of the FMS program. The prescribed administrative percentage cost for a case appears in the LOA. This percentage is applied against the case. Expenses charged directly to the FMS case (as prescribed by the LOA) are not included.

Administrative lead-time. The time interval between the initiation of procurement action and the letting of a contract or the placing of an order.

Aerospace Maintenance and Regeneration Group (AMARG). A joint service aircraft and aerospace vehicle storage, regeneration, reclamation, and disposal facility located at Davis-Monthan AFB.

Allocation. An authorization by a designated official of a DOD component making funds available within a prescribed amount to an operating agency for the purpose of making funding allotments (i.e., the first subdivision of an apportionment of funds).

Allotment. An authorization granted within and pursuant to an allocation for the purpose of incurring commitments, obligations, and expenditures in the accomplishment of an approved budget. Therefore, an allotment is a subdivision of an appropriation that provides the funding authority for an official to accomplish a specific function or mission.

Amendment. An amendment of an FMS case constitutes a scope change to an existing LOA.

Apportionment. A determination made by the Office of Management and Budget which limits the amount of obligations or expenditures which may be incurred during a specified time period. An apportionment may limit all obligations to be incurred during the specified period or it may limit obligations to be incurred for a specific activity, function, project, or a combination thereof.

Appropriation. A part of an Appropriation Act providing a specified amount of funds to be used for designated purposes. Each appropriation has a finite period of time for incurring obligations.

Appropriations act. Legislation initiated by the House and Senate Appropriations Committees, that provides authority for Federal agencies to incur obligations and to make payments out of the Treasury for specified purposes. An appropriation act is the most common means of providing budget authority. There are thirteen regular appropriation acts for each fiscal year.

Armaments. Weapons with a lethal capability (i.e., missiles, ammunition, etc.).

Armed Services Board of Contract Appeals. A board established to act as the authorized representative of the SECDEF or department Secretaries, in deciding appeals under the provisions of the disputes clause contained in USG contracts.

Arms Export Control Act (AECA). The basic US law providing the authority and general rules for the conduct of foreign military sales and commercial sales of defense articles, defense services, and training. The AECA came into existence with the passage of the Foreign Military Sales Act (FMSA) of 1968. An amendment in the International Security Assistance and Arms Export Control Act of 1976 changed the name of FMSA to the AECA. Published as 22 USC Sec. 2751 et seq.

Attrition. The loss of a resource due to natural causes in the normal course of events, such as a turnover of employees or spoilage and obsolescence of material.

Attrition [international military training]. The total destruction of a DOD capital asset (e.g., a training aircraft) when a foreign student was in physical control of the asset or as a direct result of negligence, simple or gross.

Audit. The systematic examination of records and documents to determine:

    a.   The adequacy and effectiveness of budgeting, accounting, financial, and related policies and procedures

    b.   Compliance with applicable statutes, regulations, policies, and prescribed procedures

    c.   The reliability, accuracy, and completeness of financial and administrative records and reports

    d.   The extent to which funds and other resources are properly protected and effectively used

Auditor [procurement]. A term used to represent the cognizant audit office designated by the Defense Contract Audit Agency (DCAA) or military service audit activities for conducting audit reviews of the contractor's accounting system policies and procedures for compliance with the criteria.

Authorization act. Basic, substantive, legislation that establishes or continues the legal operation of a federal program or agency, either indefinitely or for a specific period of time, or which sanctions a particular type of obligation or expenditure.

B

Back order (BO). The quantity of an item requisitioned by ordering activities that is not immediately available for issue but is recorded as a stock commitment for future issue.

Bandaria. The imaginary country used by DISAM when making an example security assistance situation. This country is not located in any real region of the world nor is it modeled after any real country. For security assistance purposes, Bandaria's country code is BN.

Base year (BY). A reference period that determines a fixed price level for comparison in economic escalation calculations and cost estimates. The price level index for the base year is 1.000.

Below-the-line-costs (obsolete terminology). Costs identified on the DD Form 1513 on lines 22 through 25. Applicable costs are added to line 21, estimated costs, to arrive at line 26, estimated total costs. Normally, DFAS–IN retains the obligational authority necessary to execute applicable costs.

Bill. A legislative proposal originating in either the House or Senate, which, if passed in identical form by both houses and signed by the president, becomes an enacted law. Bills are designated by "HR" in the House of Representatives or "S" in the Senate, according to the house in which they originate, plus a number assigned in the order in which they are introduced during the two-year period of a Congressional term. Appropriations bills always originate in the House.

Bill (or billing) code. This is a DFAS–IN country assigned code that divides FMS customer country billings into management levels lower than a US Implementing Agency or in-country service. This code often correlates to an FMS customer paying office. It appears in Block 3 of the DD Form 645. Basic alpha codes are derived from the LOA. The FMS customer should ensure that the proper bill code is indicated upon acceptance of an LOA.

Billing statement. The DD Form 645 Billing Statement represents the official claim for payment by the US government referred to in Letters of Offer and Acceptance. It also furnishes an accounting to the FMS purchaser for all costs incurred on his behalf under each agreement.

Blanket order case. An agreement between a foreign customer and the US government for a specific category of items or services (including training) with no definitive listing of items or quantities. The case specifies a dollar ceiling against which orders may be placed.

Budget authority. The authority Congress gives to government agencies, permitting them to enter into obligations that will result in immediate or future outlays (expenditures). Such budget authority does not include the authority to ensure the repayment of loans held by another person or government.

Budget year. The fiscal year following the current fiscal year, and for which the new budget estimate is prepared.

C

Canceled case. An FMS case which was not accepted or funded within prescribed time limitations, or was accepted and subsequently canceled by the requesting country or the US government. In the latter case, the US government or purchaser electing to cancel all (or part) of a case prior to the delivery of defense articles or the performance of services shall be responsible for all (or associated) termination costs.

Carrier. A military or commercial ship, aircraft, barge, train or truck, or a commercial transport company that moves material from one location to another.

Case. An FMS contractual sales agreement between the US and an eligible foreign country or international organization documented by a DD Form 1513 or an LOA. An FMS case identifier is assigned for the purpose of identification, accounting, and data processing for each offer.

Case description. A short title specifically prepared for each FMS case by the implementing agency.

Case designator. A unique designator assigned by the implementing agency to each FMS case. The designator originates with the offer of a sale, identifies the case through all subsequent transactions, and is generally a three-letter designation, comprising the last element of the Case Identifier.

Case identifier. A unique six-digit identifier assigned to an FMS case for the purpose of identification, accounting, and data processing of each LOA. The case identifier consists of the two-letter country code, a one-letter designator for the implementing agency, and a three-letter case designator.

Case modification. Modification of a case documented by an LOA modification, which constitutes an administrative or price change to an existing LOA, without revising the scope of the case.

Cash prior to delivery [FMS]. A term of sale in which the US government collects cash in advance of the delivery of defense articles and/or the performance of defense services from DOD resources.

Cash with acceptance [FMS]. A term of sale in which US dollar currency, check, or other negotiable instrument is submitted by the customer concurrent with acceptance of an FMS sales offer for the full amount shown as the estimated total cost on the LOA.

Closed case. An FMS case for which all materiel has been delivered, all services have been performed, all financial transactions, including all collections, have been completed, and the customer has received a final statement of account.

Co-development. A joint development project between the US government and foreign government to satisfy a common requirement.

Collections. Receipts in US dollars, checks, or other negotiable instruments from a purchasing country to pay for defense articles, services, or military training based on accepted FMS cases.

Combating Terrorism Fellowship Program (CTFP). Formerly known as Counterterrorism Fellowship Program, and also currently known as the Regional Defense Combating Terrorism Fellowship Program. It is a DOD security cooperation tool that provides education and training to international security personnel as part of the US global effort to combat terrorism. CTFP is authorized by section 2249C of Title 10, *US Code* which allows DOD to use up to $20 million per year to pay any costs associated with the attendance of foreign government personnel, including civilians, at selected DOD schools, conferences, centers, and other training programs.

Combined Education and Training Program Plan. Plan developed by SCO in coordination with the host country counterparts that consolidates the host country's training needs for the budget year and the planning year (i.e. Host Country Training Requirements for the next two years). Includes program objectives and justifications.

Commercial sale. A sale of defense articles or defense services made under a Department of State issued license by US industry directly to a foreign buyer, and which is not administered by DOD through FMS procedures. Also referred to as a direct commercial sale.

Commercial-type items. Any items, including those expended or consumed in use, which, in addition to military use, are used and traded in normal civilian enterprise and may be imported/exported through normal international trade channels.

Commitment [financial]. A firm administrative reservation of funds based upon firm procurement directives, orders, requisitions, authorizations to issue travel orders, or requests which authorize the recipient to create obligations without further recourse to the official responsible for certifying the availability of funds. The act of entering into a commitment is usually the first step in the process of spending available funds.

Compatibility. The characteristics or ability of two or more operational items/systems to coexist and function as elements of a larger operational system or operational environment without mutual interference. Applies also to multi-service or multi-national use.

Competent Authority Approval (CAA). An approval from the national agency responsible under a country's national law for the regulation of hazardous materials transportation. For the US, the "competent authority" (CA) is the US Department of Transportation.

Competitive proposals. A method for awarding a US government contract on a basis other than low bid, whereby the best and final offer may be obtained after discussions are concluded.

Completed case. An FMS case for which all deliveries and collections have been completed, but for which a final accounting statement (DD Form 645) has not been furnished to the purchaser.

Concurrent resolution. A concurrent resolution must be adopted by both houses, but it is not sent to the president for his signature and therefore does not have the force of law. A concurrent resolution, for example, is used as the vehicle for expressing the sense of Congress on various foreign policy and domestic issues.

Concurrent resolution on the budget. A resolution passed by both Houses of Congress but not requiring the signature of the president, setting forth, reaffirming, or revising specified congressional budget totals for the federal government for a fiscal year.

Concurrent spare parts (CSP). These are spare parts programmed as an initial stockage related to the acquisition of a major item or system. CSPs are normally shipped in advance of the release of the major item or system.

Conference committee. A meeting between representatives of the House and the Senate to reconcile differences when each chamber passes dissimilar version of the same bill. Members of the conference committee are appointed formally by the Speaker of the House and the presiding officer of the Senate from the membership of the respective standing committees having cognizance over the subject legislation.

Congressional amendment. A proposal by a member of Congress to alter the language, provisions, or stipulations in a bill or in another amendment. An Amendment usually is printed, debated, and voted upon in the same manner as a bill.

Congressional Budget Justification for Foreign Operations. The document presented annually by the Executive Branch to Congress describing the proposed annual Military Assistance, Foreign Military Sales programs, and related security assistance programs along with other foreign assistance programs for the next fiscal year (i.e., the budget year) for which

Congressional authorizations and appropriations are requested. The document is jointly produced by DOD (DSCA) and DOS (PM) and serves as a supporting document and justification for the president's annual budget request for foreign assistance. In the past, referred to as the Congressional Presentation Document (CPD).

Congressional committee. A division of the House or Senate that prepares legislation for action by the parent chamber or makes investigations as directed by the parent chamber. Most standing committees are divided into subcommittees, which study specific types of legislation, hold hearings, and report bills, with or without amendments, to a full committee. Only a full committee can report legislation to the House or Senate.

Consignee. The person or organization to whom a shipment is to be delivered, whether by land, sea or air.

Constant year dollars. A method of relating dollar values for various years by removing the annual effects of inflation and showing all dollars at the value they would have had in a selected base year. See also current year dollars.

Constructive delivery [FMS]. Completion of delivery of materiel to a carrier for transportation to a consignee, or delivery to a US post office for shipment to a consignee. Delivery is evidenced by completed shipping documents or listings of delivery at the US post office. The delivery of materiel to the customer or the customer's designated freight forwarder at a point of production, testing, or storage at dockside, at staging areas, or at airports constitutes actual delivery. Also referred to as physical delivery.

Consumption rate. The average quantity of an item consumed or expended during a given time interval, expressed in quantities by the most appropriate unit of measurement.

Continental United States (CONUS). United States territory, including the adjacent territorial waters, located within the North American Continent between Canada and Mexico. Does not include Hawaii or Alaska.

Continuing resolution (CR). Appropriations legislation enacted by Congress to provide temporary budget authority for Federal agencies to keep them in operation when their regular appropriations bill has not been enacted by the start of the fiscal year.

Continuing resolution authority (CRA). The authority to obligate funds against the FMFP, IMET, ESF, or other related security assistance appropriation for the new fiscal year under a CR granted by Congress in a Joint Resolution making temporary appropriations prior to passage of the regular appropriations act, or in lieu of such an act. Normally, however, the CRA is for a designated period less than a fiscal year, and such a CRA does not usually allow funding for the start of any new programs.

Contract. An agreement between two or more persons who are legally capable of making a binding agreement, which involves: a promise (or set of promises); a consideration (i.e., something of value promised or given); a reasonable amount of understanding between the persons as to what the agreement means; and a legal means for resolving any breach of the agreement.

Contract administration. All the activities associated with the performance of a contract, from pre-award to closeout.

Contract administration services. All those actions accomplished in or near a contractor's plant for the benefit of the US government which are necessary to the performance of a contract or in support of the buying offices, system/project managers, and other organizations, including quality assurance, engineering support, production surveillance, pre-award surveys, mobilization planning, contract administration, property administration, industrial security, and safety.

Contract administration services (CAS) charge. A surcharge applied to all FMS purchases from procurement to cover the cost of contract administration, quality assurance and inspection, and contract audit. The surcharge percentage depends upon any contract administrative reciprocal agreements with a particular purchasing country.

Contract authority. Budget authority contained in an authorization bill that permits an agency of the federal government to enter into contracts or other obligations for future payments from funds not yet appropriated by Congress. The assumption is that the necessary funds will be made available for payment in a subsequent appropriations act.

Contract award. This occurs when a contracting officer has signed and distributed a contract to a contractor.

Contract field services (CFS). These are services performed for the USG by commercial or industrial companies. These services provide instruction and training on the installation, operation, and maintenance of DOD weapons, equipment, and systems.

Contract requirements. In addition to specified performance requirements, contract requirements include those defined in the statement of work; specifications, standards, and related documents; the contract data requirements list; management systems; and contract terms and conditions.

Contract termination. Cessation or cancellation, in whole or in part, of work under a prime contract, or a subcontract there under, for the convenience of, or at the option of, the government, or a foreign purchaser (FMS), or due to failure of the contractor to perform in accordance with the terms of the contract.

Contracting officer (CO). A person with the authority to enter into, administer, and/or terminate contracts and make related determinations and findings. The term includes certain authorized representatives of the CO acting within the limits of their authority as delegated by the CO.

Conventional arms transfers (CAT). The transfer of non-nuclear weapons, aircraft, equipment, and military services from supplier states to recipient states. The USG views arms transfers as a useful foreign policy instrument to strengthen collective defense arrangements, maintain regional military balances, secure US bases, and compensate for the withdrawal of troops. US arms may be transferred by grants, leases, loans, direct commercial sales, or government-to-government cash sales under FMS.

Cooperative logistics. The logistics support provided a foreign government/agency through its participation in a United States Department of Defense logistics system, with reimbursement paid to the USG for the support provided [Joint Pub 1-02].

Cooperative logistics supply support arrangements (CLSSA). Military logistics support arrangements designed to provide responsive and continuous supply support at the depot level for US-made military materiel possessed by foreign countries and international organizations. The CLSSA is normally the most effective means for providing common repair parts and secondary item support for equipment of US origin that is in allied and friendly country inventories.

Cooperative research and development. A method by which governments cooperate to make better use of their collective Research and Development resources, to include technical data exchanges and codevelopment of new weapons systems.

Coordinating Authority. A commander or individual assigned responsibility for coordinating specific functions or activities involving forces of two or more military departments, two or more joint force components, or two or more forces of the same service. The commander or individual has the authority to require consultation between the agencies involved, but does not have the authority to compel agreement. In the event that esential agreement cannot be obtained, the matter shall be referred to the next senior in the reporting chain. This authority is given to the Senior Defense Official or the Defense Attaché (SDO/DATT) by DODD 5105.75, Department of Defense Operations at US Embassies, December 21, 2007.

Coproduction. A program implemented by a government-to-government or commercial licensing arrangement which enables a foreign government or firm to acquire the "know-how" to manufacture or assemble, repair, maintain and operate, in whole or in part, a defense item.

Cost contract. A contract that provides for payment to the contractor of allowable costs, to the extent prescribed in the contract, incurred in performance of the contract.

Country Liaison Officer (CLO). An officer or non-commissioned officer (NCO) of a foreign military establishment selected by his or her government and attached to a MILDEP or DOD agency for the primary purpose of helping administer IMS from his or her home country. For administrative purposes, the CLO is considered in a student status. In State Department terms, the CLO is the Community Liaison Officer, similar to an MWR officer in the military.

Country team. Senior members of US government agencies assigned to a US diplomatic mission overseas, and subject to the direction and supervision of the Chief, US Mission (Ambassador). Normally, such members meet regularly (i.e., weekly) to coordinate USG political, economic, and military activities and policies in the host country.

Credit case (FMS). The use of US government appropriated funds from the FMFP account to finance a foreign country's FMS purchases of US defense articles or services. Credit funds may be in the form of repayable loans or non-repayable grants.

Credit guaranty. A guaranty to any individual corporation, partnership, or other judicial entity doing business in the United States (excluding USG agencies other than the Federal Financing Bank) against political and credit risks of nonpayment arising out of their financing of credit sales of defense articles and defense services to eligible countries and international organizations.

Cross-servicing. That function performed by one military service in support of another military service for which reimbursement is required from the service receiving support.

Current fiscal year. The fiscal year in progress but not yet completed; e.g. between and including 1 October and 30 September.

Current year. The fiscal year in progress. See also budget year.

Current-year dollars. Dollar values of a given year that include the effects of inflation or escalation for that year, or which reflect the price levels expected to prevail during the year at issue. Also referred to as escalated dollars or then-year dollars.

D

Defense article. As defined in section 644(d), FAA and section 47(3), AECA, includes any weapon, weapons system, munitions, aircraft, vessel, boat, or other implement of war; any property, installation, commodity, material, equipment, supply, or goods used for the purposes of furnishing military assistance or making military sales; any machinery, facility, tool, material, supply, or other item necessary for the manufacture, production, processing, repair, servicing, storage, construction, transportation, operation, or use of any other defense article or any component or part of any articles listed above, but shall not include merchant vessels, or as defined by the Atomic Energy Act of 1954, as amended (42 US Code 2011), source material, byproduct material, special nuclear material, production facilities, utilization facilities, or atomic weapons or articles involving Restricted Data.

Defense attaché office (DAO). A DOD organization assigned to a US diplomatic mission overseas for the purposes of overt gathering of military information, representing the US Department of Defense in the conduct of military liaison activities, and performing as a component of the US country team. Several DAO's have been designated by the president as being responsible for security assistance functions in a host country.

Defense Contract Management Agency (DCMA). An agency under the direction of the Under Secretary of Defense for Acquisition, Technology and Logistics [USD (AT&L)], which provides unified contract administration services to DOD components and NASA, for all contracts except those specifically exempted.

Defense industrial cooperation. US activities performed in conjunction with selected foreign countries, which are intended to stimulate the development of foreign defense industrial capabilities, particularly in emerging technologies, for the mutual benefit of all participants.

Defense Institute of Security Assistance Management (DISAM). The centralized DOD school for the consolidated professional education of personnel involved in security cooperation management. DISAM is located at Wright-Patterson Air Force Base, Ohio, and provides an array of resident and nonresident instruction for both USG and foreign government military and civilian personnel as well as for defense contractor and industry personnel.

Defense Logistics Agency. A DOD inventory management agency responsible for approximately 95 percent of consumable items and approximately 85 percent of all spare parts in the DOD supply system.

DLA Disposition Services. An organization within DLA that provides redistribution and disposal services for DOD. FMS is one of the many programs qualified to receive DLA Disposition Services property.

DLA Logistics Information Service. An organization within DLA that serves as the US National Codification Bureau (NCB) and also provides cataloging services in support of allied defense ministries.

Defense Security Cooperation Agency (DSCA). The agency that performs administrative management, program planning, and operations functions for US military assistance programs at the DOD level under the policy direction of the Assistant Secretary of Defense (International Security Affairs).

Defense service. As defined in section 644(f), FAA and section 47(4), AECA, the term defense service includes any service, test, inspection, repair, training, publication, technical or other assistance, or defense information used for the purpose of furnishing military assistance or FMS, but does not include military education and training activities or design and construction services under section 29, AECA.

Defense stock. The term defense stock includes defense articles on hand which are available for prompt delivery. It also includes defense articles under contract and on order that would be available for delivery within a reasonable time from the date of order by an eligible foreign government or international organization without increasing outstanding contracts or entering into new contracts.

Defense Transportation System (DTS). The collection of transportation activities and carriers belonging to or under contract to the DOD. The DTS includes commercial and organic aircraft and ships, and commercial small package services under contract to the DOD, as well as the operation of US military air and ocean terminals in and outside of the US.

Defined order case. These are FMS cases characterized by orders for specific defense articles and services that are separately identified line items on the LOA.

Definitization. The process of tailoring a standard DOD system to the international partner's operational requirements, by making adjustments to the item configuration, the type and quantity of spare parts, and the logistics support package.

Diminishing Manufacturing Sources and Material Shortages (DMSMS). The loss or impending loss of manufacturers of items, suppliers of items, or raw materials needed to support and maintain a system.

Delivery. Includes constructive or actual delivery of defense articles; also, includes the performance of defense services for the customer or requisitioner, as well as accessorial services, when they are normally recorded in the billing and collection cycle immediately following performance.

Delivery forecasts. Periodic estimates of contract production deliveries used as a measure of the effectiveness of production and supply availability scheduling and as a guide to corrective actions to resolve procurement or production bottlenecks. These forecasts provide estimates of deliveries under obligation against procurement from appropriated or other funds.

Delivery Term Code (DTC). A single character code that represents how far the USG is responsible for arranging transportation of defense articles going to an international customer.

Dependable undertaking [FMS]. An excepted term and condition within the FMS case (or LOA). A firm commitment by a foreign government or international organization to pay the full amount of a contract for new production or for the performance of defense services which will assure the US against any loss on such contract and to make funds available in such amounts and at such times as may be required by the contract, or for any damages and costs that may accrue from the cancellation of such a contract, provided that in the judgment of the DOD there is sufficient likelihood that the foreign government or international organization will have the economic resources to fulfill the commitment.

Depot level maintenance. Maintenance performed on material requiring a major overhaul or a complete rebuilding of parts, assemblies, subassemblies, and end items, including the manufacture of parts, modification, testing, and reclamation as required. Provides more extensive shop facilities and equipment and personnel of higher technical skill than are normally available at the lower levels of maintenance, i.e., organizational and intermediate level maintenance.

Designated government representative (DGR). A person or persons duly authorized by a foreign government to act on behalf of that government to negotiate, commit, sign contractual agreements, and/or accept delivery of materiel.

Direct cite. Citation of the FMS Trust Fund [Account 97-11X8242] as the financing source on documents leaving the DOD system, as well as contracts with commercial firms, the General Services Administration, the Department of Transportation, etc. The term "direct cite" is not valid if any DOD organization establishes a reimbursable order to a DOD appropriation account, stock fund, or industrial fund.

Direct cost. Any cost that is specifically identified with a particular final cost objective. Such costs are not necessarily limited to items that are incorporated into the end product as labor or material.

Direct offset. A general type of industrial or commercial compensation practice required of a contractor by a purchasing government as a condition for the purchase of defense articles/services. The form of compensation, which generally offsets a specific percentage of the cost of the purchase, is directly associated with the items purchased, such as the production of components in the purchasing country for installation in the purchased end-item.

Disbursements [gross and net]. In budgetary usage, gross disbursements represent the amount of checks issued, cash, or other payments made, less refunds received. Net disbursements represent gross disbursements less income collected and credited to the appropriate fund account, such as amounts received for goods and services provided. See also outlays.

Disclosure authorization. An authorization by an appropriate US military department authority which is required prior to the disclosure of classified information to foreign nationals who are cleared by their governments to have access to classified information.

Domicile to duty transportation. Transportation from one's domicile/residence to one's place of duty/employment.

DOD components. These include all of the following: the Office of the Secretary of Defense (OSD); the military departments; the Joint Chiefs of Staff (JCS or Joint Staff); the combatant commands; the Office of the Inspector General, Department of Defense (DODIG); the Defense agencies, to include the Missile Defense Agency (MDA); and DOD field activities.

DOD field studies program. The DOD program that affords an opportunity for the International Military Student (IMS) to become familiar with the United States, the social, cultural, and political institutions of the US, and its people and their ways of life. The informational program (IP) further increases the IMSs' awareness of the US commitment to basic principles of internationally recognized human rights. Formerly the DOD informational program.

DSP-94. A DOS publication, Authority to Export Defense Articles Sold Under the Foreign Military Sales Program, which must be filed with the US Customs along with a copy of the LOA in order for defense articles to be legally exported.

E

Earmarks [appropriations]. Minimum mandatory funding levels for countries/programs established by Congress in annual foreign assistance authorization and appropriations bills. Earmarks provide Congress a means for establishing its priorities in the allocation of US foreign assistance resources.

Economic order quantity (EOQ). The most economical quantity of parts to order at one time to support a defined production rate, considering the applicable procurement and inventory costs.

Economic support fund (ESF). A USG security assistance program through which economic assistance is provided on a grant basis, to selected foreign governments with significant political or military interests for the US. The funds may be used to finance imports of commodities, capital, or technical assistance in accordance with the terms of a bilateral agreement.

Eligible recipient [security assistance]. Any friendly foreign country or international organization determined by the president to be eligible to purchase or receive (on a grant basis) US defense articles and defense services, unless otherwise ineligible due to statutory restrictions.

End item (EI). A final combination of end products, component parts, and/or materials which is ready for its intended use, e.g., aircraft, ship, tank, mobile machine shop.

Engineering change proposal (ECP). A proposal to a responsible authority recommending that a change to an original item of equipment be considered, and the design or engineering change be incorporated into the article to modify, add to, delete, or supersede original parts.

English comprehension level (ECL) examination. A test of the overall proficiency of foreign military students in English language listening and reading. A minimum entry level for each DOD course of instruction is set by the military departments (MILDEPs) on the basis of course level difficulty and hazard factors.

Environmental and morale leave. A type of leave granted to DOD personnel stationed in remote locations.

Estimated actual charges. A systematic and documented estimate of actual costs. The procedure is used in the absence of an established cost accounting system and the procedure is sometimes referred to as a cost finding technique.

Excess defense articles (EDA). Defense articles owned by the United States government which are neither procured in anticipation of military assistance or sales requirements, nor procured pursuant to a military assistance or sales order. EDA are items (except construction equipment) that are in excess of the Approved Force Acquisition Objective and Approved Force Retention Stock of all Department of Defense components at the time such articles are dropped from inventory by the supplying agency for delivery to countries or international organizations.

Execution. The operation of carrying out a program as contained in the approved budget. Often referred to as budget execution.

Executive Order. A rule or regulation, issued by the president, a governor, or some other administrative authority, that has the effect of law. Executive orders are used to implement and give administrative effect to provisions of the Constitution, to treaties, and to statutes. They may be used to create or modify the organization or procedures of administrative agencies or may have general applicability as law. Under the Administrative Procedure Act (APA) of 1946, all executive orders must be published in the Federal Register.

Expanded IMET (E-IMET). Training funded under the IMET program to the following four objectives: proper management of defense resources, improving military justice systems in accordance with internationally recognized human rights, understanding the principle of civilian control of the military, and contributing to the cooperation between police and military forces for counternarcotics law enforcement [sec. 541, FAA]. Only courses found in the Expanded IMET Handbook qualify for consideration in the Expanded IMET portion of a country's training program.

Expendable supplies and material. Supplies which are consumed in use, such as ammunition, paint, fuel, cleaning and preserving materials, surgical dressings, drugs, medicines, etc., or which lose their identity, such as spare parts, etc. Sometimes referred to as consumable supplies and material.

Expenditure authority (EA, as used in FMS). A document or authority from DFAS–IN to an FMS case implementing DOD component that allows expenditures against obligations previously recorded against an FMS case. The disbursing activity must ensure that cash is available prior to processing the disbursement.

Expenditures. The actual spending of money as distinguished from the appropriation of funds. Expenditures are made by the executive branch; appropriations are made only by Congress. The two rarely are identical in any fiscal year. In addition to some current budget authority, expenditures may represent prior budget authority made available one, two, or more years earlier. See also disbursements.

Extended training service specialists (ETSS). ETSS are DOD military and civilian personnel technically qualified to provide advice, instruction, and training in the installation, operation, and maintenance of weapons, equipment, and systems. ETSS are attached to an overseas SCO rather than assigned, and they are carried on the Joint Table of Distribution (JTD), but are not provided as an augmentation to the SCO staff. ETSS may be provided for overseas assignments for periods of up to but not exceeding one year, unless specifically approved by DSCA.

EX-number. A classification of explosive hazard assigned by the US Department of Transportation to commercial and military explosives, which determines how the explosive material may be stored and transported to comply with international safety regulations.

F

Fair Share Sustainment Programs (FSSP). US Army programs to provide hardware, software and technical support to international users of the HAWK and CHAPARRAL programs which are obsolete to the US Army.

Familiarization training. Practical experience and job-related training for specific systems, subsystems, functional areas, or other operations that require hands-on experience, to include maintenance training conducted at the depot level. This training does not provide for skill-level upgrading, which is provided under OJT when special procedures are required.

Federal Acquisition Regulation (FAR). The FAR is the primary regulation for use by federal executive agencies for the acquisition of supplies and services with appropriated funds. Besides the FAR, each agency has its supplement to describe its own particular way of doing business. The DOD supplement is called Defense FAR Supplement (DFARS).

Federal budget. The federal government's budget for a particular fiscal year transmitted in January (first Monday after January 3rd) to the Congress by the president in accordance with the Budget and Accounting Act of 1921. Includes funding requests for all agencies and activities of the executive, legislative, and judicial branches. Also termed president's budget.

Federal Logistics Information System. Central repository for all logistics identification data.

Fences. Explicit limitations (ceilings and floors) established by Congress on the use of funds provided in an appropriations act. See also earmarks.

Field Studies Program (FSP). The FSP shall provide international students and visitors the opportunity to obtain a balanced understanding of the US and to increase their awareness of the basic issues involving internationally recognized human rights.

Fiscal year [FY]. Accounting period beginning 1 October and ending 30 September of the following year. The fiscal year is designated by the calendar year in which it ends. Fiscal Year 1995 begins on 1 October 1994 and ends 30 September 1995.

Fixed costs. Costs that do not vary with the volume of business, such as property taxes, insurance, depreciation, security, and minimum water and utility fees.

Fixed price type contract. A type of contract that generally provides for a firm price or, under appropriate circumstances, may provide for an adjustable price for the supplies or services being procured. Fixed price contracts are of several types, and are so designed as to facilitate proper pricing under varying circumstances.

Follow-on training. Sequential training following an initial course of training.

Force Activity Designator (FAD). An assignment of a Roman numeral designator between I and V to international partner countries, and to US defense organizations, which determines the supply priorities that the requisitioner can use to order materiel from the DOD supply system.

Foreign Assistance Act (FAA) of 1961. The basic law providing the authority and the general rules for the conduct of foreign assistance grant activities/programs by the USG. Published as 22 USC Sec. 2151 et seq.

Foreign exchange. Foreign exchange refers to a system whereby the national currency of one country may be exchanged for the currency of another country, thereby facilitating trade between countries.

Foreign internal defense (FID). Participation by civilian and military agencies of one government in any of the programs conducted by another government to free and protect its society from subversion, lawlessness, and insurgency.

Foreign liaison officer (FLO). An official representative, either military or civilian, of a foreign government or international organization stationed in the United States normally for the purpose of managing or monitoring security assistance programs.

Foreign military sales (FMS). That portion of US security assistance authorized by the AECA, and conducted on the basis of formal contracts or agreements between the United States government and an authorized recipient government or international organization. FMS includes government-to-government sales of defense articles or defense services, from DOD stocks or through new procurements under DOD-managed contracts, regardless of the source of financing.

Foreign military sales (FMS) case. A United States of America Letter of Offer and Acceptance (LOA) or a "United States Department of Defense Offer and Acceptance," which has been accepted by a foreign country.

Foreign service national (FSN). A local hire US embassy employee, usually of the same nationality as the host country, but sometimes a third country national (TCN). The FSN fills a billet with a formal position description and is paid according to a local compensation plan developed by the embassy. FSNs are hired and employed by either State Department directly or any other embassy agency (e.g., SCO) with a validated need and billet. Typical jobs for FSNs within a SCO include budget analyst, SA training manager, administrative assistant, and vehicle driver.

Financial Management Regulation (FMR) [DOD 7000.14-R, volume 15, Security Assistance Policy and Procedures]. A manual published by the Defense Finance and Accounting Service under the authority of DODI 7000.14. It establishes basic financial procedures for security assistance activities involving management, fiscal matters, accounting, pricing, budgeting for reimbursements to DOD appropriations accounts and revolving funds, auditing, international balance of payments, and matters affecting the DOD budget.

Foreign Military Sales Forecast Report. A companion document to the Javits Report, this report provides a two-year projection by fiscal year (vice one calendar year for Javits) but only addresses potential FMS sales.

Foreign Military Sales Order (FMSO). A term used to describe DD Forms 1513 or LOAs that implement Cooperative Logistics Supply Support Arrangements. Two DD Forms 1513/LOAs are written: a FMSO I and a FMSO II.

Foreign Military Sales Order I (FMSO I). Provides for the pipeline capitalization of a cooperative logistics support arrangement, which consists of stocks on hand and replenishment of stocks on order in which the participating country buys equity in the US supply system for the support of a specific weapons system. Even though stocks are not moved to a foreign country, delivery (equity) does in effect take place when the country pays for the case.

Foreign Military Sales Order II (FMSO II). Provides for the replenishment of withdrawals of consumption-type items (repair parts, primarily) from the DOD supply system to include charges for accessorial costs and a systems service charge.

Freight Forwarder. A commercial import/export company under contract to the FMS customer who arranges transportation of materiel from a point specified in the LOA to the final destination.

Formal training [military]. Training (including special training) in an officially designated course. It is conducted or administered according to an approved program of instruction. This training generally leads to a specific skill in a certain

Glossary of Selected Terms

military occupational specialty.

Future years defense program (FYDP). The official program summarizing the Secretary of Defense approved plans and programs for the Department of Defense.

G

General English Training (GET). Defense Language Institute–English Language Center (DLIELC) courses designed to develop the English language capability of IMS so they can attend DOD schools.

Generic code (GC). A three-digit code identified in the Military Articles and Services List (MASL) and in appendix D of the SAMM, which represents the type of materiel or services to be furnished according to a specific budget activity/project account classification.

Government Accountability Office (GAO). An agency of the legislative branch, responsible solely to the Congress, which functions to audit all negotiated government contracts and investigate all matters relating to the receipt, disbursement, and application of public funds.

Government furnished equipment (GFE). Items in the possession of, or acquired by the USG, and delivered to or otherwise made available to a contractor.

Government furnished material (GFM). US government property which may be incorporated into, or attached to an end item to be delivered under a contract or which may be consumed in the performance of a contract. It includes, but is not limited to, raw and processed material, parts, components, assemblies, small tools, and supplies.

Grant. A form of assistance involving a gift of funds, equipment, and/or services which is furnished by the US government to selected recipient nations on a free, nonrepayable basis.

Grant aid (GA). Military assistance rendered under the authority of the FAA for which the United States receives no dollar reimbursement. Such assistance currently consists of the international military education and training program (IMET), and pre-1990 MAP funding.

Guidance for Employment of the Force. The GEF provides two-year direction to CCMDs for operational planning, force management, security cooperation, and posture planning. The GEF is the method through which OSD translates strategic priorities set in the NSS, NDS, and QDR into implementable direction for operational activities. It consolidates and integrates DOD planning guidance related to operations and other military activities into a single, overarching guidance document.

H

Harmonization. The process and/or results of adjusting differences or inconsistencies to bring significant features into agreement.

Holding account. An account established for each FMS country/international organization for the purpose of recording and safeguarding unidentified and certain earmarked funds for future use.

Host nation support. Civil and military assistance provided by host nations to allied forces and organizations in peace, transition to war, and wartime.

Human rights. The relationship between individuals (citizens) and governments (states) where the legal system should protect the rights of the individual from abuses by said government. Examples of fundamental human rights include the right to life, liberty, security; freedom from enslavement, torture, and cruel, inhuman, or degrading punishment; freedom from arbitrary arrest, and presumptiton of innocence until found guilty by a competent and impartial tribunal. Additionally, all citizens should have the right to participate in their governments, either directly or through free elections of their representatives.

I

Immunity from criminal prosecution. Diplomatic agents enjoy complete immunity (protection) from the criminal jurisdiction of the host State and thus cannot be prosecuted (put on trial) absent a waiver no matter how serious the offense.

Implementation date [FMS]. The date when supply action on an FMS case is initiated or directed by an implementing agency.

Implementing agency (IA). The military department or defense agency responsible for the execution of military assistance programs. With respect to FMS, the military department or defense agency assigned responsibility by the Defense Security Cooperation Agency to prepare an LOA and to implement an FMS case. The implementing agency is responsible for the overall management of the actions that will result in delivery of the materials or services set forth in the Letter of Offer and Acceptance that was accepted by a foreign country or international organization.

Impoundment. Any executive action to withhold or delay spending appropriated funds as intended by the Congress. There are two kinds of impoundments: deferrals and rescissions.

In-country training. Training offered within the geographic boundaries of a recipient purchaser country, and conducted by members of DOD, other USG organizations, or contractors.

Indirect cost. Costs which are incurred for common or joint objectives, and which are not as readily subject to treatment as direct costs. See also direct costs.

Indirect offset. A general type of industrial or commercial compensation practice required of a contractor by a purchasing government as a condition for the purchase of defense articles/services. The form of compensation, which generally offsets a specific percentage of the cost of the purchase, is unrelated to the items purchased, and may include contractor purchases of commodities and manufactured goods produced in the purchasing country.

Industrial base. The capability of US industry to respond to the needs of and produce end items for the DOD. Also, that part of the total privately-owned and government-owned industrial production and maintenance capacity located in Canada expected to be available during emergencies to manufacture and repair items required by the US military services.

Initial deposit [FMS]. Money transferred to the credit of the Treasurer of the United States or other authorized officer at the time of acceptance of an LOA as full or partial payment for defense articles, services, or training contracted for by an eligible foreign country.

Initial operational capability (IOC). The first attainment of the capability to employ effectively a weapon, item of equipment, or system of approved specific characteristics, and which is manned or operated by an adequately trained, equipped, and supported military unit or force.

Initial provisioning. The process of determining the range and quantity of items (i.e., spares and repair parts, special tools, test equipment, and support equipment) required to support and maintain an item for an initial period of service. Its phases include the identification of items of supply, the establishment of data for catalog, technical manual, and allowance list preparation, and the preparation of instructions to assure delivery of necessary support items with related end articles.

Initial spares. Spare parts procured for the logistics support of a system during its initial period of operation.

Integrated materiel management. The exercise of total DOD management responsibility for a federal supply group and class, commodity, or item by a single agency. Includes requirements, funding, budgeting, storage, issuing, cataloging, standardizing, and procurement.

Interchangeability. A condition that exists when two or more items possess such functional and physical characteristics as to be equivalent in performance, fit, and durability, and are capable of being exchanged one for the other without alteration of the items themselves or of adjoining items, except for adjustment.

Interfund billing system (IBS). Under IBS, a selling activity will credit the appropriation or fund which owns the materiel and/or finances the accessorial charges at the time of billing the ordering activity, and will charge the appropriations/funds of the ordering activity. IBS normally encompasses all supply system sales and purchases of materiel, including perishable substances, bulk petroleum, oil, lubricants, and aviation fuel. Reimbursable sales will be billed at the time items are dropped from inventory except that billings for sales under FMS and MAP will be based on constructive delivery [DODI 7420.12].

Internal defense. The full range of measures taken by a government to free and protect its society from subversion, lawlessness, and insurgency.

International armaments cooperation programs (IACP). Programs that promote rationalization, standardization and interoperability (RSI) and comprise one or more specific cooperative projects whose arrangements are defined in a written agreement between DOD and one or more countries.

International cooperative administrative support services (ICASS). The purpose of ICASS is to provide, on a reimbursable basis, needed administrative services to USG offices located overseas. The administrative support services are provided by ICASS personnel of the DOS stationed at overseas US embassies, consulates, etc. Normally, such personnel perform a variety of services including: personnel, budget and fiscal, general services, communications, security and guard, and management services. The specific services required are the basis of an agreement between DOS and the requesting agency. Charges are based on the amount of services received, with each agency, including DOS, paying its share. The ICAAS system provides an equitable method of sharing the costs of providing "common type" administrative support to the SCO and other agencies at the post.

International logistics. The planning, negotiating, and implementation of supporting logistics arrangements between nations, their forces and agencies. It includes furnishing logistics support (major end items, materiel, and/or services) to, or receiving logistics support from, one or more friendly foreign governments, international organizations, or military forces, with or without reimbursement.

International Logistics Communication System. A fee-for-service telecommunications system established for international partners to communicate supply requirements directly to the DOD supply system through the Defense Data Network.

International Logistics Control Organization. An organization within each of the military departments that is dedicated to managing logistics support programs and logistics transactions in support of foreign military sales and security cooperation programs.

International military education and training (IMET) program. That component of the US security assistance program which provides training to selected foreign military and defense associated civilian personnel on a grant basis. Training is provided at US military facilities and with US Armed Forces in the US and overseas, and through the use of Mobile Training Teams. Training also may be provided by contract technicians, contractors (including instruction at civilian institutions), or by correspondence courses. The IMET Program is authorized by the FAA.

International military student (IMS). A national of a foreign government, with military or civilian status of that government, who is receiving education or training or is touring USG activities under the sponsorship of the security assistance training program (SATP).

International military student office/manager (IMSO/IMSM). A US military office that is designated to coordinate and monitor the local SA training program and provide required administrative support for international military students in training at that activity. Also responsible for the conduct of the DOD Informational Program.

International narcotics control and law enforcement (INCLE). Counter drug bureau/programs managed by DOS, but can have materiel, services, and training support provided and managed by DOD using SC assets and procedures.

International Traffic in Arms Regulation (ITAR). A document prepared by the Directorate of Defense Trade Control (DDTC), Bureau of Political-Military Affairs, Department of State, providing licensing and regulatory provisions for the import and export of defense articles, technical data, and services. The ITAR also includes the US Munitions List. Published in the Federal Register as 22 CFR 120-130.

Interoperability. The ability of systems, units, or forces to provide services to and accept services from other systems, units or forces, and to use the services so exchanged to enable them to operate effectively together.

Inventory control point (ICP). The organizational element within a DOD system which is assigned responsibility for materiel management of a group of items including such management functions as the computation of requirements, the initiation of procurement or disposal actions, distribution management, and rebuild direction.

Inviolability of person or premises. Protections enjoyed by "diplomatic agents," which means: (1) they should not be arrested or detained; (2) they are owed a special measure of respect and protection; (3) and neither their property nor residences may be entered or searched.

Invitational travel order (ITO). A written authorization (DD Form 2285) for international military students to travel to, from, and between US activities for the purpose of training under an approved and funded IMET or FMS program.

Item identification number. A seven-character identifier assigned to each line of training in the MASL. The first character is a letter that identifies the MILDEP offering the training (B Army, P-Navy, D-Air Force). The following six characters are numbers that identify the specific item of training. The identification number is used in all FMS and IMET training programs and implementation documents.

Item manager (IM). An individual within the organization of an inventory control point or other such organization assigned management responsibility for one or more specific items of materiel.

J

Javits report. The President's estimate to the Congress of potential or proposed arms transfers during a given calendar year.

Joint resolution. A legislative resolution, designated H J Res (House) or S J Res (Senate) which requires the approval of both houses and the signature of the president, just as a bill does, and which has the force of law if approved. There is no practical difference between a bill and a joint resolution. A joint resolution generally is used to deal with a limited matter such as a single appropriation. Congressional rejection of a proposed arms transfer, lease, third country transfer, or a proposed international cooperative project takes the form of a joint resolution of disapproval.

Joint Security Assistance Training (JSAT) Regulation. Obsolete, refer to the JSCET.

Joint Security Cooperation Education and Training Regulation (JSCET). Regulation that prescribes policies, responsibilities, procedures, and administration for the education and training of international military students by the Departments of the Army, Navy and Air Force as authorized by US security assistance legislation. Regulation also is applicable to the Marine Corps and Coast Guard as well.

Joint Strategic Capabilities Plan. The JSCP is the primary vehicle through which the CJCS exercises responsibility for directing the preparation of joint plans. The JSCP provides military strategic and operational guidance to CCDRs, Service Chiefs, Combat Support Agencies, and applicable DoD agencies for preparation of campaign plans and contingency plans based on current military capabilities. It serves as the link between strategic guidance provided in the GEF and the joint operation planning activities and products that accomplish that guidance. In addition to communicating to the CCMDs specific planning guidance necessary for deliberate planning, the JSCP also translates strategic policy end states from the GEF into military campaign and contingency plan guidance for CCDRs and expands guidance to include global defense posture, security cooperation, and other steady-state activities. The JSCP is described in detail in CJCSI 3110.01G, *Joint Strategic Capabilities Plan* (classified).

L

Language training detachment (LTD). A group of personnel from the Defense Language Institute, English Language Center (DLIELC), Lackland Air Force Base, Texas, performing duty in a foreign country or in CONUS on a military installation away from DLIELC. They serve as consultants or instructors in English as a foreign language.

Lease (security assistance). An agreement for the temporary transfer of the right of possession and use of a non-excess defense article or articles to a foreign government or international organization, with the lessee agreeing to reimburse the USG in US dollars for all costs incurred in leasing such articles, and to maintain, protect, repair, or restore the article(s), subject to and under the authority of section 61, AECA (Title 22 USC 2796).

Letter of offer and acceptance (LOA). US Department of Defense letter by which the US government offers to sell to a foreign government or international organization US defense articles and defense services pursuant to the Arms Export Control Act, as amended. The LOA lists the items and/or services, estimated costs, and the terms and conditions of sale; it also provides for the signature of an appropriate foreign government official to indicate acceptance.

Letter of request (LOR). The term used to identify a request from an eligible FMS participant country for the purchase of US defense articles and services. The request may be in message or letter format.

Licensed production. Licensed production involves agreements made by US commercial firms with international organizations, foreign governments, or foreign commercial firms to produce weapon systems.

Life cycle cost. The total costs to the government of acquisition and ownership of a system over its useful life. It includes the costs of development, acquisition, support, and, where applicable, disposal.

Line item number. A three-digit alpha/numeric code that identifies a detail line item on the LOA. This code is perpetuated on the customer's bill.

Living allowance. An authorized allowance paid to an international military student while in training under the IMET program.

Glossary of Selected Terms

Loan. An agreement for the temporary transfer of the right of possession and use of a defense article or articles not acquired with military assistance funds to a foreign government or international organization, at no rental charge to the transferee, with the transferring US military department being reimbursed from MAP funds, subject to and under authority of section 503, FAA. Also, applies to loans to a NATO or major non-NATO ally of materials, supplies, or equipment for the purpose of carrying out a program of cooperative research, development, testing, or evaluation subject to and under the authority of section 65, AECA.

Locally employed staff. The general term used for Foreign Service nationals, as well as some US citizens, who ordinarily reside in the host country and are thus subject to its labor law. LE staff are employed at a US mission, or at an office of the American Institute in Taiwan by the US Government under the authority of the COM and are normally paid under the local compensation plan.

Logistics. The science of planning and carrying out the movement and maintenance of forces. In its most comprehensive sense, involves those aspects of military operations which deal with:

    a. Design and development, acquisition storage, movement, distribution, maintenance, evacuation, and disposition of materials

    b. Movement, evacuation, and hospitalization of personnel

    c. Acquisition or construction, maintenance, operation, and disposition of facilities

    d. Acquisitioning or furnishing of services

Long-lead items/long-lead time materials. Those components of a system or piece of equipment for which the times to design and fabricate are the longest, and therefore, to which an early commitment of funds may be desirable in order to meet the earliest possible date of system completion.

M

Maintenance. The upkeep of property, necessitated by wear and tear, which neither adds to the permanent value of the property nor appreciably prolongs its intended life, but keeps it in efficient operating condition. The term "preventive maintenance" involves deterring something from going wrong; the term "corrective maintenance" involves restoring something to its proper condition.

Maintenance concept/plan. A description of maintenance considerations and constraints for system/equipment under development. A preliminary maintenance concept is developed and submitted by the operating command as part of the preliminary system operational concept for each alternative solution candidate; the implementing and supporting commands provide inputs to the concept/plan.

Major defense equipment (MDE). Any item of significant military equipment on the United States Munitions List having a nonrecurring research and development cost of more than $50 million or a total production cost of more than $200 million. Also defined in section 47 (6), AECA.

Major line item. A program line for which the requirement is expressed quantitatively as well as in dollars. These lines are identified in the military articles and services list(s) (MASL) by a unit of issue (XX) other than dollars.

Major item material excess (MIMEX) offers. Involves major items of MAP equipment declared excess by the original recipient and which are offered to eligible MAP materiel recipients for application against funded current year and prior year undelivered MAP program balances.

Major non-NATO allies. Designated as Argentina, Australia, Bahrain, Egypt, Israel, Japan, Jordan, Kuwait, Morocco, New Zealand, Pakistan, Philippines, Republic of Korea, Taiwan, and Thailand [Sec. 517, FAA].

Materiel management. Direction and control of those aspects of logistics which deal with materiel, including the functions of identification, cataloging, standardization, requirements determination, procurement, inspection, quality control, packaging, storage, distribution, disposal, maintenance, mobilization planning, industrial readiness planning, and item management classification; encompasses materiel control, inventory control, inventory management, and supply management.

Memorandum of agreement (MOA) or memorandum of understanding (MOU). A written agreement between governments or a government and international organization signed by authorized representatives and signifying an intent to be legally bound.

Military articles and services list (MASL). A catalogue of materiel, services, and training used in the planning and programming of Military Assistance Program (MAP), International Military Education and Training (IMET), and Foreign Military Sales (FMS). Separate MASLs are maintained for IMET and FMS training that provides data on course identification, course availability, price, and duration of training.

Military Assistance Advisory Group (MAAG). A joint service group based overseas which primarily administers United States military assistance planning and programming in a host country. The term MAAG encompasses Joint US Military Advisory Groups, Military Missions, Military Assistance Groups, US Military Groups, and US Military Representatives exercising responsibility within a US Diplomatic Mission for security assistance and other related DOD matters. Defense Attachés are included only when specifically designated as having security assistance functions. See also security assistance organization.

Military assistance program (MAP). That portion of the United States security assistance program authorized by the Foreign Assistance Act of 1961, as amended, which provides defense articles and services to recipients on a nonreimbursable (grant) basis. Funding for MAP was consolidated under the Foreign Military Financing (FMF) Program beginning in fiscal year 1990.

Military Assistance Program Address Directory (MAPAD). The MAPAD provides clear text addresses of country representatives, freight forwarders, and customers-within-country required for releasing FMS and MAP shipments processed in accordance with military standard requisitioning and issuing procedures (MILSTRIP), and addresses required for the forwarding of related documentation.

Military civic action. The use of preponderantly indigenous military forces on projects useful to the local population at all levels in such fields as education, training, public works, agriculture, transportation, communications, health sanitation, and others contributing to economic and social development, which would also serve to improve the standing of the military forces with the population. (US forces may at times advise or engage in military civic action in overseas areas.)

Military Department (MILDEP). One of the departments within the Department of Defense created by the National Security Act of 1947, as amended. The Military Departments are: the Department of the Air Force, the Department of the Army, and the Department of the Navy.

Military Service (MILSVC). A branch of the Armed Forces of the United States, established by act of Congress, in which persons are appointed, enlisted, or inducted for military service, and which operates and is administered within a military or executive department. The Military Services are: the United States Army, the United States Navy, the United States Air Force, the United States Marine Corps, and the United States Coast Guard.

Military standard billing system (MILSBILLS). This system provides data elements, codes, standard mechanized procedures, and formats for use by DOD components for billing, collecting and related accounting for sales from system stocks, including direct deliveries. The mechanized procedures apply to MAP and FMS as outlined in DODI 7420.12 (regarding Interfund Billing System).

Military standard requisitioning and issue procedures (MILSTRIP). A uniform procedure established by the Department of Defense to govern the requisition and issue of materiel within standardized priorities.

Mobile education team (MET). A team of US DOD personnel on temporary duty in a foreign country for the purpose of educating foreign personnel in resource management. Such teams are normally funded from Expanded IMET Program funds.

Mobile training team (MTT). A team of US DOD personnel on temporary duty in a foreign country for the purpose of training foreign personnel in the operation, maintenance, or other support of weapon systems and support equipment, as well as training for general military operations. MTTs may be funded from either FMS or IMET Programs.

Modification. Modification of a case constitutes and administrative or price change to an existing LOA, without revising the scope of the case.

Munitions List. The US Munitions List is an enumeration of defense articles and defense services and is published in the Department of State's International Traffic in Arms Regulations.

N

National Defense Strategy. The NDS flows from the NSS, informs the NMS, and provides the foundation for building the legislatively mandated quadrennial defense review (QDR), which focuses the DOD's strategies, capabilities, and forces on operations of today and tomorrow. The NDS addresses how the Armed Forces of the United States will fight and win America's wars and describes how DOD will support the objectives outlined in the NSS. It also provides a framework for other DOD strategic guidance, specifically on deliberate planning, force development, and intelligence (JP 5-0).

National Military Strategy. The NMS, derived from the NSS and NDS, prioritizes and focuses the efforts of the Armed Forces of the United States while conveying the CJCS's advice with regard to the security environment and the necessary military actions to protect vital US interests. The NMS defines the national military objectives, how to accomplish these objectives, and addresses the military capabilities required to execute the strategy (JP 5-0).

National Policy and Procedures for the Disclosure of Classified Military Information to Foreign Governments and International Organizations (U) [Short Title: National Disclosure Policy (NDP-1)]. Promulgates national policy and procedures in the form of specific disclosure criteria and limitations, definitions of terms, release arrangements, and other guidance required by US departments and agencies having occasion to release classified US military information to foreign governments and international organizations.

National Security Strategy. The NSS is a comprehensive report required annually by Title 50, U.S.C., section 404a. It is prepared by the executive branch of the government for Congress and outlines the major national security concerns of the US and how the administration plans to address them using all instruments of national power. The document is purposely general in content, and its implementation relies on elaborating guidance provided in supporting documents (JP 5-0).

National stock number. A thirteen-digit stock number consisting of a four-digit federal supply classification and a nine-digit national item identification number.

NATO Codification System (NCS). A supply codification system developed by the US and adopted by NATO and non-NATO partners. The NCS standardizes item identification processes to permit item interchangeability between international partners and contributes to systems interoperability.

Net case value. Total amount of the cost reflected on line 21 of the DD Form 1513 or line 8 of the LOA.

Nonexpendable supplies and materiel. Supplies which are not consumed in use and retain their original identity, such as weapons, machines, tools, and equipment.

Nonrecurring costs (NRC or NC). Those costs funded by an RDT&E appropriation to develop or improve a product or technology either through contract or in-house effort. Also, those one-time costs incurred in support of previous production of a specified model and those costs incurred in support of a total projected production run.

Nonrecurring demands. A one-time requisition from a customer that is not used to compute demand-based requirements.

Nonrepayable credits/loans. Grant funds appropriated by Congress for use in the Foreign Military Financing Program to selected countries for their use in financing FMS acquisitions of defense articles, defense services, and training under the authority of section 23, AECA. Additionally, certain countries may be authorized these grant funds to finance direct commercial sales.

Nonstandard article. For FMS purposes, a nonstandard article is one that the DOD does not manage, either because an applicable end item has been retired or because it was never purchased for DOD components.

Nonstandard service. For FMS purposes a nonstandard service is a service that the DOD does not routinely provide for itself or for purchase.

Notice of Availability (NOA). A written notification that material requiring special handling is ready to be shipped. The NOA is sent by the shipper to the purchaser or freight forwarder for oversized, hazardous, explosive, classified or perishable material, and requires a response from the recipient with delivery instructions.

O

Obligation. A duty to make a future payment of money. The duty is incurred as soon as an order is placed, or a contract is awarded for the delivery of goods and the performance of services. An obligation legally encumbers a specified sum of money which will require an outlay or expenditure in the future.

Obligational authority (OA, as used in FMS). A document or authority passed from DFAS–IN to an implementing DOD component that allows obligations to be incurred against a given FMS case in an amount not to exceed the value specified in the obligational authority.

Observer training (OBT). Special training conducted to permit international military students to observe US military techniques and procedures.

Offer date. The date which appears on the offer portion of an LOA and which indicates the date on which an FMS offer is made to a foreign buyer.

Offset agreement. An agreement, arrangement, or understanding between a US supplier of defense articles or services and a foreign country under which the supplier agrees to purchase or acquire, to promote the purchase or acquisition by other US persons, of goods or services produced, manufactured, grown, or extracted, in whole or in part, in that foreign country in consideration for the purchase by the country of defense articles or services from the supplier [Sec. 39A(d)(1), AECA]. See also direct offset and indirect offset.

On-the-job training (OJT). A training program whereby international military students (IMSs) acquire knowledge and skills through the actual performance of duties under competent supervision in accordance with an approved, planned program.

Operation & maintenance (O&M) costs. Costs associated with equipment, supplies, and services required to train, operate, and maintain forces in a recipient country, including the cost of spare parts other than concurrent spares and initial stockages, ammunition and missiles used in training or replacements for such items expended in training or operations, rebuild and overhaul costs (excluding modernization) of equipment subsequent to initial issue, training and other services that do not constitute investment costs, and administrative costs associated with overall program management and administration.

Oral Proficiency Interview (OPI). English language test that rates English language speaking ability for international military students. Certain courses require an OPI test be taken and a specific OPI score to be met before an IMS can attend the course.

Ordering activity. An activity that originates a requisition or order for procurement, production, or performance of work or service by another activity.

Ordnance. Explosives, chemicals, pyrotechnic and similar stores, e.g., bombs, guns, ammunition, flares, smoke, and napalm.

Orientation tour (OT). A tour arranged for key foreign personnel that may be funded under FMS or IMET to acquaint them with US organizations, equipment, facilities, or methods of operation at various locations.

Outlays. Actual expenditures. Checks issued, interest occurred on the public debt, or other payments. Total budget outlays consist of the sum of the outlays from appropriations and other funds in the budget, less receipts (i.e., refunds and reimbursements).

Outside CONUS. All geographic areas not within the territorial boundaries of the continental United States. OCONUS includes Hawaii and Alaska.

Overseas training. Training provided foreign nationals at training installations outside the US.

P

Packing, crating, handling, & transportation (PCH&T). The resources, processes, procedures, design considerations, and methods to ensure that all system, equipment, and support items are preserved, packaged, handled, and transported properly, including: environmental considerations, equipment preservation requirements for short-and-long-term storage, and transportability. One of the principal elements of integrated logistics support (ILS).

Paramilitary forces. Forces or groups which are distinct from the regular armed forces of any country, but resemble them in organization, equipment, training, or mission.

Payment on delivery [FMS]. An FMS term of sale in which the US government issues a bill to the FMS purchaser at the time of delivery of defense articles or the rendering of defense services from DOD resources. This term may only be used pursuant to a written statutory determination by the Director, DSCA, who may find it in the national interest to authorize such payment. Based on presidential action, this term may also be modified to read "Payment 120 Days After Delivery."

Payment schedule. List of dollar amounts and when they are due from the foreign customer. The payment schedule supplements the Letter of Offer and Acceptance (LOA) presented to the customer. After acceptance of the LOA, the payment schedule generally serves as the basis for billing to the customer. Changes in the estimated costs of an FMS case may require changes in the accompanying payment schedule.

Performing activity. An activity which is responsible for performing work or service, including the production of material and/or the procurement of goods and services from other contractors and activities.

Performance-Based Logistics. The DOD strategy of purchasing support in terms of systems readiness and performance outcome, rather than simply acquiring and stocking material on demand. DOD contracts with a manufacturer who is responsible for ensuring optimum system performance by providing complete logistics support to the customer.

Planning, programming, and budgeting system (PPBS). An integrated system for the establishment, maintenance, and revision of the Future Years Defense Program (FYDP) and the DOD budget.

Port of Debarkation (POD). A military or commercial air or ocean port at which materiel is offloaded. Also referred to as the Port of Discharge.

Port of Embarkation (POE). A military or commercial air or ocean port at which a carrier begins the journey to deliver materiel to the consignee. This is also referred to as the Port of Exit.

Price and availability (P&A) data. Prepared by the MILDEPs, DSAA, and other DOD components in response to a foreign government's request for preliminary data for the possible purchase of a defense article or service. P&A data are not considered valid for the preparation of an LOA. Furnishing of this data does not constitute a commitment for the USG to offer for sale the articles and services for which the data are provided.

Procurement lead time. The interval in months between the initiation of procurement action and receipt into the supply system of the production model (excluding prototypes) purchased as the result of such actions; procurement lead time is composed of two elements, production lead time, and administrative lead time.

Procuring contracting officer (PCO). The individual authorized to enter into contracts for supplies and services on behalf of the government by detailed bids or negotiations and who is responsible for overall procurement under such contracts.

Production lead time. The time interval between the placement of a contract and receipt into the supply system of materiel purchased.

Professional military education (PME). Career training designed to provide or enhance leadership and the recipient force's capabilities to conduct military planning, programming, management, budgeting, and force development to the level of sophistication appropriate to that force.

Program management review (PMR). A management level review held by a Systems Program Office or Systems Program Manager for the purpose of determining the status of an assigned system. PMRs are designed as tools to identify problems, if any, and to develop appropriate follow-up actions as required.

Progress payments. Those payments made to contractors or DOD industrial fund activities as work progresses under a contract; payments are made on the basis of cost incurred or percentage of work completed, or of a particular stage of completion accomplished prior to actual delivery and acceptance of contract items.

Provisioning. See initial provisioning.

Q

Quadrennial Defense Review. Existing legislation requires the Secretary of Defense to conduct a QDR and to submit a report on the QDR to Congress every four years. The QDR articulates a national defense strategy consistent with the most recent NSS by defining force structure, modernization plans, and a budget plan allowing the military to successfully execute the full range of missions within that strategy (JP 5-0).

Quality assurance (QA). A planned and systematic pattern of all actions necessary to provide confidence that adequate technical requirements are established, that products and services conform to established technical requirements, and that satisfactory performance is achieved.

R

Ratification. The formal action of the president in giving effect to a treaty that has been approved by the Senate. The treaty then is officially proclaimed and becomes legally enforceable.

Rationalization, standardization and interoperability (RSI). Any action that increases the effectiveness of NATO Forces through more efficient or effective use of defense resources committed to the Alliance.

Reapportionment. A revision of an annual apportionment of funds either upwards or downwards, accomplished within the fiscal year for which the original apportionment applied.

Reappropriation. The congressional carrying over of funds unused in one year to the following year. For example, ESF or IMET funds which at the end of the fiscal year are not reserved or obligated, are customarily made available by the Congress for use in the subsequent fiscal year.

Reciprocal defense procurement. Procurement actions which are implemented under memoranda of understanding/ memoranda of agreement (MOU/MOA) between the US and various participating nations whereby the participants agree to effect complementary acquisitions of defense articles from each other's country.

Recoverable item. An item that is normally not consumed in use and is subject to return for repair or disposal. See also reparable item.

Recoupments. Adjustments or cancellations of outstanding MAP orders in prior year program accounts that generate additional funds for the current year operations.

Reimbursable expenditure. An expenditure made for another agency, fund, appropriation, or for a private individual, firm or corporation, which subsequently will be recovered.

Reimbursements. Amounts received by an activity for the cost of material, work, or services furnished to others, for credit to an appropriation or their fund account.

Reliability. A fundamental characteristic of an item of material expressed as the probability that it will perform its intended function for a specified period of time under stated conditions.

Reorder point. The point at which time a stock replenishment requisition is submitted to maintain the predetermined stock age objective.

Repair and replace [FMS]. Programs by which eligible Cooperative Logistics Supply Support Arrangement (CLSSA) customers return repairable carcasses to the US and receive a serviceable item without awaiting the normal repair cycle time frame.

Repair and return. Programs by which eligible foreign countries return unserviceable repairable items for entry into the US military department repair cycle. Upon completion of repairs, the same item is returned to the country and the actual cost of the repair is billed to the country.

Reparable item. An item that can be reconditioned or economically repaired for reuse when it becomes unserviceable

Replenishment spare parts. Items and equipment, both repairable and consumable, purchased as spares by inventory control points and which are required to replenish stocks for use in the maintenance, overhaul, and repair of equipment, such as ships, tanks, guns, aircraft, engines, etc.

Reprogramming. The transfer of funds between program elements or line items within an appropriation.

Rescission of budget authority. The permanent cancellation of budget authority prior to the time when the authority officially terminates. The rescission process begins when the president proposes a Rescission to the Congress for fiscal or policy reasons. Unlike the deferral of budget authority, which occurs unless Congress acts to disapprove the deferral, rescission of budget authority occurs only if both Houses of Congress approve the rescission, by simple majority, within forty-five days of continuous session.

Research and development. Those program costs primarily associated with research and development efforts, including the development of a new or improved capability to the point where it is ready for operational use.

Resolution. A "simple" Congressional resolution, designated H. Res (House) or S. Res (Senate), deals with matters entirely within the prerogatives of one house or the other. It requires neither passage by the other chamber nor approval by the president, and it does not have the force of law. Most such resolutions deal with the rules or procedures of one house. They also are used to express the sentiments of a single house, such as condolence to the family of a deceased member, or to comment on foreign policy or executive business. A simple resolution is the vehicle for a "rule" from the House Rules Committee. See also Concurrent Resolution and Joint Resolution.

Retainable Instructional Material (RIM). Unclassified books, pamphlets, maps, charts, or other course material issued to and retained by the international military student and their US classmates. It also includes official Field Studies Program materials.

Revolving fund. A fund established to finance a cycle of operations to which reimbursements and collections are returned for reuse in a manner that will maintain the principal of the fund; e.g., working capital funds and industrial funds.

Rule of Law. A fundamental component of a democratic society where all members of said society—both citizens and rulers—are bound by a set of clearly-defined and universally-accepted laws. In a democracy, this is manifested in an independent judiciary, a free press, and a system of checks and balances on leaders through free elections.

S

Safety level. The quantity of materiel, in addition to the operating level of supply required to be on hand to permit continuous operations.

Security assistance (SA). A group of programs authorized by the Foreign Assistance Act (FAA) of 1961, as amended, and the Arms Export Control Act (AECA) of 1976, as amended, or other related statutes by which the United States provides defense articles, military training, and other defense related services, by grant, loan, cash sale, or lease, in furtherance of national policies and objectives [Joint Pub 1-02, as amended through 14 April 2006]. Table C1.T1, SAMM, provides a listing of twelve major security assistance programs, of which seven are administered by DOD and five are administered by DOS. The seven programs managed by DOD are included in the DOD-defined security cooperation program.

Security Assistance Management Manual (SAMM) [DSCA 5105.38M]. A manual published by the Defense Security Cooperation Agency. It sets forth the responsibilities, policies, and procedures governing the administration of security assistance within the Department of Defense [available online: http://www.dsca.mil/samm/].

Security assistance management review (SAMR). A management review led by a security assistance organization, for the purpose of determining the status of one or more specific programs. Such reviews may include the entire range of a purchaser's security assistance program.

Security assistance network (SAN). An Internet-based network developed for the SA community to provide access to the world wide web, identification of web sites of interest to the SA community, an E-mail system (primarily for overseas users), a library function for the storage and conveyance of large data files, a bulletin board function for viewing SA documents, and the hosting of SA training and budgetary data.

Security cooperation. Activities undertaken by the DOD to encourage and enable international partners to work with the US to achieve strategic objectives. It includes all DOD interactions with foreign defense and security establishments, including all DOD-administered security assistance programs, that: build defense and security relationships that promote specific US security interests, including all international armaments cooperation activities and security assistance activities; develop allied and friendly military capabilities for self-defense and multinational operations; and provide US forces with peacetime and contingency access to host nations.

Security Cooperation Education and Training Working Group (SCETWG). An annual geographic combatant command conference conducted for the purpose of establishing the SA and SC training program for each country. Attendees are the SCO training manager and representatives from DSCA, the MILDEP, training agencies , and other key SC training management personnel. Actual IMET and FMS training programs are submitted, reviewed and determinations made as to training availability. The CTFP program is also a major focus of the SCETWG.

Security Cooperation Information Portal (SCIP). A DOD managed web-based system that provides access to FMS and security cooperation case-related data extracts as well as numerous other capabilities.

Security cooperation organization (SCO). Those DOD organizations permanently located in a foreign country and assigned responsibilities for carrying out of security cooperation management functions under section 515 of the Foreign Assistance Act and under Joint Publication 1-02, regardless of the actual name given to such DOD Component. The generic term SCO replaces the former term security assistance office (SAO).

Security Cooperation Officer Token Administrator. The individual designated, in writing, by the security cooperation office Chief to oversee and maintain the custody of each SCIP token within the security cooperation office.

Security force assistance (SFA). DOD activities that contribute to the unified action by the USG to support the development of the capacity and capability of foreign security forces (FSF) and their supporting institutions. (DODI 5000.68, Oct 2010)

Senior Defense Official (SDO) and Defense Attaché (DATT). Principal DOD official in a US embassy, as designated by the Secretary of Defense. The SDO or DATT is the Chief of Mission's principal military advisor on defense and national security issues, the senior diplomatically accredited DOD military officer assigned to a diplomatic mission, and the single point of contact for all DOD matters involving the embassy or DOD elements assigned to or working from the embassy. The SDO or DATT is considered the dual-hatted chief of both the security cooperation organization (SCO) and defense attaché office (DAO) in the embassy. This position was established by DODD 5105.75, Department of Defense Operations at US Embassies, December 21, 2007. The same document gives coordinating authority (see glossary definition) to the SDO or DATT for the purpose of ensuring that all DOD elements in a country are working in consonance with each other and under the guidance of the Chief of Mission. The SDO or DATT program replaces the now defunct US Defense Representative (USDR) model.

Security Risk Categories (SRC). Categories designated by the security community that determine the transportation security requirements for movement of sensitive Arms, Ammunition, and Explosives (AA&E), based on capability, portability and volatility of the explosive.

Sensitive Materiel. Volatile and dangerous explosives which require special handling and transportation arrangements. The term sensitive also applies to highly desirable selected technologies which are not explosive, but which require special security procedures for transportation.

Sequestration. Refers to the issuance of a presidential order canceling budgetary spending in order to reduce the deficit by the required amount for that year.

Services. Includes any service, test, inspection, repair, training, publication, technical or other assistance, or defense information furnished as military assistance under the FAA, or furnished through FMS under the AECA.

Significant military equipment (SME). Defense articles for which special export controls are warranted because of the capacity of such articles for substantial military utility or capability. These items are identified on the United States Munitions List in the *International Traffic in Arms Regulations* (ITAR) by an asterisk preceding the item category listing.

Shipper. The commercial or military manufacturer, vendor, supply depot, or repair facility that ships material in support of security cooperation programs on behalf of the DOD.

Single Vendor Integrity (SVI). The requirement that all replacement spares and support equipment for a specific weapon system are provided by the same manufacturer that provided the original equipment.

Site Survey. A team of US personnel who assess the FMS customer's logistics capabilities and shortfalls to determine the optimum type and quantity of logistics support to be included in the Total Package Approach.

Sole source acquisition. A contract for the purchase of supplies or services that is entered into or proposed to be entered into by an agency after soliciting and negotiating with only one source.

Solicitation. The formal document used in negotiating acquisitions to communicate government requirements to prospective contractors and to solicit proposals.

Source selection. The process wherein the requirements, facts, recommendations, and government policy relevant to an award decision in a competitive procurement of a system/project are examined and the decision made.

Spares/spare parts. An individual part, subassembly, or assembly supplied for the maintenance or repair of systems or equipment.

Glossary of Selected Terms

Special Assignment Airlift Mission (SAAM). A dedicated US military aircraft, chartered to deliver sensitive, classified or explosive defense articles to a specific customer location, when no commercial delivery capability exists.

Specialized English training (SET). Nine weeks of Specialized English Training at DLIELC provides intensive practice in the functional English language skills and technical terminology identified by Military Service as essential for success in technical training courses and professional military education. Focuses on terminology the international military student will need to know in follow on courses.

Staging cost. The cost incurred by the Department of Defense in consolidation of materiel before shipment to an FMS customer. Includes costs incident to storage and control of inventory, consolidation of incoming articles into a single shipment, and a break in CONUS transportation.

Standardization. The process by which DOD achieves the closest practicable cooperation among the military services and defense agencies for the most efficient use of research, development, and production resources.

Standardization agreement [NATO]. The record of an agreement among several or all of the members nations of NATO to adopt like or similar military equipment, ammunition, supplies and stores; and operational, logistics, and administrative procedures. National acceptance of a NATO allied publication issued by the Military Agency for Standardization may be recorded as a Standardization agreement.

Standardized training list (STL). List of all the Security Cooperation training courses that a country has requested from DOD and the status of the courses.

Supplemental appropriations. An act appropriating funds in addition to those provided for in the annual appropriations acts. Supplemental appropriations provide additional budget authority beyond the original estimates for programs or activities (including new programs authorized after the date of the original appropriations act) in cases where the need for funds is too urgent to be postponed until enactment of the next regular appropriations bill.

Supply Discrepancy Report (SDR). A process for international customers to file a complaint with the DOD for product loss, quality deficiencies, damage, and various other problems associated with the delivery of material under the FMS program.

Surface Deployment and Distribution Command (SDDC). A US Army organization serving as the single DOD manager for military traffic, land transportation, and common-user ocean terminals. The SDDC provides transportation planning and support for the surface movement of passengers and cargo within the Defense Transportation System, including within CONUS.

Systems acquisition process. The sequence of acquisition activities starting from an agency's reconciliation of its mission needs with its capabilities, priorities, and resources, and extending through the introduction of a system into operational use or the otherwise successful achievement of program objectives.

System Support Buyout. An opportunity for international partners to make a final purchase of major items and associated spares and support equipment of a major system that is being terminated in the DOD inventory, prior to the contracts or production being discontinued.

T

Technical assistance field team (TAFT). A team of US DOD personnel deployed on PCS status, normally for one year or longer, to a foreign country to provide technical assistance and training to foreign military personnel in the operation, maintenance, and employment of specific equipment, technology, weapons, supporting systems, or in other special skills related to military functions.

Technical assistance team (TAT). A team of US DOD personnel deployed to a foreign country on TDY status (i.e., up to 179 days) to place into operation, operate, maintain, and repair equipment provided under the FMS or MAP programs.

Technical Coordination Group (TCG). A US Air Force aviation support program that provides technical assistance for specific aircraft and engines. The TCG provides dedicated technical and engineering support to international partners who have purchased the aircraft or engines through the FMS program.

Technical data (TD). Recorded information of a scientific or technical nature, regardless of form or characteristic. Examples of technical data packages include research and engineering drawings and associated lists, specifications, standards, process sheets, manuals, technical reports, catalog item identifications, and related information and computer software documentation.

Technical data package (TDP). Normally includes technical design and manufacturing information sufficient to enable the construction or manufacture of a defense item component modification, or to enable the performance of certain maintenance or production processes. It may include blueprints, drawings, plans, or instructions that can be used or adapted for use in the design, production, manufacture, or maintenance of defense items or technology.

Technical manual. A publication containing instructions designed to meet the needs of personnel responsible for (or being trained in) the operation, maintenance, service, overhaul, installation, and inspection of specific items of equipment and materiel.

Test control officer (TCO). US military or civilian personnel designated to administer, supervise, and control ECL testing and test materials. Must be a US citizen, not a foreign national "local hire" civilian, or foreign military officer or NCO.

Theater Campaign Plans. Plans developed by geographic combatant commands that focus on the command's steady-state activities, which include operations, security cooperation, and other activities designed to achieve theater strategic end states. It is incumbent upon geographic combatant commanders to ensure any supporting campaign plans address objectives in the Global Environmental Fund global planning effort and their respective theater campaign plans. Contingency plans for responding to crisis scenarios are treated as branch plans to the campaign plan.

Theater Security Cooperation Strategy. The document of a geographic combatant commander which plans, prioritizes, and proposes allocation of DOD resources across the full spectrum of military engagement within an area of operations. Normally, the TSCS is augmented by individual plans for each country, routinely termed country campaign plans. The TSCS responds to the OSD-level Security Cooperation Guidance and, when approved, serves as the roadmap for the execution of security cooperation activities by the combatant command staff, the component commands, and the assigned SCOs.

Third country/party transfers. The transfer of US defense articles, services, and training to a country (a third country) from a country that originally acquired such items from the United States. As a condition of the original sale or transfer, the recipient government must obtain the consent of the President of the United States for any proposed third country/party transfer.

Total obligational authority (TOA). TOA is the total amount of funds available for programming in a given year, regardless of the year the funds are appropriated, obligated, or expended. TOA includes new obligational authority, unprogrammed, or reprogrammed obligational authority from prior years, reimbursements not used for replacements of inventory in kind, advanced funding for programs to be financed in the future, and unobligated balances transferred from other appropriations.

Total package approach (TPA). A means of ensuring that FMS customers are aware of and are given the opportunity to plan for and obtain needed support items, training, and services from the US government contractors, or from within the foreign country's resources which are required to introduce and operationally sustain major items of equipment or systems.

Training management system (TMS). A MS Access computer program developed by DISAM for use in the SCO to manage the SA training program. TMS uses STL and MASL data downloaded from the SA Network to produce IMET and FMS management reports, invitational travel orders, and other training management documents. Versions of TMS are also available for use by international military student offices at training activities and at the annual training program management review.

Training/training support. Formal or informal instruction of IMSs in the United States or overseas by officers or employees of the United States, contract technicians, contractors (including instruction at civilian institutions), or by correspondence courses, technical, educational or information publications and media of all kinds, training aids, orientations, training exercises, and military advice to foreign military units and forces. [Sec. 47(5), AECA]

Training program management review (TPMR). Obsolete term. See Security Cooperation Education and Training Working Group (SCETWG).

Tranche. A portion of an appropriation to be allocated to a foreign country. At times, Congress will direct that security assistance funds for a particular country or program be allocated in two or more portions (i.e., tranches), and will generally specify the timing of such allocations as well as the conditions which must be met before the sequential tranches may be allocated.

Transportation Plan. A document that details the transportation and security arrangements for moving classified or sensitive material, and identifies individuals responsible for providing security at various points during transportation.

Travel and living allowance (TLA). Those costs associated with transportation, excess baggage, and living allowances (per diem) of IMSs which are authorized for payment under the IMET Program.

Treaty. A formal agreement entered into between two or more countries. The treaty process includes negotiation, signing, ratification, exchange of ratifications, publishing and proclamation, and treaty execution. Treaties having only two signatory states are called bilateral, whereas those with more than two parties are multilateral.

Trust fund. A fund credited with receipts which are earmarked by law and held in trust, or in a fiduciary capacity, by the government for use in carrying out specific purposes and programs in accordance with an agreement.

Type of address code. One of several codes used in the MAPAD to identify a plain language address to which to ship a specific category of documents or material.

Type of assistance code. A code used to reflect the type of assistance (if any) and/or the planned source of supply for items/services identified on the Letter of Offer and Acceptance. Also known as a type of finance code.

U

Unaccepted case. An FMS letter of offer that was not accepted or funded within the prescribed time shown on the LOA.

Uniform Materiel Movement and Issue Priority System (UMMIPS). A DOD system of ranking materiel requirements and time standards for requisition processing and materiel movement through the use of a two-digit priority designator. It identifies the relative importance of competing demands for logistics resources.

Unified command (UCOM). A command with a broad continuing mission under a single commander and composed of significant assigned components of two or more US services, and which is established and so designated by the president, through the secretary of defense with the advice and assistance of the Joint Chiefs of Staff, or, when so authorized by the Joint Chiefs of Staff, by a commander of an existing unified command established by the president. Now referred to as combatant commands.

US Army Corps of Engineers (USACE). The US Army's principal engineering design, construction, research and development organization. USACE is an implementing agency responsible for accepting Letters of Request and developing Letters of Offer and Acceptance.

United States Code (U.S.C.). A consolidation and codification of the general and permanent laws of the United States arranged according to subject matter under fifty title headings. The U.S.C. sets out the current status of the laws, as amended. It presents the laws in a concise and usable form without requiring recourse to the many volumes of the Statutes at Large containing the individual amendments.

V

Veto. Disapproval by the president of a bill or joint resolution (other than one proposing an amendment to the Constitution). When Congress is in session, the president must veto a bill within ten days (excluding Sundays) of receiving it; otherwise, the bill becomes law without the president's signature. When the president vetoes a bill, it must be returned to the house of origin with a message stating the president's objections.

W

War reserve stocks for allies. A DOD program whereby the services procure or retain in their inventories those minimum stockpiles of materiel such as munitions, equipment, and combat essential consumables to ensure support for selected allied forces in time of war, until future in-country production and external resupply can meet the estimated combat consumption.

Worldwide Warehouse Redistribution Service (WWRS). A tri-service program that redistributes excess spare parts and support equipment acquired by foreign military sales customers.

INDEX

I

Immigration Customs Enforcement (ICE), 3-8

Implementing Agency (IA), 5-1, 5-22

   Code, 5-24, 6-6

Indemnification, 8-3, 8-9

Industry, 4-19

Information Exchange Program (IEP), 1-14, 13-12, 13-16

Initial Deposit, 12-12

Insurance, 8-14, 11-4

Interest Bearing Accounts (IBA), 12-6

International

   Acquisition Career Path (IACP), 13-25

   Agreement, 13-15

   Agreements, 8-20

   Air and Trade Shows, 1-15

   Armaments Cooperation (IAC), 1-13, 13-1, 13-11

   Logistics Communication System (ILCS), 10-14

   Logistics Control Organization (ILCO), 5-24, 10-6, 10-37, 10-41, 10-42, 10-43, 10-46, 11-14, 11-27

   Military Education and Training (IMET), 1-3, 14-1

      Expanded IMET, 1-4

   Military Student Office(r) (IMSO), 14-26, A1-3

   Narcotics Control and Law Enforcement (INCLE), 1-6

   Peacekeeping Capabilities (EPIC), A2-18

   Program, 7-1

      Security, 7-1, 7-4, 7-33

   Security Agreements, 7-14

   Security Assistance Network web (I-SANweb), A1-3

   Traffic in Arms Regulations (ITAR)

      DSP-85 (classified), 10-27

      Exemption 123.4 (unclassified), 10-27

   Training Management (ITM), A1-15

   Visit Program (IVP), 7-21, 7-23

   Authorization, 7-23

Inventory Control Point (ICP), 10-2, 10-4

Invitational Travel Order (ITO), 14-11, 14-33

Iraq Security Forces Fund (ISFF), 1-8

ISANweb, 14-29

Israeli Cooperative Programs, 1-15

Item Manager (IM), 9-4

J

Javits Report, 2-22

Joint

   Capabilities Integration and Development System (JCIDS), 13-2

   Combined Exchange Training, 1-21

   Combined Exchange Training (JCET), 14-4

   Security Cooperation Education and Training (JSCET) Regulation, 14-4

   Staff, 3-10

   Strategic Capabilities Plan (JSCP), 19-3

Jordan, 1-12

L

Latin America Training Waiver, 1-19

Leahy Amendment, 2-10, 14-24, 16-9

Lease, 1-3, 8-18

Legal Status Overseas, 4-24

Lend-Lease Program, A2-4

Letter of Offer and Acceptance (LOA), 5-1, 5-3, 6-1

   Data, 5-7, 5-10

Letter of Request (LOR), 5-3, 5-5, 5-7, 5-8, 5-9, 5-22

   Advisory, 5-8

   Format, 5-4

License, 7-18

   Exemption, 7-19

Life Cycle Logistics Support Planning Process, 10-15

U

W